David and Ruth
Whitehouse

Atlas of the World

with 103 maps
drawn by
John Woodcock
and
Shalom Schotten

W. H. Freeman and Company

San Francisco

Library of Congress Cataloging in Publication Data

Whitehouse, David.
    Archaeological atlas of the world.

    Bibliography: p.
    Includes index.
    1. Archaeology—Maps.   I.   Whitehouse, Ruth, joint
author.   II.   Woodcock, John.   III.   Schotten, Shalom.
IV.   Title.
G1046.E15W5   1975   912   75–2028
ISBN 0–7167–0274–6
ISBN 0–7167–0273–8 pbk.

Originally published in Great Britain 1975 by Thames and
Hudson.
Printed in Great Britain

Contents

Introduction

This Atlas has been carefully planned to meet the requirements of professional archaeologists, students, and the ever-increasing numbers of amateurs and interested laymen who wish to become familiar with the current archaeological scene both at home and abroad. It contains 103 maps covering the whole world and accurately pinpointing some 5,000 pre- and proto-historic sites. Each map is accompanied by explanatory notes. The map section is divided into seven parts, each prefaced by a commentary. The greater part of this introduction is devoted to a brief survey of the origin and growth of archaeological research, and is intended to serve as background information to the Atlas proper.

Although the Atlas is restricted to prehistoric and proto-historic archaeology, we have applied no hard-and-fast rule to the upper chronological date line; for, as Professor Grahame Clark's *World Prehistory: a New Outline* (London/N.Y., 1969) so clearly shows, civilization and the historical record reached different parts of the globe at widely differing dates. In compiling the Atlas we have taken as a general criterion the importance of archaeology in the study of an ancient people or place: if archaeology plays a major role (as in the study of recent 'aboriginal' peoples in Australia), then we have included that culture; if it plays only a secondary role (as in the study of Classical Rome), we have omitted it. Even so, we have had to make exceptions. Thus, Classical Greece appears, although the historian provides much of our information, because Greek influence was of considerable importance in Iron Age Europe.

Each of the maps has superimposed on it a standardized grid the coordinates of which provide the precise location of each site. At the end of the book will be found an index of sites, each entry bearing the page number of the map, and the grid references. The spellings used conform as closely as possible to those in the Site Index of the Institute of Archaeology, University of London. In addition to the sites themselves, the maps show important topographical features such as rivers and mountain ranges, and larger towns and cities are marked as a further aid to orientation. Coastlines, river courses and national boundaries are those of present times. Specially selected symbols are used throughout to indicate the type of site, in accordance with the table below:

✚ Undifferentiated sites and find-spots
● Settlements
▼ Funerary monuments
△ Religious monuments
○ Caves and rock shelters
◎ Cave art and rock reliefs
∴ Hoards and votive deposits
▢ Mineral sources
◆ Mineral workings
✪ Sites which combine several of the above categories

Prehistory and absolute dates

One of the problems confronting the archaeologist is that of chronology, for unless he knows the chronological relationships of different civilizations, cultures or sites he cannot evaluate the significance of similarities or differences between them.

The oldest written chronologies – the king lists of Egypt and Mesopotamia – stretch back only as far as *c.* 3000 BC and apply to small geographical areas. By noting similarities between datable finds from these areas and otherwise undatable finds from neighbouring regions, such scholars as Montelius and Childe constructed approximate chronologies for the later prehistory of peripheral areas like western Europe. Meanwhile, following the lead of Thomsen and Worsaae, archaeologists were assembling local relative chronologies, which enabled them to determine the order, but not the absolute dates, of prehistoric events, while sequences of geological deposits offered a similar relative chronology for more remote periods.

These methods, of course, are only approximate and for years archaeologists sought a method of obtaining accurate dates for prehistoric material. Dendrochronology, or tree-ring dating, provided a partial solution, but the real breakthrough came in 1949, when Professor Willard Libby announced the discovery of the radiocarbon technique. Briefly, Libby and his colleagues discovered that a radioactive isotope of carbon, C^{14}, which is assimilated by all living organisms, decayed after death at a fixed and measurable rate. Libby calculated that C^{14} had a half-life of 5270 ± 47 years (it has since been recalculated), that is to say, after 5270 years only half the original amount of C^{14} remained, after 10,540 years only a quarter, and so on. The amount remaining after about 30,000 years is extremely small and difficult to assess; older material, therefore, cannot be dated with accuracy and beyond about 60,000 BC the technique is useless. Nevertheless 'Carbon 14' caused a revolution in archaeological thought; despite the margin of error attached to *all* dates, whatever their antiquity, a reliable time-scale emerged for prehistory and relationships between prehistoric cultures snapped into place with a precision previously unknown.

Carbon 14, moreover, is not the only dating technique which depends on the decay of a radioactive isotope. One of the isotopes of potassium (K^{40}), for example, changes to argon (A^{40}) with a half-life of 1300 million years, making it invaluable for dating material older than about 500,000 years. Thus, while C^{14} provides dates for recent prehistory and the later Palaeolithic period, potassium-argon has yielded dates for the Early Palaeolithic at such sites as Olduvai Gorge, in Tanzania.

Unhappily, a difficulty has arisen recently over the interpretation of dates derived from Carbon 14, for it appears that in the past the amount of C^{14} assimilated by living organisms has fluctuated. For the archaeologist this means that the time-scale of radiocarbon years deviates from the 'real' time-scale of calendar years by different amounts at different periods. Fortunately, thanks

to an investigation of a tree known as bristlecone pine (*Pinus aristata*), we are able now to correct the most recent carbon dates, up to about 6500 years ago. The bristlecone pine grows in California and is extraordinarily long-lived. Using both living and dead specimens, scientists constructed a sequence of annual growth rings extending back to 4500 BC. By counting backwards from new growth to old, they were able to give a reliable date, *in calendar years*, for every ring. Dated samples were taken at regular intervals and C^{14} dates were obtained for them. It was then possible to compare the 'real' calendar dates with C^{14} determinations, tabulate the degree of divergence and correct the carbon dates.

These problems emerged only recently and uncertainties still remain. Archaeologists have agreed, therefore, that for the time being uncorrected dates should remain in use, with corrected dates quoted also, whenever necessary. We follow what has become established practice and use the letters bc in lower case for uncorrected C^{14} dates; the upper-case letters BC are used both for corrected C^{14} dates and for historical dates (in other words, all dates that are thought to represent calendar years).

The development of archaeology

Archaeology is the study of the material remains of the past, whether they belong to a remote period of prehistory or the early years of the Industrial Revolution. While the first principle of archaeological research is always to assemble as objectively as possible all the available evidence, the ultimate goal is not simply to collect objects but to draw conclusions about human behaviour. In Sir Mortimer Wheeler's words: 'The archaeological excavator is not digging up *things*, he is digging up *people*'. Where the study of prehistory is concerned, the archaeologist is the only person able to collect the evidence, and for nearly two million years of human development all our information derives from archaeological research. Nevertheless, archaeological techniques are applicable to historical societies; in the British Isles and Europe archaeology is now one of the sharpest tools available to the student of medieval towns and cities.

Archaeology, then, is a method of enquiry and its techniques are available to students of any period or place for which material evidence survives. Today these techniques take a wide variety of forms. The field archaeologist, searching for new sites or evaluating an unexcavated site which has been known for years, may call in the aerial photographer and the magnetometer- and resistivity-surveyor. The excavator may require assistance from the soil scientist, hydrologist and pollen analyst before he can interpret the features he has uncovered. In the finds hut, and later the laboratory, specialists may examine samples of flora and fauna, stone, metal and even coprolites or dung. Just a cursory glance down the list of contents of Don Brothwell and Eric Higgs (eds) *Science in Archaeology* (London, second edition 1969) will indicate the formidable battery of techniques brought to bear on archaeological problems.

In the paragraphs that follow we shall examine briefly the three main factors that have contributed to the present advanced state of archaeological knowledge: (1) the establishment of the antiquity of man, (2) the construction of a model for prehistory – a framework which allowed the archaeologist to explain his discoveries, and (3) the development of archaeological techniques in the field.

The antiquity of man

Man has speculated about his past for centuries. Belshazzar's sister, in the sixth century BC, had a private museum of antiquities; in the first century AD Chinese savants divided the past into Ages of Stone, Bronze and Iron; the *virtuosi* of the Renaissance collected Classical antiques and, in the wilder parts of Europe, debated the age of prominent sites, such as Stonehenge and Silbury Hill, and the origin of curiosities like flint arrowheads and axes. This, however, was antiquarianism not archaeology, and it is only in the last two hundred years that men and women have studied the past systematically.

A major obstacle to the development of archaeology in Europe was the prevailing view about the antiquity of man. In 1650 Archbishop Ussher had calculated from the Old Testament that the earth was created in 4004 BC. All educated Europeans knew of the ancient civilizations of Greece and Rome, Persia, Assyria and Egypt; before these there were barely three millennia to absorb the whole of man's early development and, indeed, of geological time.

Geology, moreover, appeared to corroborate the biblical account. Geology had emerged as a science in the late eighteenth century, stimulated by the observation of stratified deposits in canal cuttings and other excavations made by the engineers of the Industrial Revolution. Geological stratigraphy suggested that great changes had taken place during the earth's history and fossils seemed to indicate that sudden catastrophes had overtaken the world. What better explanation could there be than the Flood described in Genesis? Hence the 'Catastrophist' view of antiquity, expounded at length and with great authority by William Buckland (1784–1856) who was successively Professor of Geology at Oxford and Dean of Westminster. Buckland's *Reliquiae Diluvianae* (1823) reconciled Genesis and geology by maintaining that both indicated the occurrence of a Universal Deluge, which explained the remains of extinct animals then being reported in growing numbers – they had been caught in the cataclysm and drowned.

Catastrophism was not, however, the only possible interpretation of geological stratigraphy. James Hutton (1726–97) and later the great Charles Lyell (1797–1875) argued that ancient deposits could be understood only in terms of processes observable today; indeed, Lyell subtitled his *Principles of Geology* (1830–33) 'an attempt to explain the former changes of the Earth's surface by reference to causes now in action'. Granted this view, the great age of the earth became an almost inescapable conclusion and 4004 BC a geological absurdity. And granted the antiquity of the earth, the antiquity of *man* became a distinct possibility.

By the time Lyell published *Principles of Geology*, several writers had reported discoveries of human remains or stone tools in association with extinct animals and apparently of great antiquity. Initially, such finds were explained satisfactorily in Catastrophist terms; it was the evidence collected by a Frenchman, Boucher de Perthes, which first demonstrated that man had a long prehistory. For years, Boucher had collected flint implements from the ancient gravels of the Somme, publishing his results in 1838 and 1847, when he produced *Antiquités celtiques et anté-diluviennes*. Boucher argued that his discoveries could not be explained simply by reference to the Flood; indeed, they were literally *ante*-diluvian. In 1859, after visiting Boucher, the British scholars Evans and Prestwich announced their conviction that man had already existed 'in a period of antiquity remote beyond any of which we have hitherto found traces'.

In the same momentous year, Charles Darwin published *The Origin of Species*, setting out at length the theory of evolution which he and Wallace had postulated separately in 1858. The implications of evolutionary theory were explored first by T. H. Huxley in *Man's Place in Nature* (1863) and by Darwin himself in *The Descent of Man* (1871). Thus, by the 1860s man had acquired not only a history far longer than Ussher allowed, but also an even longer ancestry in the animal kingdom. He was no longer the product of a Special Creation and archaeologists now faced the problem of finding out just what his history had been.

Models for prehistory

By the eighteenth century, many Europeans believed that prehistory should be divided into three ages, on the basis of technological change; the ages of stone, bronze and iron. It was not until 1816–19, however, that the 'Three Age' system was put to practical use, when Christian Jurgensen Thomsen (1788–1865) arranged and opened to the public the new Danish National Museum of Antiquities in Copenhagen. In his guide to the collections, published in 1836, Thomsen explained that the Three Age system offered a relative chronology – still, he emphasized, conjectural – for prehistoric antiquities. This conjecture was soon verified by excavation. J. J. A. Worsaae (1821–85), with Thomsen's encouragement and support from the king of Denmark, began a series of excavations, during which he not only showed that the Three Age system was (broadly speaking) correct in north-west Europe, but also established archaeological principles: the need for methodical excavation, a clear record of the results and for the careful collection and recording of all discoveries.

Five years later, Sven Nilsson (1787–1883) published the first part of *Skandinaviska Nordens Urinvånare*, later translated as *The Primitive Inhabitants of Scandinavia*. Nilsson put forward a different scheme for human development – a sociological and economic model, with four stages beginning with (1) savagery, progressing through (2) nomadic pastoralism and (3) settled agriculture to (4) civilization. Thus, archaeology now possessed two approaches to prehistory: the purely typological approach of the Three Ages and the sociological model, influenced by observation of living 'primitive' peoples. Both approaches were seminal. On the one hand, John Lubbock (1834–1913) in *Prehistoric Times* (1865), one of the landmarks of nineteenth-century archaeology, modified the Three Ages, introducing the terms 'Palaeolithic' and 'Neolithic', while Oscar Montelius (1843–1921) subdivided the Neolithic and Bronze Ages on the basis of implement typology and correlated contemporary phases in different regions. On the other hand, E. B. Tylor (1832–1917) and Lewis Morgan (1818–81) constructed new sociological models which, in Morgan's case, had a profound influence on the work of Marx and Engels, and on four generations of Marxist thought. For example, Gordon Childe (1890–1957), one of the greatest interpreters of prehistory, used Morgan's sequence of savagery–barbarism–civilization, in many works, notably *What Happened in History* (1942; reprinted, Harmondsworth, 1964).

Archaeology in the field

Although Worsaae and others – including in the eighteenth century Thomas Jefferson, third President of the United States, and in the nineteenth century Heinrich Schliemann (1822–90), the discoverer of Troy, and Sir Flinders Petrie (1835–1942) – were pioneers of archaeology in the field, it was General Pitt-Rivers (1827–1900) who transformed excavation into a precise and meticulous technique. Between 1880 and 1890 he conducted a series of excavations on Cranborne Chase in southern England and published his results in four detailed monographs (1887–98). Pitt-Rivers insisted on careful, disciplined excavation and a total record of the finds. 'Excavators', he wrote, 'as a rule record only those things which appear to them important at the time, but fresh problems . . . are constantly arising. *Every detail* should, therefore, be recorded in the manner most conducive to facility of reference . . .'. (The italics are ours.)

The last seventy years have seen, of course, considerable refinement of excavating techniques. Sir Mortimer Wheeler, in a series of brilliant excavations, beginning at Caernarvon in 1921 and continuing through Maiden Castle (where work began in 1934) and sites in India and Pakistan, set a new standard of efficiency in the field. Other archaeologists, in various parts of the world, have carried the process further. Nevertheless, the objectives described by Pitt-Rivers remain the same. The excavator must collect all the available evidence in an objective, methodical fashion. If he fails, then all the natural sciences put together cannot correct his errors.

Thus, by the end of the last century, archaeology had come of age. The antiquity of man was accepted as a fact, scholars had experimented with different models for prehistory, and the field worker was acquiring a sound methodology. Together these developments formed a springboard for the archaeology of the twentieth century.

FURTHER READING

BIBBY, G. 1956, 1957. *The Testimony of the Spade*, New York and London.

BROTHWELL, D. and E. HIGGS (eds) 1969. *Science in Archaeology²*, London and New York.

CLARKE, D. L. 1968. *Analytical Archaeology*, London and New York.

DANIEL, G. 1950. *A Hundred Years of Archaeology*, London and New York.

——— 1967. *The Origins and Growth of Archaeology*, Harmondsworth and New York.

HEIZER, R. F. 1959. *The Archaeologist at Work*, New York.

PALLOTTINO, M. 1968. *The Meaning of Archaeology*, London and New York.

RENFREW, C. 1973. *Before Civilization*, London and New York.

Palaeolithic sites in the Old World

In this first section we are concerned with the emergence and early development of man in the Old World: with his place in the animal kingdom and his material culture, from the earliest tools of Australopithecus to the relatively sophisticated equipment, burial rites and art of the late Pleistocene hunters of Europe and Asia – in short, with the whole of the Old Stone Age, or Palaeolithic period.

Man, despite his accomplishments, is an animal, distinguished from his nearest relatives by the ability to make tools rather than by any metaphysical quality. This ability, of course, is directly related to physical characteristics – upright posture, which frees the forelimbs to manipulate tools; stereoscopic vision; the facility to grip with finger and thumb and, above all, co-ordination of eyes, brain and limbs. Thus, modern man (*Homo sapiens*) and his most recent ancestors are separated from other animals by both anatomical and cultural criteria, and man's early development is, therefore, the concern of archaeologists and physical anthropologists alike.

The criteria which distinguish man emerged during the periods of the earth's history known as the Pliocene and Pleistocene. According to recent estimates, based on the potassium-argon method of dating, the Pleistocene (or Quaternary) period lasted some two million years, ending about ten thousand years ago. It was an age of repeated climatic change, probably on a global scale. In Europe at least four major cold, or *glacial*, periods occurred, characterized by massive extensions of the polar ice-sheets and mountain glaciers. Tropical and sub-tropical regions experienced wet, or *pluvial*, periods, most likely corresponding in time to the glacial maxima to the north and south. Warm and relatively dry phases separated the glacial and pluvial periods, and these are known as *interglacial* or *interpluvial* phases. This sequence of fluctuating climate, clearly illustrated in the geological record, forms the background to the emergence of man. Indeed, the fluctuations may have stimulated man to evolve new patterns of behaviour in response to new environmental conditions.

Man is a Primate; that is, biologists classify him as a member of the Primate order, which includes, among other creatures, all monkeys and apes. He belongs to the sub-order *Anthropoidea* and within this to the family *Hominoidea*. Biologists divide the Hominoidea into apes (*Pongidae*) and hominids (*Hominidae*), and one question which exercises the anthropologist is: when did the hominids emerge as a distinct family? The answer appears to be: at least 15 million years ago. One of the first undoubted hominids was a creature known as *Ramapithecus*, found in India and Kenya in deposits 5–15 million years old. Ramapithecus lacked the long dagger-like canine teeth of the nut- and fruit-eating apes, having instead canines no longer than his incisors – a feature found also in man.

Our first close ancestors, however, belonged to the genus *Australopithecus*, known from early Pleistocene deposits two million years old. Australopithecus walked erect; by 2·6–1·75 million years ago he was making tools and simple working platforms or shelters. Nearly all the Australopithecines known to us come from Africa and it seems likely that they evolved on the savannah of east and southern Africa. At the most famous of all palaeolithic sites in Africa, Olduvai Gorge, the late Dr Louis Leakey investigated a sequence of deposits which began about 1·9 million years ago and contains remains of Australopithecus, primitive 'chopper' tools and a crude shelter, in addition to rich industries of a later date.

Modern man belongs to the genus *Homo* and his nearest ancestors, including Neandertal man, are now placed in the same category. The earliest member of the genus, *H. erectus*, comprises all the fossils previously classified as *Pithecanthropus*, including the finds from Java, Chou K'ou Tien and Ternifine. *Homo erectus* had a larger brain than Australopithecus, and smaller teeth. His remains belong to the Middle Pleistocene period, as do the earliest examples of the best-known palaeolithic tool – the hand-axe. Indeed, during the Middle Pleistocene two distinct traditions of toolmaking emerged: the Acheulian (named after St Acheul, near Amiens in France) with abundant hand-axes, and the Clactonian (named after Clacton in south-east England) with flake tools and choppers.

The second member of the genus *Homo* is *H. sapiens*. Contrary to earlier opinion, which saw him as a brutish ape-like creature, most anthropologists now classify Neandertal man as a member of the species *H. sapiens*, as of course is modern man. The remains of Neandertal man, which are widely distributed in the Old World, from the English Channel to southern Africa, Uzbekistan and Java, vary considerably in physical type. The so-called 'classic' Neandertaler, found in Europe, was short and stocky, with a large head, receding chin and pronounced brow ridges; the 'generalized' type had less-pronounced features, although the receding chin and brow ridges remained. If we include the finds from Swanscombe and Steinheim (the exact status of neither is clear), men of Neandertal type appeared in Europe during the penultimate, or Holstein, interglacial and survived well into the last major glacial period, about 30,000 years ago.

The culture associated with Neandertal man during the last glaciation is known as the Mousterian (named after Le Moustier in Dordogne), a general term which embraces several regional and chronological variants. Neandertal man frequently lived in caves and excavation has revealed much about his way of life. He made regular use of fire. He had a standardized kit of stone tools, usually made on flakes. Although we have no evidence of art or personal adornment, we do know that Neandertal man buried his dead with some ceremony; a cemetery of ten graves was found at Mount Carmel and at Teshik-Tash in Uzbekistan a child was buried in a circle of goat horns.

Neandertal man disappeared about 30,000 years ago and was replaced by modern man, the subspecies *H. sapiens sapiens*. Why he vanished we do not know; anthropologists have suggested that he was outside the direct line of human evolution, or simply that he evolved into the modern type, perhaps by the process of neoteny, in which juvenile features survive into full maturity, thus eliminating pronounced characteristics (such as brow ridges) which normally appear in their most emphatic form only in adult life.

Physically, the earliest 'modern' men did not differ significantly from their immediate predecessors. However, their culture contained many new elements, notably a tool-kit of small stone implements (blades and burins), bone tools and weapons, personal ornament – and art. In many areas, notably in Russia, we have evidence of encampments comprising tent-like huts and shelters, used by bands of hunters in pursuit of horses, reindeer and mammoth. Nevertheless, art is probably the most familiar achievement of the Upper Palaeolithic (or Leptolithic) period, and the discovery of painted caves, such as Altamira and Lascaux, probably did more than anything else to convince popular opinion that 'stone age man' was more than a mere semi-ape.

FURTHER READING

Bordes, F. 1968. *The Old Stone Age*, London and New York.
Butzer, K. 1971. *Environment and Archaeology*, London and Chicago.
Clark, G. 1969. *World Prehistory: a New Outline*², London and New York.
Coles, J. M. and E. S. Higgs 1969. *The Archaeology of Early Man*, London and New York.
Dobzhansky, T. H. 1962. *Mankind Evolving*, Yale.
Giedion, S. 1962. *The Eternal Present*, Oxford and New York.
Oakley, K. 1966. *Frameworks for dating Fossil Man*² (revised edn), London and Chicago.
Pilbeam, D. 1970. *The Evolution of Man*, London and New York.

Pre-Neandertal hominid fossils

Man belongs to the Primate Order, the sub-order *Anthropoidea*, the super-family *Hominoidea* and the family *Hominidae*. His nearest relations among living animals are the apes (*Pongidae*), who belong to the same super-family.

Modern man, *Homo sapiens sapiens*, is the only surviving member of the hominid family, but we have fossil evidence of several extinct species. These are usually divided into two genera: Australopithecus and Homo. The earliest substantial group of hominid remains, reckoned to date from between *c.* 5·5 million years (at Lothagam) and less than one million years ago, belongs to Australopithecus. Finds are abundant in south and east Africa and a single example is known from Java. Compared with man, Australopithecus was relatively small; he possessed a small brain but, like man, he walked erect and his teeth had many human characteristics. At least two contemporary species of Australopithecus are recognized: the larger, more robust and perhaps vegetarian *A. robustus*, and the more slender, partly carnivorous and probably tool-making *A. africanus*. The important hominid remains found near Lake Rudolf and reckoned to be *c.* 2·6 million years old may well belong to this latter type. The evolutionary position of Australopithecus is hotly disputed. Some authorities maintain that he belongs to a line distinct from modern man and in this context we should note that one of the hominids from Bed I at Olduvai Gorge has been designated not Australopithecus but Homo (*H. habilis*) and considered man's true ancestor; a similar claim has been made for one of Richard Leakey's new hominid finds from Rudolf East. Others believe all these early hominid finds could be part of a single variable (Australopithecine) population and that either all the Australopithecines, or just *A. africanus*, are the ancestors of man.

For the period *c.* 900,000–300,000 years ago we have hominids now unanimously assigned to the genus Homo (*H. erectus*). They are found in north and east Africa (including Olduvai), southeast Asia (Java and Pekin) and even in Europe (near Heidelberg and Budapest). *H. erectus* was taller than Australopithecus and had a larger brain, a smaller face and smaller teeth; his skull, however, was thicker.

Only two important fossils from the period *c.* 250,000–100,000 BC are known: the skull fragments from Swanscombe (England) and Steinheim (West Germany). They belong to creatures closer to modern man than to *H. erectus*.

FURTHER READING

COLLINS, D. *et al.* 1973. *Background to Archaeology*[2], London and New York.

DOBZHANSKY, T. 1962. *Mankind Evolving*, Yale.

OVEY, C. 1964. *The Swanscombe Skull*, London (Royal Anthropological Institute Occasional Papers, No. 20).

PILBEAM, D. 1970. *The Evolution of Man*, London and New York.

——— 1972. *The Ascent of Man*, New York and London.

WASHBURN, S. (ed.) 1963. *Classification and Human Evolution*, New York (Viking Fund Publications in *Anthropology*, No. 37) and London.

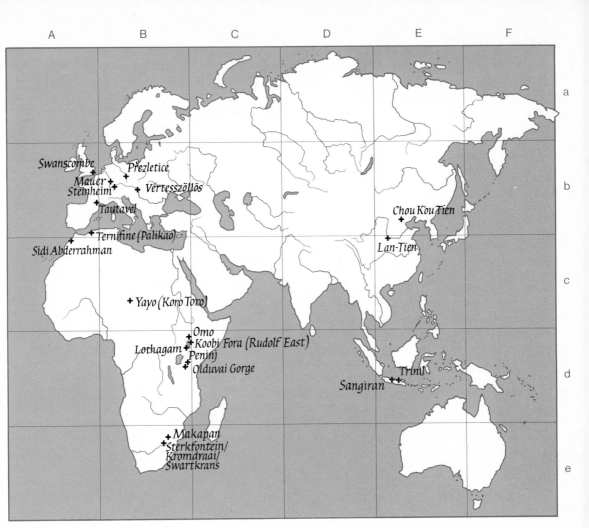

Swanscombe
Přezletice
Mauer
Steinheim
Vértesszöllös
Tautavel
Ternifine (Palikão)
Sidi Abderrahman
Chou Kou Tien
Lan-Tien
Yayo (Koro Toro)
Omo
Koobi Fora (Rudolf East)
Lothagam
Peninj
Olduvai Gorge
Sangiran
Trinil
Makapan
Sterkfontein/
Kromdraai/
Swartkrans

Neandertal fossils

The type of man named after a find at Neandertal near Düsseldorf in West Germany is the latest fossil hominid to differ significantly from modern man.

Human fossils of the period *c.* 100,000–30,000 years ago are much more numerous than from earlier in the Pleistocene and have a wide distribution in Europe, Africa and Asia. All are usually classified as Neandertalers for, although they display considerable variation, there are several important characteristics they share: a large cranial capacity, low foreheads, brow ridges, a receding chin and heavy facial architecture. Anthropologists recognize two broad groups of Neandertal fossils: the so-called 'classic' Neandertalers, characteristic of western Europe, who were stockily built, had pronounced brow ridges and massive jaws (features, however, which were exaggerated in early reconstructions, based on a chronically arthritic skeleton from La Chapelle-aux-Saints); and the 'generalized' Neandertalers, whose heavy features were less pronounced than those of the 'classic' type and who therefore appear closer to modern man. The earliest Neandertalers from Europe and finds from Africa and Asia belong to this latter type.

The place in human evolution of the Neandertalers as a whole is a matter of dispute. Until recently the most popular view was that they died out and that modern man descended from another line, represented only by isolated (and early) finds, such as the fragments from Swanscombe. Today, however, most authorities believe that the Neandertalers were direct ancestors of modern man, occupying an intermediate position between *Homo erectus* and *H. sapiens sapiens*; indeed they are often described as a subspecies of *sapiens* – *H. sapiens neanderthalensis*. However, opinion is still divided on the question whether the western 'classic' Neandertalers became extinct, leaving only the 'generalized' group as our ancestors, or whether both types survived to father different races of modern man.

Two achievements of Neandertal man are particularly significant. He was the first man to extend the range of human settlement outside the frost-free zone and (as far as we know) he was the first to bury his dead.

FURTHER READING

Collins, D. *et al.* 1973. *Background to Archaeology*², London and New York.

De Beer, B. 1950. *Embryos and Ancestors*, Oxford and New York.

Pilbeam, D. 1970. *The Evolution of Man*, London and New York.

—— 1972. *The Ascent of Man*, New York and London.

Vallois, H. 1954. Neanderthals and Praesapiens. *Journal of the Royal Anthropological Institute* 84, 111–30.

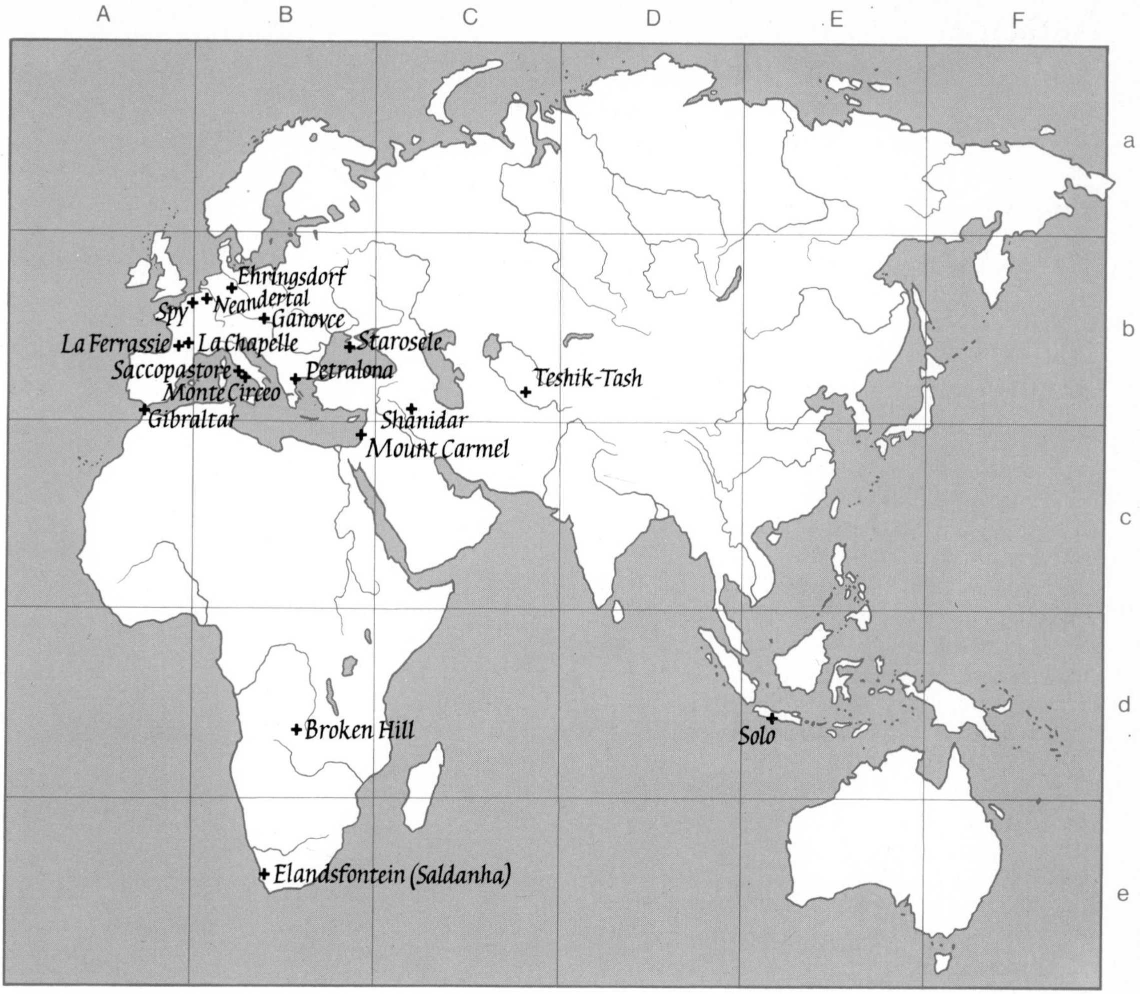
A
B
C
D
E
F
a
b
c
d
e
Ehringsdorf
Spy
Neandertal
Ganovce
La Ferrassie
La Chapelle
Starosele
Saccopastore
Petralona
Monte Circeo
Teshik-Tash
Gibraltar
Shanidar
Mount Carmel
Broken Hill
Solo
Elandsfontein (Saldanha)

Early man in Africa

It is often said that Africa was the cradle of mankind and this claim is very strongly supported by archaeological discoveries. If we follow Oakley's convenient definition and regard man as the tool-making animal, we find in east Africa two sites near Lake Rudolf with stone tools dated by the potassium-argon method to between two and three million years ago and a third site, Olduvai Gorge, with tools about 1·85 million years old – more than a million years older than dated tools found anywhere else in the world. Moreover, anatomical criteria also point to Africa as the cradle of man, for this was the homeland of *Australopithecus*, the vegetivorous *A. robustus* and the more slender *A. africanus* who probably was both a meat-eater and a tool-maker and may have been the ultimate ancestor of Homo. (Following many anthropologists, we take Louis Leakey's *H. habilis* to be a member of the species *A. africanus*.)

Perhaps the most important of all palaeolithic sites in Africa is Olduvai Gorge in Tanzania, where a long sequence of Pleistocene deposits is exposed in a ravine 40 km long and 100–130 m deep. In the earliest deposits, Bed I, bones of both types of *Australopithecus* occur, associated with stone tools of an industry named the Oldowan after the site; the most characteristic type is a chopping tool flaked in two directions to produce a cutting edge. The meat diet of the Oldowan hunters was small game: young animals, lizards, crabs, etc. In Bed II at Olduvai, deposited about a million years ago, Oldowan tools still occur, but they are associated with new types, including multi-facetted stone balls.

By half a million years ago, man had become a proficient big-game hunter and sites of this age contain the remains of large animals – elephants, giant sheep, rhinoceros, etc. – together with improved stone tools, the earliest 'hand-axes'. These important developments were probably associated with the emergence of a new human type, *Homo erectus*, whose remains occur in the upper levels of Bed II at Olduvai Gorge.

FURTHER READING

COLLINS, D. *et al.* 1973. *Background to Archaeology*[2], London and New York.
LEAKEY, L. S. B. 1951. *Olduvai Gorge*, Cambridge.
LEAKEY, M. 1971. *Olduvai Gorge. Excavations in Beds I and II, 1960–1963*, Cambridge.
OAKLEY, K. P. 1967. *Man the Tool-maker*[5], London.
TOBIAS, P. V. 1967. *Olduvai Gorge, Volume II: the cranium and maxillary dentition of Australopithecus (Zinjanthropus) boisei*, Cambridge.

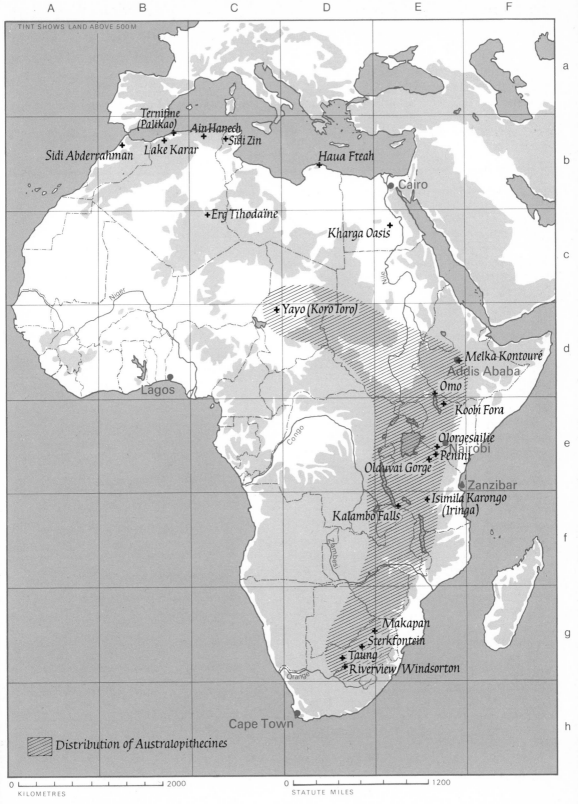

TINT SHOWS LAND ABOVE 500M

Ternifine (Palikao)
Ain Hanech
Sidi Zin
Sidi Abderrahman
Lake Karar
Haua Fteah
Cairo
Erg Tihodaïne
Kharga Oasis
Yayo (Koro Toro)
Melka Kontouré
Addis Ababa
Omo
Koobi Fora
Lagos
Olorgesailie
Nairobi
Peninj
Olduvai Gorge
Zanzibar
Isimila Karongo (Iringa)
Kalambo Falls
Makapan
Sterkfontein
Taung
Riverview/Windsorton
Cape Town

Niger
Congo
Zambesi
Orange
Nile

Distribution of Australopithecines

0 _____ 2000
KILOMETRES

0 _____ 1200
STATUTE MILES

Early man in Africa 21

Old World sites earlier than the Holstein interglacial

Throughout the Lower Palaeolithic (indeed, until some 40,000 years ago), *Homo sapiens* and his ancestors were confined to the Old World: Africa, Europe and Asia. Some of the most important sites earlier than the Holstein interglacial are in Africa, where at the world-famous site of Olduvai Gorge, Dr Louis Leakey revealed a long sequence of Pleistocene deposits beginning nearly two million years ago. The deposits contain a rich fauna, artifacts, working and living areas and several hominid fossils. In 1970 another early Pleistocene site was found in east Africa, at the north-east end of Lake Rudolf. Here, Richard Leakey has uncovered hominid fossils and stone tools about 2·6 million years old – older than Bed I at Olduvai Gorge. The earliest hominids from east Africa fall into two major groups, usually regarded as separate species of *Australopithecus*. The earliest tools are pebbles flaked bifacially to form crude 'Oldowan' chopping tools, named after the industry in Bed I at Olduvai. New types appear in Bed II including, high in the deposit, the first hand-axes. In southern Africa, the early Pleistocene site at Sterkfontein contains chopping tools, perhaps associated with *Australopithecus*. A few early sites in north Africa have yielded chopping tools and other simple stone artifacts.

In Asia, the earliest published sites are later than those in Africa, beginning about half a million years ago. The most informative sites are in China – at Chou K'ou Tien and Lan-Tien – and both have yielded remains of *Homo erectus*, associated with chopping tools, evidence of big-game hunting and with the use of fire. In the Punjab, a flake and chopper tool industry from the Soan Valley may be earlier than the Holstein interglacial, while in western Asia the site at Ubeidiya in the Jordan Valley has yielded another chopper industry, possibly associated with remains of *Homo erectus*. Chopper tool industries are known from several other sites, including Gerasimovka in southern Russia.

Among the earliest sites in Europe, Vallonet in France has yielded flakes and pebble tools, while Vértesszöllös in Hungary contains a flake and chopper industry of a slightly later date. Elsewhere, sites like Abbeville and Torralba have hand-axe industries, sometimes associated with evidence for big-game hunting.

FURTHER READING

BORDES, F. 1968. *The Old Stone Age*, London and New York.
COLES, J. M. and E. S. HIGGS 1969. *The Archaeology of Early Man*, London and New York.
COLLINS, D. M. *et al.* 1973. *Background to Archaeology²*, London and New York.
PILBEAM, D. 1972. *The Ascent of Man*, New York and London.

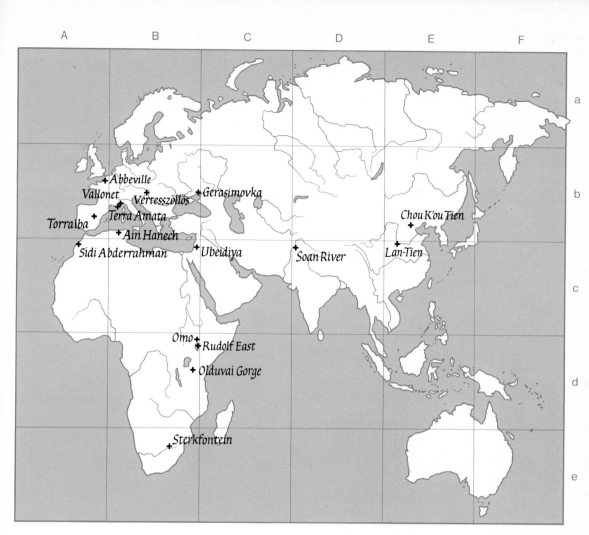

Old World sites earlier than the Holstein interglacial   23

Palaeolithic sites in India

The Indian Palaeolithic is usually divided into three phases: the Early, Middle and Late Stone Ages. After more than a century of collecting, often from sites on river terraces, we possess a great quantity of material, but its chronology is not yet fully understood.

The Early Stone Age contains two distinct cultural traditions. The first comprises industries characterized by choppers and cleavers, best known from sites in the Soan valley, which probably form part of the east Asian 'chopper/chopping tool' complex described by Movius. The second tradition incorporates hand-axes of Acheulian type. This is known sometimes as the Madrasian and the key site is Attirampakkam. Early Stone Age implements were usually made of quartz. Bands lived mainly in the open and the rare cave deposits indicate temporary occupation.

In the Middle Stone Age, for which we have C^{14} dates between 40,000 and 20,000 bc, flake industries replaced most of the choppers and hand-axes of the Early Palaeolithic. Jasper and chalcedony, chosen for their conchoidal fracture, were worked into scrapers and other tools with careful retouching. Several regional cultures are recognized. Among the most important sites is Sanghao in Pakistan, a cave containing four phases of occupation represented by deposits 3 m deep. Recent reports indicate that blade and burin industries of classic leptolithic type – hitherto unknown in India – occur in several provinces, notably Andhra Pradesh.

The Late Stone Age, which is entirely post-Pleistocene in date, comprises numerous microlithic industries, found at open camp or factory sites and in caves and rock shelters. Among the most notable sites are Adamgarh cave and a large open settlement at Bagor. Bands of hunters and gatherers using microlithic industries survived well into the Neolithic and metal-using periods; a late microlithic industry at Lekhania, for example, has a C^{14} date of 1710 bc, while at Bagor phase III, which has a food-producing economy but microlithic tools, is dated c. 600 BC–AD 200.

FURTHER READING

ALLCHIN, B. and R. 1968. *The Birth of Indian Civilization*, Harmondsworth and San Francisco.

COLES, J. M. and E. S. HIGGS 1969. *The Archaeology of Early Man*, London and New York.

CORVINUS, G. K. 1973. Excavations at an Acheulian site at Chirki-on-Pravara in India. In Hammond, N. (ed.), *South Asian Archaeology*, London and Park Ridge.

MISRA, V. N. 1973. Bagor – a late mesolithic settlement in north-west India. *World Archaeology* 5, no. 1, 92–110.

MOVIUS, H. L. 1948. The Lower Palaeolithic cultures of southern and eastern Asia. *Trans. American Philosophical Soc.* 38, 329–420.

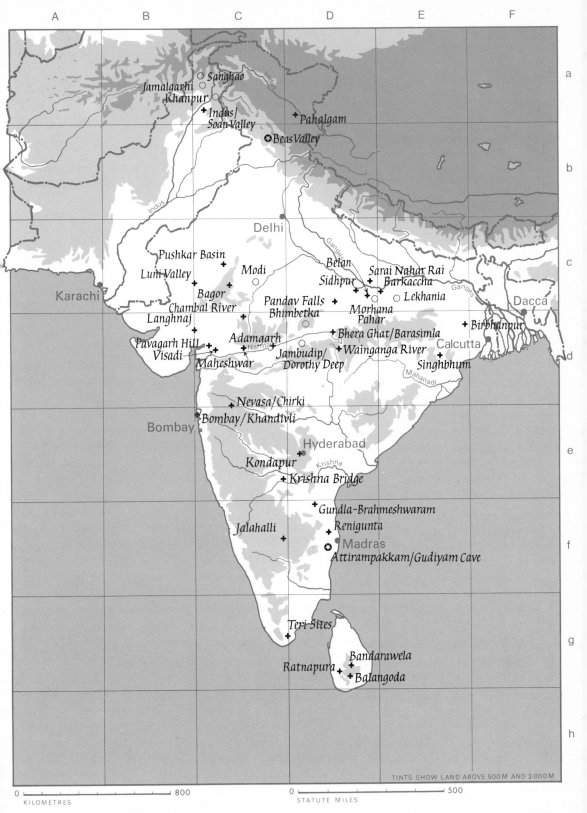

Palaeolithic sites in India **25**

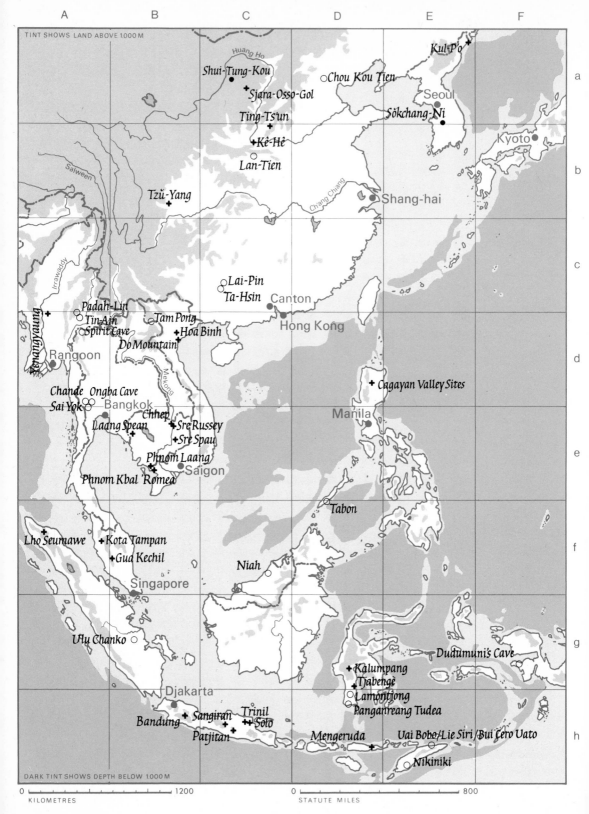

TINT SHOWS LAND ABOVE 1,000 M

Huang Ho

a

Shui-Tung-Kou ●

○ Chou Kou Tien

Kul-P'o +

+ Sjara-Osso-Gol

Seoul

Ting-Ts'un
+

Sökchang-Ni
●

+ Kê-Hê

b

○ Lan-Tien

Salween

Kyoto ●

Tzŭ-Yang +

Ch'iang Chiang

Shang-hai ●

c

○ Lai-Pin

Irrawaddy

○ Ta-Hsin

Canton ●

Padah-Lin ○

Tam Pong ○

Hong Kong

○ Tin-Ain

+ Hoa Binh

○ Spirit Cave

Do Mountain

d

Yenangyaung

Rangoon ●

Mekong

+ Cagayan Valley Sites

Chande Ongba Cave

Manila

Sai Yok ○○

Bangkok ●

Chhep

+ Sre Russey

Laang Spean ●

+ Sre Spau

e

Phnom Laang +

Saigon ●

Phnom Kbal 'Romea +

○ Tabon

Lho Seumawe +

+ Kota Tampan

f

+ Gua Kechil

Niah ○

Singapore

g

Ulu Chanko ○

Dudumuni's Cave +

+ Kalumpang

Djakarta

+ Tjabenge

Trinil

○ Lamontjong

Bandung ●

+ Sangiran   +● Solo

Panganreang Tudea

h

Patjitan +

Mengeruda

Uai Bobo/Lie Siri/Bui Cero Uato

+

○ Nikiniki

DARK TINT SHOWS DEPTH BELOW 1,000 M

0 ————————————————— 1200
KILOMETRES

0 ————————————————— 800
STATUTE MILES

Palaeolithic sites in east and south-east Asia

Palaeolithic sites in east and south-east Asia

Most lower palaeolithic sites in eastern Asia yield industries comprising chopper tools and flakes. At the rich site of Chou K'ou Tien, for example, locality 13 yielded chopping tools associated with the bones of *Homo erectus pekinensis* (see p. 16), and those of a large number of game animals, datable either to the Mindel glaciation or the Mindel/Riss interglacial. Locality 15, usually dated to the Riss glaciation, yielded flakes with prepared platforms. Elsewhere in China, the Fenho complex of Shansi and Honan, which belongs to the Riss or Riss/Würm period, contains tools with bifacial flaking. Farther south, in the Irrawaddy valley of Burma, the Anyathian industries occur in Riss/Würm and Würm contexts. Earlier Anyathian industries include choppers, often made of silicified wood; later assemblages lack the choppers. In Malaysia another industry with choppers, the Tampanian, is named after the site at Kota Tampan. The only assemblages of Mousterian type in this area occur in China, at such sites as Shui-Tung-Kou in the Ordos region. Here an evolved 'Mousterian' industry displays not only the Levallois technique, but also features of the Leptolithic in Eurasia. True leptolithic sites occur in China at Chou K'ou Tien (in the upper cave) and elsewhere, including Sjara-Osso-Gol in the Ordos.

In south-east Asia the most important late palaeolithic culture is the Bacsonian or Hoabinhian, named after sites in the DRV (North Vietnam). Hoabinhian sites have a wide distribution from China to Malaysia and similar assemblages occur in Java, Borneo and elsewhere. It is hardly surprising that the subsistence economy varied considerably from region to region; hunters and gatherers occupied caves or rock shelters, while on the Sumatran coast large shell middens accumulated. In recent years one of the most exciting discoveries relating to south-east Asian prehistory has been the excavation of Spirit Cave, where a Hoabinhian industry is associated with the remains of domesticated or semi-domesticated plants (leguminous beans, water chestnuts and bottle gourds) dated by C¹⁴ to *c.* 9750–7500 bc – apparently some of the earliest domesticated plants in the world. At a later date numerous Hoabinhian sites yield evidence of cultivation.

FURTHER READING

BORDES, F. 1968. *The Old Stone Age*, London and New York.
GLOVER, I. C. 1973. Late Stone Age traditions in South-East Asia. In Hammond, N. (ed.), *South Asian Archaeology*, London and Park Ridge.
GORMAN, C. F. 1972. Excavations at Spirit Cave, North Thailand. *Asian Perspectives* XIII, 79–108.
MOVIUS, H. L. 1948. The Lower Palaeolithic cultures of southern and eastern Asia. *Trans. American Philosophical Soc.* 38, 329–420.
—————— 1960. *Asian Perspectives* I. (A special Palaeolithic issue).

Middle palaeolithic and leptolithic sites in Africa

see map p. 28

During the Middle Palaeolithic two distinct cultural provinces emerged in Africa: (1) north of the Sahara, with Mousterian industries comparable with those of Europe (see pp. 34/35) and (2) south of the Sahara, where true Mousterian industries were lacking, although certain 'Mousteroid' traits occur.

Mousterian industries have been found throughout north Africa, but few sites have been studied in detail. Of the latter, the best known is Haua Fteah, a cave in Cyrenaica, where Mousterian levels are dated to *c.* 45,000–41,000 bc. Another important site is El Guettar in Tunisia.

In Cyrenaica the Mousterian was succeeded by the Dabban industry, characterized by backed blades, gravers and end-scrapers. These features, which may occur as early as 30,000 bc at Haua Fteah, are characteristic of leptolithic technology in Europe. West of Cyrenaica, especially in Algeria and Tunisia, we find the Aterian industry, named after the Tunisian site of Bir el-Ater. This was a local development of the Mousterian;

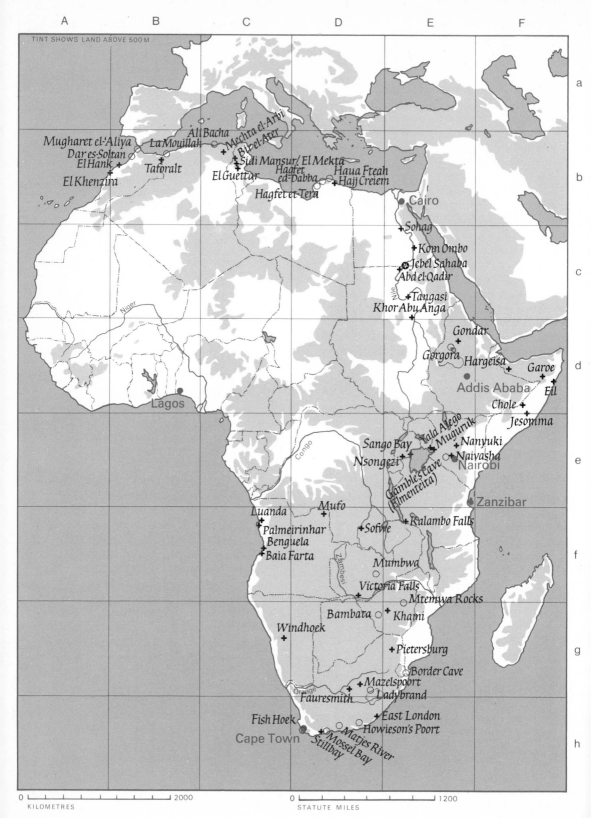

28 *Middle palaeolithic and leptolithic sites in Africa*

blades were not used and the most distinctive stone tool was a tanged point. In the western Maghrib the earliest blade industry, the Oranian or Ibero-Maurusian, dates from very late Pleistocene or Neothermal times. An 'eastern Oranian' variant occurs in Cyrenaica. Later still, in the seventh millennium bc, these industries were replaced by the Capsian, a blade industry with a strong microlithic element.

South of the Sahara different traditions prevailed. The 'First Intermediate' stage contained two major industries: the Fauresmith of southern Africa and the Sangoan of east and central Africa. Both developed out of the Acheulian. The Fauresmith culture represents an adaptation for living in open country, the Sangoan for forest conditions. The succeeding 'Middle Stone Age' is roughly contemporary with the Leptolithic of north Africa and Europe. In the Congo forests the Lupemban culture, characterized by woodworkers' axes and adzes, as well as bifacial points, developed out of the local Sangoan. To the south and east the grasslands supported the Stillbay culture, in which bifacial leaf-shaped points are typical. The culture that developed in the Transvaal is known as the Pietersburgian. Blade industries are not known in southern Africa and throughout the 'Middle Stone Age' the region developed in isolation.

FURTHER READING

CLARK, J. D. 1965. *The Later Pleistocene Cultures of Africa*. *Science* 150, 833–47.
——— 1967. *Atlas of African Prehistory*, Chicago.
——— 1970. *The Prehistory of Africa*, London and New York.
McBURNEY, C. B. M. 1967. *The Haua Fteah and the Stone Age of the South-east Mediterranean*, Cambridge.

The Mousterian complex is well represented in numerous caves and rock shelters in the Near and Middle East. They occur in the Zagros region (e.g. the caves of Shanidar and Hazar Merd in Iraq and several caves in the Khorramabad valley in western Iran) and in the Levant, where sites are especially abundant. Levantine sites of particular importance include Jabrud in Syria, Ksar Akil in Lebanon, caves on Mount Carmel and near Lake Tiberias in Israel and caves in Jordan. Neandertal remains occur in both the Zagros region and the Levant; indeed at Shanidar and Mugharet es-Skhūl on Mount Carmel small 'cemeteries' have been excavated.

The Leptolithic, too, is well known in both regions. In the Zagros the earliest leptolithic culture, the Baradostian, comprises simple and polyhedral burins, rods, backed blades and endscrapers. It is found at Shanidar and several sites in Iran. C^{14} dates for the Baradostian range from c. 40,000 to 21,000 bc. The Baradostian was followed by the Zarzian industry and at Pa Sangar in Iran the excavators demonstrated that it developed directly out of the earlier industry. The Zarzian is characterized by small round endscrapers, backed blades and notched bladelets, with geometric microliths in the latest levels. It probably survived until the beginnings of farming in the Zagros region.

The Levantine sequence of leptolithic cultures is well understood, for numerous sites are known. The earliest phase in the Levant, the Emiran, has many Mousterian types, such as points and side-scrapers, which occur in association with blades – a combination which recalls the north African Dabban culture, known from the Cyrenaican cave of Haua Fteah. The Emiran was succeeded by the Antelian which contains many traits found also in the Aurignacian of western Europe. (Indeed, 'Aurignacian' features occur as far east as Kara Kamar in Afghanistan.) The last two phases of the Levantine sequence are known as the Atlitian and the Kebaran and represent local regional cultures.

The first leptolithic cultures in the Near East are among the earliest in the world to contain

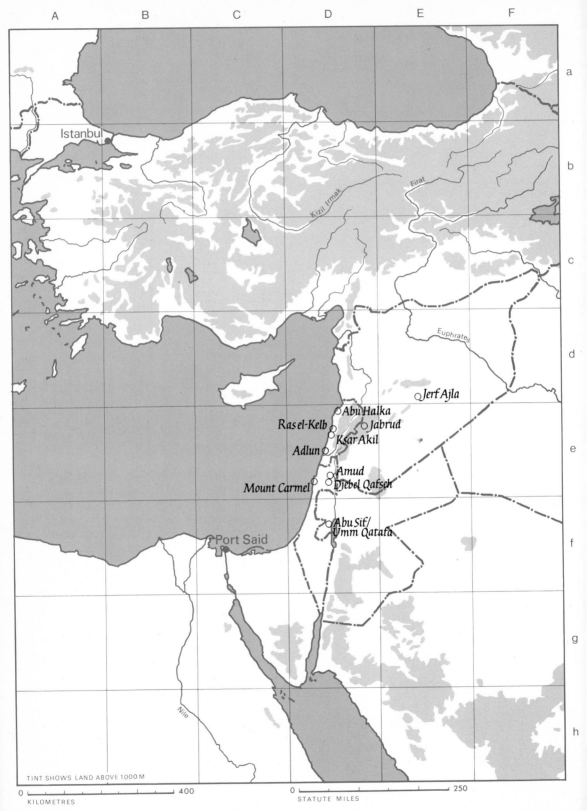

Istanbul

Kizil Irmak

Firat

Euphrates

Jerf Ajla

Abu Halka
Ras el-Kelb ○ ○ Jabrud
Ksar Akil
Adlun ○

Amud
Mount Carmel ○ ○ Djebel Qafseh

Abu Sif/
Umm Qatafa

Port Said

Nile

TINT SHOWS LAND ABOVE 1000 M

0   400
KILOMETRES

0   250
STATUTE MILES

30   *Middle palaeolithic and leptolithic sites in the Near East*

blades and burins. Consequently some authorities believe that the Leptolithic of Europe originated in western Asia and was introduced from that area by the first modern men (*Homo sapiens sapiens*) to live in Europe. Others, however, believe that leptolithic technology developed independently in several areas.

FURTHER READING

BINFORD, S. R. 1968. Early upper Pleistocene adaptations in the Levant. *American Anthropologist* 70, 707–17.
GARROD, D. A. E. and D. M. BATE 1937. *The Stone Age of Mount Carmel*, Oxford.
HOLE, F. and K. V. FLANNERY 1967. The Prehistory of Southwestern Iran: a Preliminary Report. *Proceedings of the Prehistoric Society* 33, 147–206.
SOLECKI, R. S. 1963. Prehistory in Shanidar Valley, Northern Iraq. *Science* 139, 179–93.
—— 1972. *Shanidar. The humanity of Neanderthal man*, London.

European sites between the Holstein and Eemian interglacials

see map pp. 32/33

Although Europe was inhabited before the Holstein (Mindel-Riss) interglacial, it was only at this time, and especially in the succeeding Riss glaciation, that settlement became relatively common. The earliest inhabitants of Britain arrived in the Holstein interglacial and are represented at the important sites of Clacton-on-Sea, Hoxne and Swanscombe. The last-named site yielded the famous skull fragments which, together with another skull from Steinheim in Germany, probably of Riss date, constitute the only human fossils of the period *c.* 250,000–100,000 years ago; they probably represent an evolutionary stage between *Homo erectus* and Neandertal man (*H. sapiens neanderthalensis*).

During the Holstein two traditions of toolmaking existed side by side: the Acheulian, with hand-axes as the most characteristic implement, and the Clactonian, characterized by tools made on thick flakes and with the distinctive 'Clactonian notch'. The Acheulian industry developed

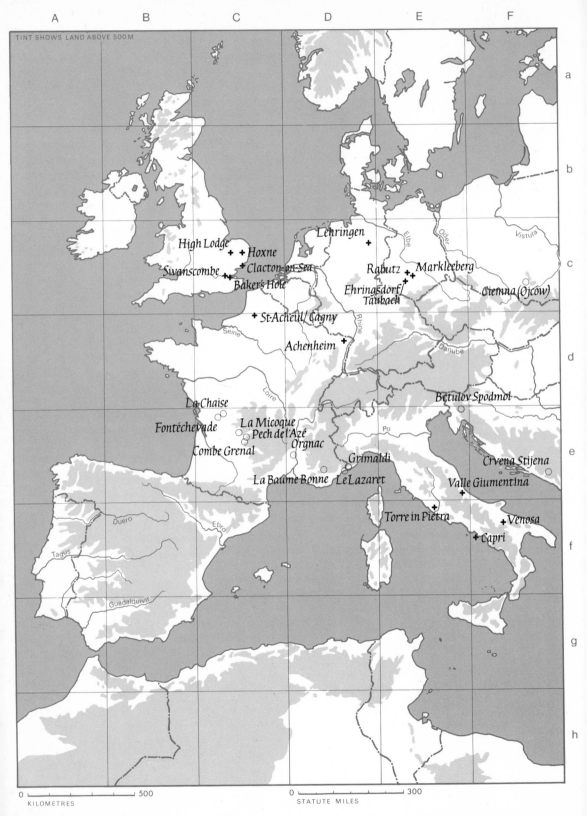

32 *European sites between the Holstein and Eemian interglacial*

out of the chopping-tool tradition of Oldowan type and has a basically African and south European distribution. The Clactonian, which may also have a chopping-tool ancestry, but perhaps of Asiatic or European background, is best known in northern Europe, although related industries are widely scattered over Eurasia. At Swanscombe, where both industries occur, the Acheulian is later than the Clactonian, although both are dated to the Holstein interglacial.

In the succeeding Riss (Saale) glaciation we find the earliest evidence of man's presence during an ice age in the tundra zone north of the temperate forests: at such sites as Baker's Hole and Ebbsfleet in southern England and Markleeberg in East Germany. Stone technology is characterized by the 'Levallois' style of flaking, in which cores were prepared in advance to predetermine the shape of the flakes to be detached. Cave habitation, which became customary in the last (Würm or Weichsel) glaciation, began during Riss, with occupation attested in caves like La Baume Bonne and La Chaise in France and rock shelters such as that outside Grotta Paglicci in south-east Italy.

FURTHER READING

BORDES, F. 1968. *The Old Stone Age*, London and New York.
COLLINS, D. 1969. Culture traditions and environment of early man. *Current Anthropology* 10, 267–316.
COLLINS, D. *et al.* 1973. *Background to Archaeology*², London and New York.
OVEY, C. 1964. *The Swanscombe Skull*, Royal Anthropological Institute, London.

Middle palaeolithic sites in Europe

see map pp. 34/35

The Middle Palaeolithic is the term traditionally applied to the period between the last (Eemian) interglacial and the middle of the last (Würm or Weichsel) glaciation, i.e. from *c.* 100,000 to 35,000 bc. Fossil man of this period is named after the site of Neandertal near Düsseldorf and his cul-

TINT SHOWS LAND ABOVE 500 M

Lebenstedt

Wylotne

Oldbury

Engis
Spy
Wallertheim
Kúlna

Kent's Cavern

Mauern

La Cotte de St-Brelade

Tata
Erd

Krapina

Fontmaure

Grotta Pocala
Betulov Spodmol

La Quina
Le Moustier
Quinzano
Visoko Brdo

La Ferrassie
Combe Grenal
Grotta di Broion

Combe Capelle

Toirano

El Castillo

Baume les Peyrards
Grimaldi

Crvena Stijena

Romani
Saccopastore

Bisceglie

Monte Circeo
Polignano a Mare

Furninha
Palinuro
Castro

Cova Negra, Bellús
Cueva del Cochino

Carigüela de Piñar

Gibraltar

0   500
KILOMETRES

0   300
STATUTE MILES

34   *Middle palaeolithic sites in Europe*

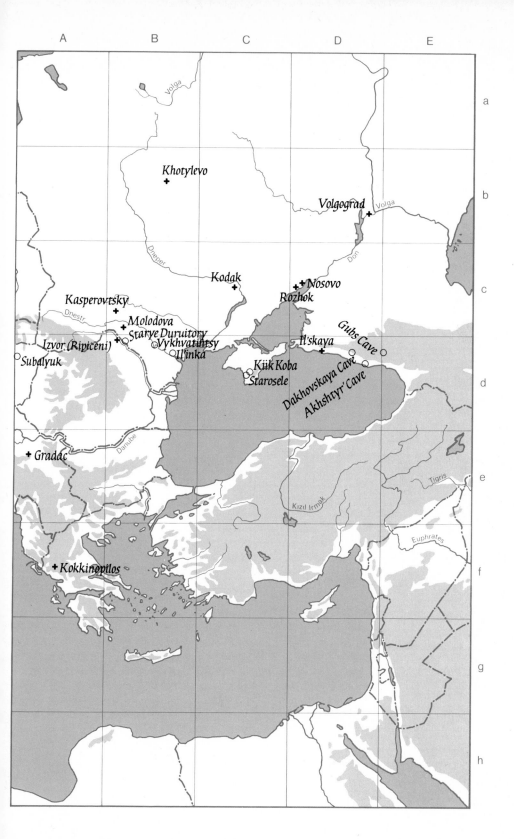

tures are grouped – perhaps wrongly – under the name Mousterian, after the rock shelter at Le Moustier in the Dordogne. Living in caves, begun in the previous (Riss or Saale) glaciation, was now characteristic and we have evidence for long-burning fires; indeed, perhaps it was in the Middle Palaeolithic that man developed sufficient control over fire to permit intensive cave occupation and therefore expansion into the tundra zone north of the temperate forests.

Unlike earlier hominids, Neandertal man buried his dead with some ceremony, although the burials at European sites, such as La Ferrassie, are less elaborate than the most spectacular sites in Asia, like Teshik-Tash.

The term Mousterian is applied to a group of industries which share several important characteristics: the use of flakes struck from a prepared core, and the common occurrence of scrapers, perhaps used for preparing skins. The best known of the several Mousterian industries are: the 'Typical' Mousterian, the Ferrassie and Quina variants (both probably derived from the earlier Charentian tradition), the Mousterian of Acheulian tradition (derived from the Acheulian) and the Denticulate Mousterian. Although these groups were defined in south-west France, they also occur elsewhere in Europe. In Italy an additional variant, the Pontinian, occurs, characterized by tools made from small pebbles.

In a controversial interpretation of the various Mousterian industries Binford has suggested that differences might be explained in functional terms, whilst Bordes and others believe that the variations were determined by partly chronological and partly cultural causes.

FURTHER READING

BINFORD, L. K. and S. R. 1966. A preliminary Analysis of Functional Variability in the Mousterian of Levallois Facies. *American Anthropologist* 68, no. 2, pt. 2, 238–95.
BORDES, F. 1968. *The Old Stone Age*, London and New York.
COLES, J. M. and E. S. HIGGS 1969. *The Archaeology of Early Man*, London and New York.
COLLINS, D. *et al.* 1973. *Background to Archaeology*², London and New York.
MELLARS, P. A. 1969. The Chronology of Mousterian Industries in the Perigord Region. *Proceedings of the Prehistoric Society* 35, 134–71.

Mousterian industries are well represented in the USSR. Sites are concentrated mainly in the Caucasus and the Crimea, but also occur far to the north on the steppes; however, none has been found north of the 49th parallel. Many of the sites are caves, but there are also extremely important open sites as at Sukhaya Mechetka near Volgograd (formerly Stalingrad) and on the Dnestr at Molodova I.

Neandertal remains have been found at several sites. At Kiik Koba in the Crimea an adult and a child were buried in trench graves in a cave, and another Crimean cave, Starosele, contained an infant burial. In the cave of Teshik-Tash in Uzbekistan the body of a Neandertal boy was surrounded by several pairs of goat horns.

Leptolithic cultures are both rich and varied on Russian territory and sites are known in European Russia, the Caucasus, Soviet central Asia and in Siberia. Although archaeologists often apply European designations to Russian finds, industries in the two areas were not closely related. Of particular interest are the open sites of European Russia, which yield industries often described as 'eastern Gravettian', associated with traces of domestic structures. They include Gagarino and several localities at Kostienki on the Don and Pushkari and Mezin in the Desna basin. Dwellings consist of irregular oval hollows, surrounded by piles of large animal bones, usually mammoth. We assume that they had a covering of skins supported on bones and tusks. In Siberia similar structures occur at Mal'ta and Buret'.

'Venus' figurines are relatively common on leptolithic sites; indeed a high proportion of all the known Venuses come from the USSR. By contrast, parietal art has been found at only one site: Kapova Cave in the southern Urals, which contains paintings.

FURTHER READING

BORDES, F. 1968. *The Old Stone Age*, London and New York.
COLES, J. M. and E. S. HIGGS 1969. *The Archaeology of Early Man*, London and New York.
MONGAIT. A. L. 1961. *Archaeology in the USSR*, Harmondsworth and Baltimore.
SULIMIRSKI, T. 1970. *Prehistoric Russia. An Outline*, London and New York.

Middle palaeolithic and leptolithic sites in Russia 37

TINT SHOWS LAND ABOVE 500M

A   B   C   D   E   F

a
b
c
d
e
f
g
h

Creswell Crags

Aveline's Hole
Cheddar
Kent's Cavern

Maisières
Chaleux

Jerzmanowice

Předmosti

Dolní Věstonice/
Pavlov

Pincevent

Vogelherd
Petersfels

Willendorf

Schussenquelle

Arcy-sur-Cure

Angles-sur-l'Anglin

Potočka Zijalka

Les Cottés

Solutré

Betulov Spodmol

Pair-non-Pair

La Madeleine

Colli Berici

Cueva Morín   El Castillo

Salpetrière

Finale Ligure

Crvena Stijena

Isturitz

Niaux

Grimaldi

Grotta Paglicci

Reclau Viver

Monte Circeo

Grotta di Uluzzo
Romanelli

Parpalló

Grotta di San Teodoro

Cueva Ambrosio

Carigüela de Piñar
Hoyo de la Mina
Gibraltar

Levanzo
(Cala dei Genovesi)

Seine

Loire

Rhine

Elbe

Oder

Vistula

Danube

Po

Duero

Ebro

Tagus

Guadalquivir

0 ──────── 500
KILOMETRES

0 ──────── 300
STATUTE MILES

38   *Leptolithic sites in Europe*

Leptolithic sites in Europe

The Upper Palaeolithic, or Leptolithic, of Europe lasted from *c.* 35,000 to 10,000 bc. Leptolithic deposits are often found overlying Mousterian levels of the Middle Palaeolithic, and today many authorities believe that the tool-making traditions of the Leptolithic developed locally out of regional variants of the Mousterian and leptolithic man (of the modern species, *Homo sapiens sapiens*) was the direct descendant of the Neandertalers. Such a view contrasts strongly with the earlier opinion that the leptolithic cultures were brought to Europe by an immigration from the Near East of *H. sapiens*, who wiped out the earlier and 'inferior' Neandertal population.

The Leptolithic is much better understood than any earlier period and archaeologists have worked out detailed regional culture sequences. The most famous is that of south-west France, but comparable sequences are available for regions such as Spain, Italy and eastern Europe.

By any criterion the leptolithic tool-kit was superior to that of the earlier periods: flake tools were replaced by thinner, more regular blades and specialized tools, like the burin (engraver), were invented. Projectile points, sometimes pressure-flaked, indicate the use of the spear. Specialized bone tools also appeared: split- and bevel-based points and, towards the end of the period, barbed harpoons. Before the end of the Leptolithic the bow may have been in use.

The most spectacular achievement of leptolithic man was his art. Cave paintings and engravings occur first in France *c.* 32,000 bc, but by general consent the finest art was produced during the Magdalenian phase, *c.* 14,000–11,000 bc. In addition to cave art, leptolithic societies produced engraved and painted designs on small objects of bone and stone, and carved or modelled figurines in stone, bone and clay.

FURTHER READING

Bordes, F. 1968. *The Old Stone Age*, London and New York.
Coles, J. M. and E. S. Higgs 1969. *The Archaeology of Early Man*, London and New York.
Collins, D. *et al.* 1973. *Background to Archaeology*[2], London and New York.
Ucko, P. and A. Rosenfeld 1967. *Palaeolithic Cave Art*, London and New York.

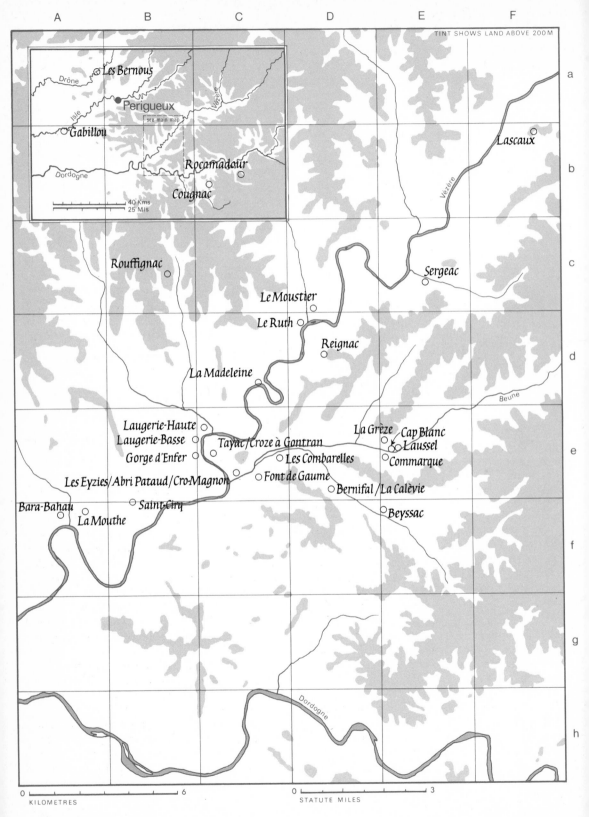

A B C D E F

TINT SHOWS LAND ABOVE 200M

a

Drône
○ Les Bernous
● Perigueux
Isle
see main map
Vézère
Gabillou ○

b
○ Rocamadour
Dordogne
Cougnac ○
40 Kms
25 Mis

Lascaux ○

Rouffignac ○

c
Sergeac ○

Vézère

Le Moustier ○

d
Le Ruth ○

Reignac ○

La Madeleine

Beune

e
Laugerie-Haute ○
Laugerie-Basse ○   Tayac / Croze à Gontran ○
Gorge d'Enfer ○
Les Combarelles ○
Les Eyzies / Abri Pataud / Cro-Magnon ○
Font de Gaume ○
La Grèze ○ Cap Blanc
Laussel
Commarque ○
Bernifal / La Calèvie ○

Bara-Bahau ○   Saint-Cirq ○
La Mouthe
Beyssac ○

f

g

Dordogne

h

0 _____ 6
KILOMETRES

0 _____ 3
STATUTE MILES

40 *Palaeolithic sites in the Dordogne*

Palaeolithic sites in the Dordogne

The Périgord region of south-west France, most of which falls within the Department of Dordogne, contains an exceptionally large number of important palaeolithic sites. The greatest concentration lies in the valley of the Vézère, near the village of Les Eyzies. Although many open sites also exist, the area is especially famous for its caves and rock shelters, many of which contain art. In addition to their intrinsic importance, many sites in the Dordogne have historical significance in the development of palaeolithic studies. These sites were first investigated systematically in the 1860s. In 1863 the French geologist Edouard Lartet began a series of excavations in the Dordogne in collaboration with the English banker and ethnologist, Henry Christy. The two men's express intention was to work out the sequence of archaeological cultures (and thereby the course of man's development) through the examination of stratified deposits containing artifacts and other remains. This approach, now commonplace, was at that time revolutionary. Indeed we realize how forward-looking was the approach of Lartet and Christy when we remember that in 1863 it was only four years since the antiquity of man had been accepted – and by no means unanimously.

Lartet and Christy were remarkably successful. From finds at a number of sites they constructed a sequence of leptolithic cultures. At Le Moustier they extended the sequence backwards in time, first to the Middle Palaeolithic (for this became the type site of the Mousterian culture) and later to the Lower Palaeolithic, for they discovered deposits with hand-axes comparable with those from the gravels of the Somme and the Thames. This was the first detailed sequence of palaeolithic cultures and, although we know now that it does not have the universal validity assumed by Lartet and Christy, it was a considerable achievement.

The sites of the Dordogne were the scene of further important discoveries thirty years later when the authenticity of cave paintings was hotly disputed. Although the paintings at Altamira had been published in 1880, they were widely re-garded as fraudulent. However in 1894–5 engravings of undoubted authenticity were found at La Mouthe: the lower parts of the engravings were actually covered by undisturbed leptolithic deposits. The discovery was a turning point in the dispute over the authenticity of leptolithic art.

FURTHER READING

BIBBY, G. 1956, 1957. *The Testimony of the Spade*, New York and London.
DANIEL, G. 1950. *A Hundred Years of Archaeology*, London and New York.
LARTET, E. and H. CHRISTY 1865–75. *Reliquiae Aquitanicae*, London.
SIEVEKING, A. and G. 1962. *The Caves of France and Northern Spain: a guide*, London.

Leptolithic art
see map pp. 42/43

The art of the Leptolithic falls into three main categories: *cave* or *parietal art*, comprising paintings and engravings on the walls and roofs of caves and rock shelters; *mobiliary art* (French: *art mobilier*), comprising paintings and engravings – nearly always the latter – on tools and other small objects of stone, bone and ivory; and *figurines*, comprising animals and human females (the latter known as 'venuses') carved in stone, bone or ivory and occasionally modelled in clay. Such effigies may also take the form of larger clay models and rock reliefs.

The region most rich in leptolithic art, especially in engraved and painted caves, is the Franco-Cantabrian area (see map on p. 44), but sites occur in other parts of the Mediterranean basin: elsewhere in Iberia (e.g. Parpalló and Escoural) and in Sicily and the Italian mainland (e.g. Levanzo, Addaura, Romanelli and Paglicci caves). Also, cave art has been found much farther east, in the

TINT SHOWS LAND ABOVE 500 M

Balver Höhle
Maszycka
Trou de Chaleux
Oberkassel
Andernach
Předmosti
Trou Magrite
Pekarna
Pavlov/
Klause
Dolní Věstonice
Hohlenstein
Vogelherd
Arcy-sur-Cure
Petersfels/Kesserloch/Schweizersbild
Saint-Marcel
Solutré
La Colombière
Roc de Sers
Le Veyrier
Lascaux
Les Hoteaux
La Ferrassie
Pech-Merle
Ebbou/Oullins/Chabot
Très Colombres
Covalanas
Bruniquel
La Baume Latrone
Isturitz
Altamira
Niaux
Tuc d'Audoubert
Tivoli
Paglicci
Casares
Monopoli
Romanelli
Maltravieso
Parpalló
Escoural
Addaura
Pileta
Ardales
Levanzo
Niscemi
Cala
Nerja
Palomas

Seine
Loire
Rhine
Elbe
Oder
Vistula
Danube
Po
Duero
Ebro
Tagus
Guadalquivir

0   500
KILOMETRES

0   300
STATUTE MILES

42   Leptolithic art

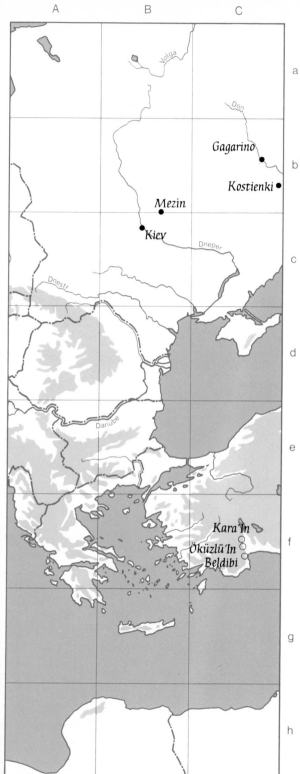

Kapova Cave in the southern Urals and in southern Anatolia in the caves of Kara'In and Oküzlü'In and the rock shelter of Beldibi. Venus figurines have an even wider distribution, from Siberia (e.g. Buret' and Mal'ta) to western Europe. Mobiliary art is found in all the areas where cave art or figurines occur.

The earliest leptolithic art probably dates from before 30,000 bc, and it continued until at least the beginning of the Neothermal period. Indeed in several areas, but not the central Franco-Cantabrian zone, art of leptolithic type was produced in the 'Mesolithic'.

The motivation of leptolithic art has been much discussed. Although mobiliary art may have been primarily decorative, both cave art, which is often hidden in dark and barely accessible recesses, and venuses with their exaggerated breasts, buttocks and swollen bellies suggest a ritual function. Indeed it is generally held that venuses were associated with a cult of fertility, while cave art, with its preoccupation with animals, should be explained in terms of hunting magic – a pattern of behaviour abundantly documented in the ethnographic record.

FURTHER READING

GIEDION, S. 1962. *The Eternal Present*, Oxford and New York.
GRAZIOSI, P. 1956. *L'Arte dell'Antica Età della Pietra*, Florence.
LEROI-GOURHAN, A. 1965. *Préhistoire de l'Art Occidental*, Paris.
UCKO, P. and A. ROSENFELD 1967. *Palaeolithic Cave Art*, London and New York.

43

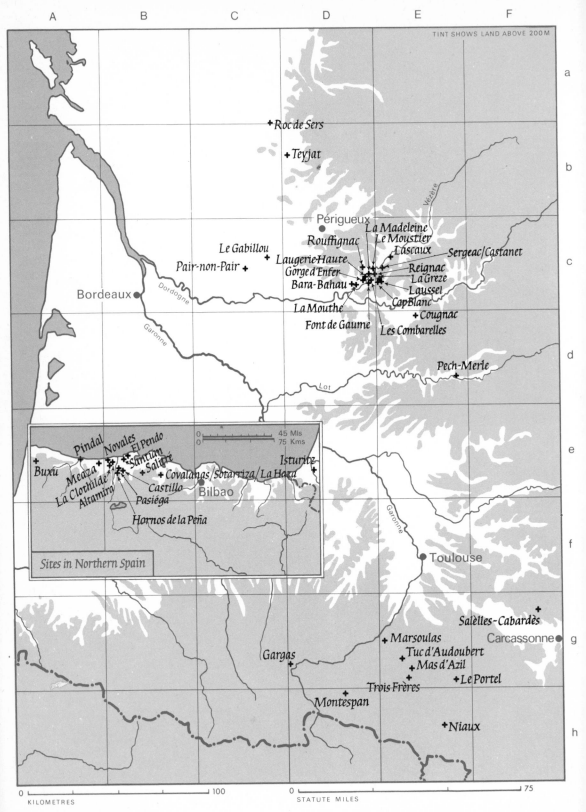

A   B   C   D   E   F

a

+ *Roc de Sers*

+ *Teyjat*

b

Vézère

Périgueux

+ *La Madeleine*
+ *Le Moustier*

Rouffignac + + *Lascaux*

+ *Le Gabillou* + *Sergeac/Castanet*

Pair-non-Pair + + *Laugerie-Haute*
+ *Reignac*
Gorge d'Enfer + *La Greze*
Bara-Bahau + + *Laussel*

Bordeaux + *Cap Blanc*

Dordogne

+ *La Mouthe* + *Cougnac*

Garonne

Font de Gaume + + *Les Combarelles*

c

d

+ *Pech-Merle*

Lot

Sites in Northern Spain

0   45 Mls
0   75 Kms

Pindal *Novales* *El Pendo*
+ + + *Santian*
Buxu *Meaza* *Salitré* + *Isturitz*
+ *La Clothilde* + *Covalanas/Sotarriza/La Haza*
Altamira *Castillo*
Pasiega Bilbao

Hornos de la Peña

Garonne

e

f

Toulouse

+ *Salèlles-Cabardès*

+ *Marsoulas*
Gargas + *Tuc d'Audoubert* Carcassonne
+ *Mas d'Azil*

Trois Frères + + *Le Portel*

g

Montespan +

+ *Niaux*

h

0 ———————————— 100
KILOMETRES

0 ——————— 75
STATUTE MILES

Franco-Cantabrian art

Cave art is perhaps the most spectacular achievement of the leptolithic cultures of Europe and the most abundant and magnificent examples occur in the Franco-Cantabrian region. More than one hundred decorated caves are known in this area – the great majority in southern France – and the number of sites which have yielded portable decorated objects (mobiliary art) is even greater.

The earliest representational art is found in the Aurignacian I stage, dating from before 30,000 bc. It includes animals engraved in outline or painted in red or black without perspective (e.g. Castanet and Covalanas). During the later Aurignacian and Perigordian phases (c. 29,000–20,000 bc) the quality of both engraving and painting improved and the first 'Venuses' appeared. We know little about the art of the succeeding Solutrean stage, although the large bas-reliefs at Roc de Sers and other sites belong to this period.

However, the climax of artistic activity came in the Magdalenian period (c. 16,000–10,000 bc) and many of the most important decorated caves – Altamira, Les Combarelles, Niaux, Font de Gaume – are of this date. The paintings at Lascaux may be earlier, but the evidence is not clear. Magdalenian art was often highly accomplished: artists mastered the use of perspective, they produced polychrome paintings and complete scenes now filled whole walls or ceilings, where previously isolated animals were drawn with no sense of composition. Mobiliary art was also both common and elaborate and we have several Magdalenian bas-reliefs, such as those at Cap Blanc and Angles-sur-l'Anglin. Indeed, the abundance of art in the late Magdalenian caves conveys an impression of hunting communities living under exceptionally favourable environmental conditions – an impression borne out by the evidence concerning the climate and the economy of the Magdalenians and by the fact that when conditions changed art virtually disappeared. Thus, in the mesolithic Azilian culture which succeeded the Magdalenian in the Franco-Cantabrian region, the only vestiges of art were pebbles engraved or painted with simple geometric motifs; cave art had vanished.

FURTHER READING

BREUIL, H. and F. WINDELS 1952. *Four Hundred Centuries of Cave Art*, Montignac.
GIEDION, S. 1962. *The Eternal Present*, Oxford and New York.
GRAZIOSI, P. 1956. *L'Arte dell'Antica Età della Pietra*, Florence.
LEROI-GOURHAN, A. 1965. *Préhistoire de l'Art Occidental*, Paris.
UCKO, P. and A. ROSENFELD 1967. *Palaeolithic Cave Art*, London and New York.

'Venuses' and other leptolithic figurines
see map pp. 46/47

Over sixty female statuettes of the Leptolithic period, known as 'Venuses', have been found in Europe and Asia. The focus of distribution is eastern central Europe: Austria, Czechoslovakia and East Germany, where the earliest examples occur. Here also are some of the best known find-spots, including Dolní Věstonice, Pavlov, Předmostí and Willendorf. Venuses also occur farther west, in France (e.g. Lespugue) and Italy (e.g. Savignano), and farther east, in the Ukraine (e.g. Kostienki) and Siberia, where several highly stylized examples are known (e.g. Mal'ta). The figurines are associated with the culture still usually known as the Gravettian in eastern Europe and Italy and as the Perigordian (but formerly Gravettian) in France. In the east, Venuses were being made before c. 25,000 bc, while in France they occur first in the Noailles stage of the Perigordian sequence, dated c. 25,000–21,000 bc.

Leptolithic figurines are made of mammoth ivory, soft stone or (as in some cases in Czechoslovakia and Russia) of clay mixed with ash and hardened by fire. Usually the figurines are

'Venuses' and other leptolithic figurines

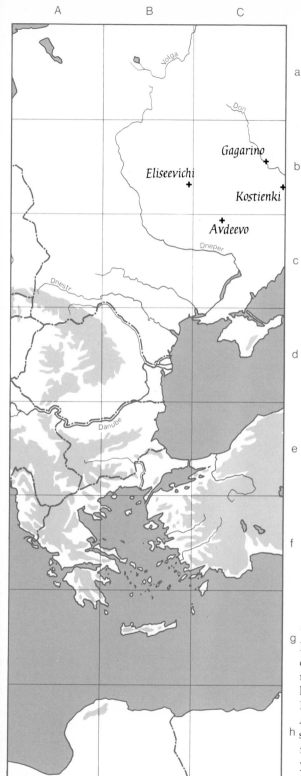

modelled in the round. The Venuses are nearly always naked, their faces are either featureless or nearly so and the breasts, buttocks and abdomen are emphasized; many are clearly pregnant. It is generally agreed that they indicate a fertility cult. Although most figurines take this form, there are exceptions. For instance, a Venus from Předmostí is not modelled at all, but consists of an engraved ivory rod, while on two miniature female heads from Dolní Věstonice and Brassempouy (France) the facial features are clearly defined.

In the central area, especially Moravia, we find animal figurines made of ivory or clay, including mammoth, bear, ibex, lion and horse. Like the Venuses, the famous limestone relief at Laussel (France), which depicts a fat lady holding a horn, presumably relates to a leptolithic fertility cult.

FURTHER READING

CLARK, G. 1969. *World Prehistory: a New Outline*², London and New York.
COLLINS, D. *et al.* 1973. *Background to Archaeology*², London and New York.
NEUSTUPNY, J. and E. 1961. *Czechoslovakia before the Slavs*, London and New York.
POWELL, T. G. E. 1966. *Prehistoric Art*, London and New York.

Post-glacial hunters and gatherers in Europe

see map pp. 48/49

The Würm glaciation came to an end and the Flandrian stage of the Neothermal period began *c.* 8300 bc. As the temperature rose, the ice sheets retreated, revealing extensive new territories for human exploitation. In the low-lying areas of Europe, forest rapidly replaced open grassland. After the end of the Pleistocene, hunting cultures survived until the introduction of farming, i.e. for some 3000 years in eastern Europe, 4000 years in most of western Europe and for even

TINT SHOWS LAND ABOVE 500 M

Oban
Morton
Larne
Star Carr
Peacock's Farm
Thatcham
+ Broxbourne
Farnham
Horsham
Fère-en-Tardenois
Téviec
Hoëdic
Rouffignac
Sauveterre-la-Lémance
Mas d'Azil
Cogul
Barranco de Valltorta
Prado del Navazo
Cueva de la Cocina
Parpalló
Minateda
Muge
Hoyo de la Mina

Ertebølle
Klosterlund
Mullerup
(Maglemose)
Bromme
Holmegaard
Duvensee
Stellmoor
+ Pesse
Janislawice
Zatýni
Ofnet
Sered'
Birsmatten-Basishöhle
Betulov Spodmol
Grotta Azzurra di
Samartorza
Colli Berici
Arene Candide
Crvena Stijena
Gudnja
Grotta Maritza
Grotta delle Mura
Monte Circeo
Grotta la Porta
Termini Imerese
Grotta Corruggi

Duero
Tagus
Guadalquivir
Ebro
Seine
Loire
Rhine
Po
Elbe
Oder
Vistula
Danube

0   500
KILOMETRES

0   300
STATUTE MILES

48 *Post-glacial hunters and gatherers in Europe*

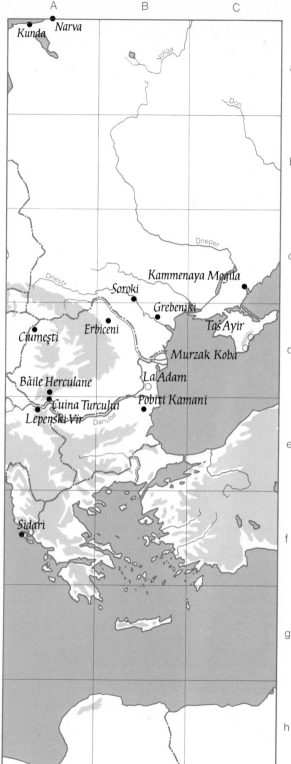

longer in the extreme north and west of the continent. This continuation of hunting and gathering economies in the Flandrian period took several regional forms, usually described collectively as the 'Mesolithic'.

In the main centres of the Leptolithic, such as south-west France and the middle Danube, the disappearance of the grasslands which had supported vast herds of grazing animals probably led to a considerable decline in population and certainly to the abandonment of many features of late leptolithic culture, notably art. Thus the Azilian, Sauveterrian and Tardenoisian cultures of the Flandrian are impoverished in comparison with the Magdalenian. In northern Europe, round the shores of the Baltic and the North Sea, various adaptations to the new forest environment appeared (the Maglemosean in the west and the Kunda culture in the east), characterized by axes and other wood-working tools. Other groups concentrated on gathering shellfish. Perhaps the best known of these is the Ertebølle ('kitchen midden') culture of Denmark, but shellfish-gatherers also existed in Scotland, Ireland and Brittany and on the shores of the Mediterranean in Iberia, southern France and Italy.

Two significant developments took place in the Flandrian period: the widespread adoption of the bow, which is first reliably attested in Europe at Stellmoor in north Germany in very late glacial times, and the domestication of the dog (which is represented *c.* 7500 bc at Star Carr in eastern England). Both innovations led to improved hunting techniques, but no far-reaching culture change.

FURTHER READING

CLARK, G. 1936. *The Mesolithic Settlement of Northern Europe*, Cambridge.

CLARK, G. and S. PIGGOTT 1965. *Prehistoric Societies*, London and New York.

COLLINS, D. *et al.* 1973. *Background to Archaeology*[2], London and New York.

KOZŁOWSKI, S. K. (ed.) 1973. *The Mesolithic in Europe*, Warsaw.

TRINGHAM, R. 1971. *Hunters, Fishers and Farmers of Eastern Europe 6000–3000 BC*, London.

Africa

The period in which Africa made a unique contribution to human development was the Early Palaeolithic; indeed, the emergence of man himself and the first million years or more of his development apparently took place in Africa, and Africa alone. In the later Pleistocene and the Neothermal period the continent lost this leading role and in some ways (for example in its technology) Sub-Saharan Africa remained backward in comparison with other regions. Nevertheless, one of the earliest civilizations in the world, that of Egypt, arose in Africa and flourished there for some three millennia.

In the early Neothermal period the characteristic stone industries were microlithic and they occur in most parts of the continent. They were produced by bands of hunters and gatherers adapting to the increasingly warm climatic conditions. Of particular interest is the development in the Nile valley, where the population increased sharply in the late Pleistocene and early Neothermal, probably because groups abandoned the surrounding desert as food resources diminished. In addition to hunting buffalo, hartebeeste, gazelle and hippopotamus, sedentary communities along the Nile caught fish and gathered wild cereals.

Unfortunately there is a gap in our knowledge of the culture sequence in the Nile valley between the microlithic industries and the earliest agricultural communities, dated to the mid-fifth millennium bc in the Faiyum. It seems unlikely, however, that food production was invented independently in Egypt, since the earliest domesticated species – wheat, barley, sheep and goats – are indigenous not to Africa, but to western Asia. It seems probable, therefore, that farming was introduced from the early agricultural centres in Asia. However, the sedentary economy of the earlier Nile communities and their exploitation of wild cereals may have predisposed them to adopt farming with alacrity. The neolithic inhabitants of the Faiyum not only cultivated emmer wheat and flax and bred sheep, goats, cattle and swine, but also continued to hunt and fish. The earliest occupation at Merimde, a settlement of wattle-and-daub houses on the edge of the Delta, also belongs to the fifth millennium bc. There were other communities of simple farmers in Upper Egypt; the best known site is the settlement and cemetery at Badari.

The food-producing economy appeared relatively early throughout north Africa. It existed in Cyrenaica by 4800 BC and in the Maghrib during the fourth millennium bc. In these areas communities kept sheep and goats and used pottery, but we have no evidence that they practised agriculture. Their tool-kits show continuity with earlier traditions and it is thought that no significant population change occurred. The introduction of stock-rearing and pottery was probably due to diffusion, either westwards from the Nile or south from the islands and peninsulas of the Mediterranean.

While the rest of Africa was occupied by pastoralists and hunters and gatherers, the civilization of Dynastic Egypt developed in the Nile valley. The Predynastic period, which lasted for most of the fourth millennium BC and apparently developed directly out of the local Neolithic, is usually divided into two stages: Naqada I (or Amratian) and Naqada II (or Gerzean). Throughout the period technology and economy improved and society became more complex. Thus, by the end of Naqada II a wealthy society had come into existence, stratified into classes and with marked economic specialization. The Predynastic period ended c. 3200 BC with the unification of Upper and Lower Egypt, allegedly by the legendary ruler Menes, who founded the first dynasty of pharaohs. The ensuing Dynastic period saw the arrival of true civilization, characterized by writing, monumental art and architecture and other sophisticated traits. The degree to which contact with Mesopotamia influenced, or even brought about, the emergence of Egyptian civilization has long provoked controversy. The undoubted presence of Mesopotamian features, especially decorative motifs, in the period immediately preceding the unification of Upper and Lower Egypt shows that there was *some* influence; on the other hand, mature Egyptian civilization possessed a distinctive character, having little in common with those of Asia. Indeed, Mesopotamian influence may have acted simply as a catalyst, which stimulated a process which had already begun in the Nile valley.

The civilization of Dynastic Egypt lasted for two and a half millennia and its main elements were preserved for almost another thousand years in the Meroitic kingdom on the Upper Nile. It changed remarkably little during this long history; isolated in a rich environment surrounded by desert and having achieved a successful ecological and social equilibrium, the Egyptians had little incentive to change. While this extra-ordinary conservatism enabled the civilization to survive, it did restrict its influence on other cultures. Indeed, the prehistory of most of Africa remained almost totally free of Egyptian influence.

The practice of farming in one form or another gradually spread over most of the continent. During the fifth and fourth millennia bc the Sahara was occupied by 'neolithic' pastoralists who bred cattle, sheep and goats, but who also hunted extensively. These pastoralists probably did not practise agriculture. Much of our knowledge of their activities is derived from the paintings and engravings they made on rock faces. Increasing desiccation of the Sahara in the third millennium bc caused the displacement of many pastoralist groups.

In west Africa traits which are often termed 'neolithic', such as pottery and ground stone axes, appeared in the third millennium bc. Although we have no direct evidence, it is thought that the inhabitants may also have engaged in farming. It is suggested, largely on analogy with later cultures in the region, that third-millennium communities may have grown indigenous millets, sorghum and Guinea rice. In the rain forests, yam and oil palm may have been domesticated early. Domesticated animals, however, would have been of ultimately Asian origin – sheep, goats and cattle.

Meanwhile, a pastoralist economy spread southwards from the Sudan into the Horn of Africa, Kenya and adjacent regions. This probably occurred in the second and first millennia bc.

Except for Egypt and Mauritania (where copper ores were exploited from an early date), Africa passed directly from the Stone Age to the Iron Age. Iron was used in the first millennium BC both in the Nile valley and in the Phoenician colonies on the Mediterranean coast. Iron metallurgy may have reached most of the African continent by way of the Meroitic kingdom in the Nile valley, bringing with it improved means of forest clearance (thus encouraging the spread of agriculture) as well as more efficient equipment for hunting and warfare. One of the earliest iron-using cultures in Sub-Saharan Africa was the Nok culture of Nigeria, which developed in the last few centuries bc. Elsewhere iron-working appeared in the first millennium AD.

In the late prehistoric period Africa received influences from several directions. The north coast was incorporated in successive Mediterranean civilizations; the coast of east Africa and Malagasy were influenced by traders and settlers from elsewhere in the Indian Ocean: Arabia, the Persian Gulf, even Indonesia. In the fifteenth century the Portuguese established factories all round the African coast. In spite of these influences on the coast, the vast hinterland of Africa continued to support cultures which were distinctively African. The Zimbabwe culture of Rhodesia, for example, whatever diffusionists and white racialists may claim, is wholly African in character, although some believe that the monumental architecture (which is later than *c.* AD 1200) may have been inspired by Arabian prototypes (which are considerably earlier).

FURTHER READING

ALDRED, C. 1961. *The Egyptians*, London and New York.
ALIMEN, H. 1957. *The prehistory of Africa* (transl. A. H. Broderick), London.
CHILDE, V. G. 1952. *New Light on the Most Ancient East* (revised edn), London and New York.
CLARK, J. D. 1970. *The Prehistory of Africa*, London and New York.
FAGAN, B. M. 1965. *Southern Africa during the Iron Age*, London and New York.
MCBURNEY, C. B. M. 1960. *The Stone Age of northern Africa*, Harmondsworth.

Late Stone Age and neolithic sites

During the late Pleistocene and early Neothermal periods Africa was occupied by various specialized hunting and gathering groups, most of whom produced microlithic stone industries. The earliest rock art of the Sahara may have been created by hunting and gathering groups before *c.* 5000 bc.

The practice of farming, introduced from western Asia, appeared early in north Africa, from *c.* 5000 bc, but was slow to spread south of the Sahara. It appeared in the savanna belt in the third, and in east Africa in the second millennium bc. The equatorial forest was colonized by farmers only in the first millennium bc, while in southern Africa agriculture arrived at approximately the same time as iron, in the early centuries A D. In many areas, especially in the south, 'stone age' communities who lived by hunting and gathering survived alongside iron-using farmers until very recent times. These late hunting communities in Tanzania, Rhodesia, south and southwest Africa have left an impressive pictorial record in the form of abundant paintings and engravings on rock faces and in caves.

In the Nile valley the introduced farming economy which became the basis on which Egyptian civilization grew, was of specifically Asiatic type with all the important domesticates indigenous to Asia. West of the Nile valley, in the Sahara, Cyrenaica and the Maghrib, the Neolithic took a pastoralist form, based on the rearing of sheep and goats and sometimes cattle. There is no evidence that agriculture was practised till a late date. South-east of the Nile valley, in the Horn of Africa and in Kenya, neolithic communities also practised pastoralism, and we have no firm evidence of agriculture.

The situation was different in other parts of the continent. It seems probable, though unproven, that the earliest Neolithic in the savanna belt was already based on the cultivation of local plants, including millets, sorghum and Guinea rice, while in the west African rain forests indigenous yams and oil palms may also have been cultivated at an early date. It was these African plants, as well as others of south Asian origin (different yams, taro and bananas), introduced through the Arab entrepots of the east coast, that were cultivated in southern Africa during the Iron Age.

FURTHER READING

ALIMEN, H. 1957. *The prehistory of Africa* (transl. A. H. Broderick), London.
CLARK, J. D. 1967. *Atlas of African Prehistory*, Chicago.
——— 1970. *The Prehistory of Africa*, London and New York.
DAVIES, O., H. J. HUGOT and D. SEDDON 1968. Origins of African agriculture. *Current Anthropology* 9, 479–509.
McBURNEY, C. B. M. 1967. *The Haua Fteah (Cyrenaica) and the Stone Age of the South-east Mediterranean*, Cambridge.

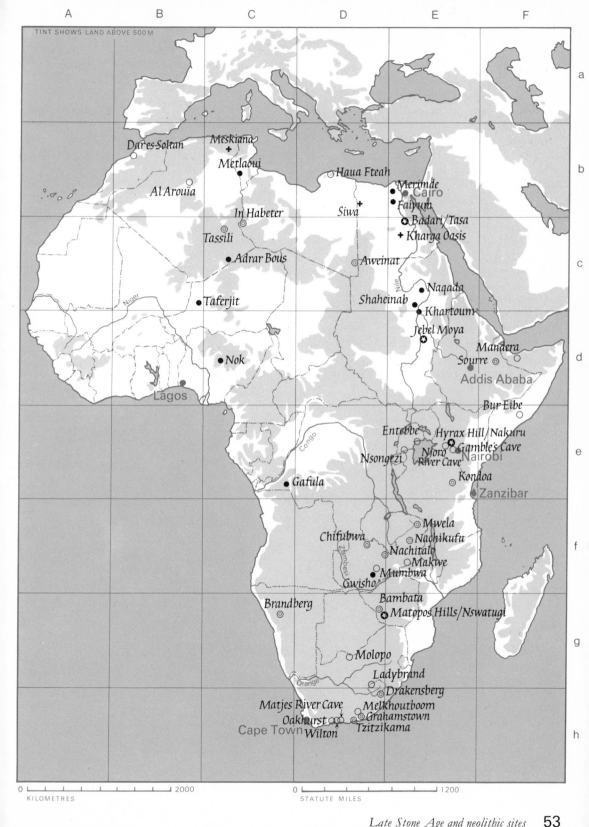

TINT SHOWS LAND ABOVE 500M

A B C D E F

a

b

Dar es-Soltan

Meskiana +

Metlaoui

Haua Fteah

Al Arouïa

Merimde
Cairo
Faiyum

In Habeter

Siwa

Badari/Tasa

Kharga Oasis +

Tassili

Adrar Bous

Aweinat

c

Taferjit

Shaheinab

Naqada

Khartoum

Jebel Moya

Nok

Mandera
Sourre

d

Lagos

Addis Ababa

Bur Eibe

Entebbe

Hyrax Hill/Nakuru
Gamble's Cave

Nsongezi

Njoro
River Cave
Nairobi

Kondoa

e

Gafula

Zanzibar

Mwela
Nachikufu

Chifubwa

Nachitalo

Makwe

Mumbwa

f

Gwisho

Brandberg

Bambata
Matopos Hills/Nswatugi

Molopo

g

Ladybrand
Drakensberg

Matjes River Cave

Melkhoutboom
Grahamstown

Oakhurst

Cape Town

Wilton

Tzitzikama

h

0 ——————— 2000
KILOMETRES

0 ——————— 1200
STATUTE MILES

Late Stone Age and neolithic sites 53

Iron Age and recent sites

Iron-working was introduced to Africa from western Asia in the first half of the first millennium BC: the Phoenicians used it in their colonies along the north coast and the Assyrians brought it to Egypt, whence it spread up the Nile to the kingdom of Meroe. It may have been from Meroe that iron-working spread to most of the continent, though it could also have been carried across the Sahara by nomadic groups or invented locally. The first iron-using group known in Sub-Saharan Africa is the Nigerian Nok culture, which flourished between c. 500 bc and AD 200. Elsewhere iron-working appeared in the first few centuries AD, in association with dimple-based pottery in Kenya, Ruanda, Uganda and Tanzania, and with channelled ware in Zambia and Rhodesia. In southern Africa the earliest iron-using peoples belong to the ninth or tenth centuries AD; here farming and iron-working seem to have been introduced at the same time. Indeed it may have been the use of iron that first made farming sufficiently easy in these areas to compete with hunting and gathering as a way of life. Hunting and gathering communities in fact survived alongside farming ones until very recent times, continuing to produce abundant rock art.

From the first millennium BC the northern part of the continent was largely civilized: the coastal fringe and Egypt were incorporated in the successive Mediterranean civilizations, while the Meroitic state flourished on the upper Nile and the Axumite kingdom developed in Ethiopia. Farther south, however, 'prehistoric' societies survived until the colonial era. After c. AD 1000 this area was characterized by the growth of powerful centralized autocracies. The best known groups are the Luba and Luanda empires of the Katanga and Kasai, the kingdom of Kongo and the empire of Monomatapa. The most important site of the last group is Zimbabwe, which was occupied throughout the Rhodesian Iron Age, from its beginnings as a small village before AD 300 through the phase associated with the empire of Monomatapa with its impressive stone architecture, into the Portuguese period and until 1833, when the settlement was finally destroyed.

Communities such as that at Zimbabwe traded local ivory, tortoise-shell, gold, iron and slaves first with the Arab communities on the east coast and later with the Portuguese. However, the cultural influence of the Arabs and Portuguese was marked only on the coast; the cultures of the interior remained wholly African until very recent times.

FURTHER READING

ARKELL, A. J., B. FAGAN and R. SUMMERS 1966. The Iron Age in Sub-Saharan Africa. *Current Anthropology* 7, 451–84.

CLARK, J. D. 1970. *The Prehistory of Africa*, London and New York.

FAGAN, B. M. 1965. *Southern Africa during the Iron Age*, London and New York.

GARLAKE, P. S. 1973. *Great Zimbabwe*, London and New York.

SHINNIE, P. L. 1967. *Meroe. A Civilisation of the Sudan*, London and New York.

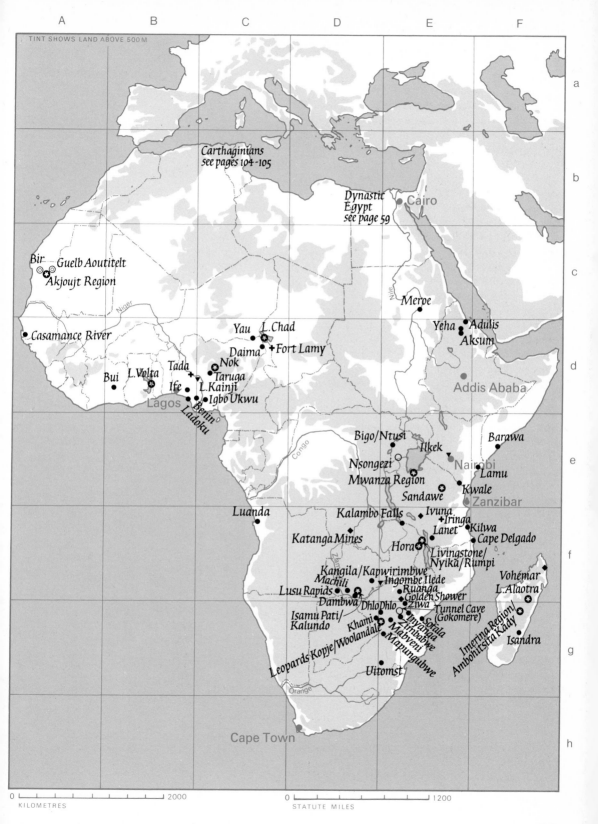

TINT SHOWS LAND ABOVE 500M

Carthaginians
see pages 104-105

Dynastic
Egypt
see page 59

Cairo

Bir
Guelb Aoutitelt
Akjoujt Region

Meroe

Yau L.Chad
Daima Fort Lamy

Yeha Adulis
Aksum

Casamance River

Addis Ababa

Tada Nok
Bui L.Volta Taruga
Ife L.Kainji
Benin Igbo Ukwu
Lagos Ladoku

Barawa

Bigo/Ntusi Ilek
Nsongezi Nairobi
Mwanza Region Lamu
Sandawe Kwale
Zanzibar

Luanda

Kalambo Falls Ivuna
Katanga Mines Iringa
Hora Lanet
Livingstone/ Kilwa
Nyika/Rumpi Cape Delgado

Kangila/Kapwirimbwe
Machili Ingombe Ilede Vohémar
Lusu Rapids Ruanga L.Alaotra
Dambwa Golden Shower
Isamu Pati/ Dhlo Dhlo Ziwa
Kalundo Khami Inyanga Tunnel Cave
Leopards Kopje/Woolandale Mabveni (Gokomere)
Mapungubwe Zimbabwe Imerina Region/ Isandra
Sofala Ambohitsita Kādy

Uitomst

Cape Town

Iron Age and recent sites 55

0   2000
KILOMETRES

0   1200
STATUTE MILES

Predynastic Egypt

The latest palaeolithic inhabitants of the Nile valley, known from such sites as Abd el-Qadir and Jebel Sahaba and dated between *c.* 15,000 and 8000 bc, were hunters, fishermen and collectors. By *c.* 12,500 some communities may have developed relatively stable settlements, supported by the intensive exploitation of natural resources. Thus, while certain sites indicate an emphasis on fishing (e.g. Catfish Cave), others depended largely on wild cereals (e.g. near Kom Ombo); site 117 at Jebel Sahaba is a cemetery with 58 burials, and similar, but smaller, cemeteries are known from other contemporary sites. In the immediately post-Pleistocene period some groups probably began to experiment with incipient domestication of local plants and animals, a situation that recalls the sequence of events in western Asia.

By the later sixth millennium bc, agricultural settlements, apparently with flimsy palm-frond and matting huts, are well-attested in both Lower and Upper Egypt. In Lower Egypt, the Faiyum A settlements (with C^{14} dates of 4441–3860 bc) contained underground grain silos lined with matting and the bones of domesticated cattle and sheep/goat, while Merimde (with C^{14} dates beginning 4300 bc) apparently extended over an area of 180,000 square metres. In Upper Egypt, where more evidence (but little in the way of carbon dates) is available, we have a sequence of three main cultures: Badari, Amri (Naqada I) and Gerza (Naqada II). The Badari culture was broadly contemporary with Faiyum A and the Merimde settlement. Several settlements are known and these reveal that hunting and fishing still played a significant role in the economy, while among the domesticated plants emmer was important. During the period of the Naqada I and II cultures (with C^{14} dates of 3794–2270 bc) large settlements evolved, probably supported by intensive irrigation agriculture.

FURTHER READING

ALDRED, C. 1965. *Egypt to the End of the Old Kingdom*, London and New York.
ARKELL, A. J. and P. J. UCKO 1965. Review of Predynastic Development in the Nile Valley. *Current Anthropology* 6, 145–66.
CHILDE, V. G. 1952. *New Light on the Most Ancient East* (revised edn), London and New York.
CLARK, J. D. 1971. A Re-examination of the Evidence for Agricultural Origins in the Nile Valley. *Proceedings of the Prehistoric Society* 37, 34–79.

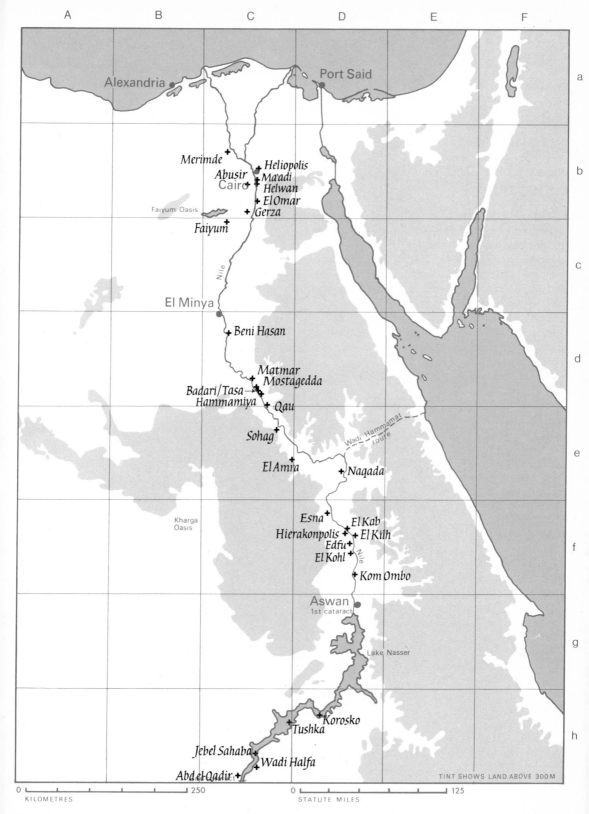

A B C D E F

a

Alexandria   Port Said

b

Merimde
Heliopolis
Abuṣir   Ma'adi
Cairo   Helwan
El Omar
Faiyum Oasis   Gerza
Faiyum

Nile

c

El Minya

Beni Hasan

d

Matmar
Mostagedda
Badari/Tasa →
Hammamiya   Qau

Sohag

Wadi Hammamat route

e

El Amra   Naqada

Kharga
Oasis

Esna   El Kab
Hierakonpolis   El Kilh
Edfu
El Kohl   Nile

f

Kom Ombo

Aswan
1st cataract

g

Lake Nasser

h

Korosko
Tushka

Jebel Sahaba
Wadi Halfa
Abd el-Qadir

TINT SHOWS LAND ABOVE 300M

0   250
KILOMETRES

0   125
STATUTE MILES

Predynastic Egypt   **57**

Dynastic Egypt

During the late Gerzean period (*c.* 3400–3200 BC) the rival kingdoms of Upper and Lower Egypt emerged in the Nile valley and the Delta region. Monumental architecture and the first rudimentary hieroglyphs appeared, while cylinder seals and other objects point to stimulating contacts with western Asia.

The two kingdoms were unified *c.* 3200 BC by a ruler from Upper Egypt, traditionally known as Menes. Egyptologists identify Menes with Narmer, who erected monuments at Hierakonpolis and Abydos. Herodotus recounts that Menes founded Memphis at the frontier between Upper and Lower Egypt. The first two dynasties of pharaohs constitute what is usually known as the Archaic Period. Among its chief surviving monuments are royal burials at Saqqara, and a notable invention was papyrus.

In the succeeding Old Kingdom (Dynasties III–VI, *c.* 2660–2180 BC) Egypt began to exert influence beyond her frontiers, especially in Palestine. At home, massive building projects indicate strong central control; in Dynasty III Djoser's step pyramid was built at Saqqara, and in Dynasty IV the great pyramids of Giza and Maidum.

The First Intermediate Period (Dynasties VII–X, *c.* 2180–2080 BC) was marked by grave internal dissent and incursions from Libya and Sinai. It was followed by the Middle Kingdom (Dynasties XI–XIII, *c.* 2080–1640 BC), during which stability was restored by pharaohs who ruled from Thebes, although in Dynasty XII the capital was moved to El Lisht. Once again the frontiers were secured and under Sesostris III Egyptian forces advanced up the Nile, while a chain of forts was built on the Asian frontier. Trade with Palestine, Syria and Crete flourished. Among the pharaohs who carried out ambitious building projects in places such as Heliopolis, Thebes and other cities, was Sesostris I.

In the Second Intermediate Period (Dynasties XIV–XVII, *c.* 1640–1570 BC) Egypt was disrupted by the so-called Hyksos – apparently not the 'Shepherd Kings' described by Manetho (*c.* 250 BC), but Semitic immigrants who set up a short-lived state in Lower Egypt. Among other crafts the Hyksos introduced bronze technology to the Nile valley.

With the New Kingdom (Dynasties XVIII–XV, *c.* 1570–1075 BC) Egypt was reunited and under Tuthmosis III the Egyptians began a series of campaigns in Palestine. However, in the twelfth century BC, convulsions in the Levant and the invasions of the 'sea peoples' forced the Egyptians back to their former frontier. Thanks partly to the spectacular contents of Tutankhamun's tomb, the New Kingdom impresses us as a period of sophistication and wealth. In the Late Period (Dynasties XXI–XXXI, 1075–332 BC), on the other hand, Egypt decayed under the impact of Assyrian and Persian invasions.

FURTHER READING

ALDRED, C. 1961. *The Egyptians*, London and New York.

CERNY, J. 1952. *Ancient Egyptian Religion*, London and New York.

EDWARDS, I. E. S. 1960. *The Pyramids of Egypt* (revised edn), London and New York.

ELGOOD, P. G. 1951. *The Later Dynasties of Egypt*, Oxford and New York.

SMITH, W. S. 1958. *Art and Architecture of Ancient Egypt*, London and Baltimore.

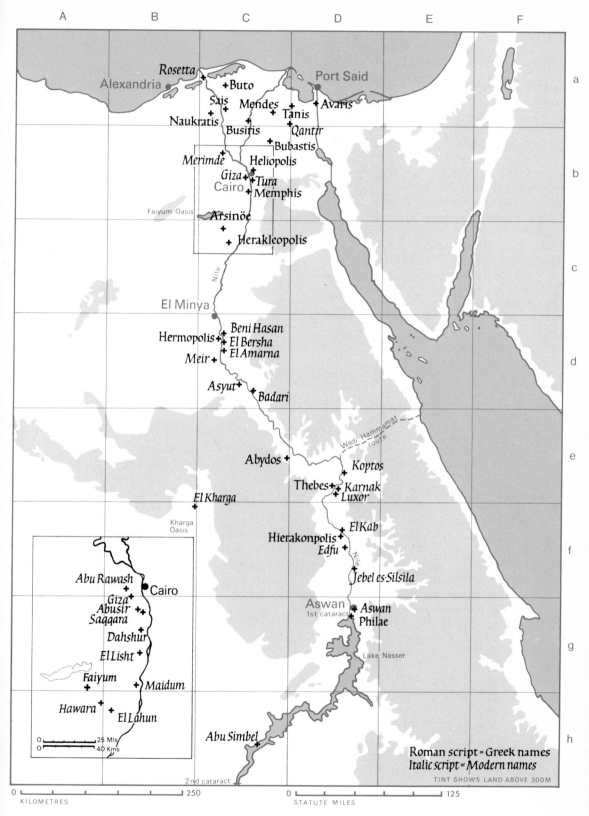

A B C D E F

Rosetta
Alexandria
Port Said
a
Buto
Sais Mendes Avaris
Naukratis Busiris Tanis
Qantir
Bubastis
Merimde Heliopolis
b
Giza Tura
Cairo Memphis
Faiyum Oasis
Arsinöe
Herakleopolis

Nile

c

El Minya

Beni Hasan
Hermopolis El Bersha
Meir El Amarna
d

Asyut
Badari

Wadi Hammamat route

Abydos Koptos
e
Thebes Karnak
El Kharga Luxor

Kharga
Oasis

El Kab
Hierakonpolis
Edfu
f

Nile

Jebel es-Silsila

Aswan Aswan
1st cataract Philae
g
Lake Nasser

h
Abu Simbel

Roman script = Greek names
Italic script = Modern names

TINT SHOWS LAND ABOVE 300M

2nd cataract

0   250
KILOMETRES

0   125
STATUTE MILES

Abu Rawash
Giza Cairo
Abusir
Saqqara
Dahshur
El Lisht
Faiyum Maidum
Hawara El Lahun

0   25 Mls
0   40 Kms

Dynastic Egypt   **59**

Western Asia

It is in western Asia that two of the greatest advances in the history of man are believed to have originated: (1) the transition from an economy based on hunting and gathering to one based on the cultivation of crops and the breeding of animals, sometimes called the Neolithic, or Food-producing, Revolution, and (2) the evolution of urban civilization, sometimes called the Urban Revolution. These two developments were of such far-reaching importance to western Asia, the Mediterranean region and Europe that here we shall concentrate on them exclusively. They did not, of course, occur in western Asia alone. Prehistoric societies in Mesoamerica, the Far East and elsewhere independently developed food-producing economies; urban civilization arose independently in the Americas and eastern Asia, and perhaps in Europe.

The food-producing revolution

When men learnt to grow crops and domesticate animals he gained partial control over his food supply and thereby freed himself from total dependence on nature. The increased availability of food gave rise to a rapid increase in population and provided the surplus of man-power and materials that enabled society to develop new cultural activities: the new farming economy was, in fact, the basis on which urban civilization arose. Although undoubtedly 'revolutionary' in its effects, the change from a food-collecting to a food-producing economy did not occur overnight. It was a long process, which took place in at least three different areas of western Asia, as well as in other regions, taking different forms in each.

We can distinguish three main phases through which the farming economy developed in western Asia:

(1) The development began with a stage of incipient food production before 7000 bc on the Zagros flanks, in the Levant and in southern Anatolia. These communities had domesticated plants – einkorn and emmer wheats, barley and some leguminous crops – and some of them also reared domesticated sheep or goats or both, but not at this stage cattle or swine. They all still depended to varying degrees on wild foods. The early farming economies of this stage were clearly viable alternatives to traditional hunting and gathering economies, but initially not noticeably superior: strictly hunting and gathering communities survived alongside the new farming communities.

(2) The first stage developed imperceptibly into one of settled village farming, initially in the areas of incipient food-production, but occurring throughout much of western Asia by 5000 bc. These communities possessed domesticated plants and animals, but concentrated on cereal production by dry farming. Cattle and swine had been added to the domesticated animals and the plant repertory now included improved strains of wheat and barley. By this stage the superiority of the farming economy had become apparent and the role of hunting and gathering diminished sharply; if hunting communities as such survived, they can have done so only in marginal zones. At this time the farming economy began to spread outside the natural habitat zone of the wild prototypes of the domesticated plants and animals and it is to this stage that the spread of farming into Europe belongs.

(3) After c. 5000 bc the dry farming of stage 2 was replaced in many areas by irrigation agriculture. Indeed irrigation may have begun on a modest scale, with simple modifications of existing stream courses, before this date, but it became widespread in the fifth millennium bc. The importance of irrigation was twofold. In the first place it allowed the production of much higher crop yields and could therefore support considerably increased populations and secondly it made it possible to grow crops on land which could not be cultivated at all by the dry-farming method. Thus it provided the means for the extension of the farming economy into the alluvial plains of the great river valleys and thereby laid the foundation for the growth of urban civilization, which forms the subject of the next section.

III

The urban revolution

The second 'revolution' in western Asia saw the transformation of largely self-sufficient neolithic villages into cities with an economy based on intensive food-production, secondary industries and external trade. Whereas farming had developed on the hills and plains of the Near East, the earliest urban communities arose in the river valleys where fertile soils, if irrigated, gave high crop yields and so supported exceptionally large populations. Thus, the three great ancient civilizations of the Old World outside China rose on the alluvial soils of major river systems: the Tigris–Euphrates, the Nile and the Indus. Meanwhile, in smaller valleys a comparable development towards urban life sometimes occurred. Early urban sites are known, for example, in Turkmenia, notably at Namazga and Altin-depe, and in south-east Iran at Shahr-i Sokhta and at Tepe Yahya. However, although initially urban communities developed in a number of river valleys, it was only in the extremely large alluvial systems that the development was sustained and full civilization emerged. Elsewhere, the towns were either abandoned or declined, and civilization was introduced later from outside.

The earliest of the three civilizations mentioned above, and the only one to arise in western Asia, was that of the Sumerians in southern Mesopotamia, which had emerged by the late fourth millennium B C. Its origins are better understood than those of Egypt or the Indus Valley civilization, since archaeological discoveries present a clear record of the process whereby villages of the fifth millennium B C gradually grew in size and complexity until they emerged as the extensive cities of the third millennium: Ur, Eridu, Erech, Nippur, Lagash and others. Factors contributing to the evolution of civilization in Mesopotamia included the high crop yields obtained by irrigating fertile alluvial soils, technological developments (such as metallurgy and the invention of the wheel), the harnessing of animal and wind power, and social elements, including co-operation in important community projects, notably large-scale irrigation and expeditions in search of raw materials unavailable on the alluvial plains. The interaction of these and other factors had a 'multiplying' effect, so that once under way the process of increasing the efficiency of primary production, increasing economic specialization and increasing centralization gathered momentum until the 'revolution' was accomplished.

Early Sumerian civilization was characterized by cities with large populations, supported by a highly productive form of agriculture. Administration was in the hands of the temple priests, who collected and redistributed surplus wealth. The urban society contained numerous specialists: craftsmen and merchants, and priests and 'civil servants' who organized the complex community. Indeed, it was the mounting complexity of urban administration which stimulated the invention of writing, and this in turn permitted developments in mathematics, astronomy and other fields of knowledge.

Thus, before 3000 B C a full urban civilization existed in the Tigris–Euphrates valley. It is probable that the civilizations of Egypt and the Indus valley evolved independently of Mesopotamia, but throughout western Asia itself the influence of the Sumerians and their successors, the Akkadians and Babylonians, was profound, and all subsequent civilizations in the region were in some sense derivative. Indeed, through these later civilizations and subsequently through the Roman Empire and Christianity some of the practices, knowledge and beliefs of the Sumerians were eventually incorporated into 'Western' culture.

FURTHER READING

BRAIDWOOD, R. J. and B. HOWE 1960. *Prehistoric Investigations in Iraqi Kurdistan*, Chicago.
BRAIDWOOD, R. J. and G. R. WILLEY (eds) 1962. *Courses Towards Urban Life*, Edinburgh and Chicago.
HALLO, W. W. and W. K. SIMPSON 1971. *The ancient Near East. A history*, New York.
KRAMER, S. N. 1961. *History begins at Sumer*[2], London and New York.
MELLAART, J. 1965. *Earliest Civilizations of the Near East*, London and New York.
OPPENHEIM, A. L. 1964. *Ancient Mesopotamia*, Chicago.

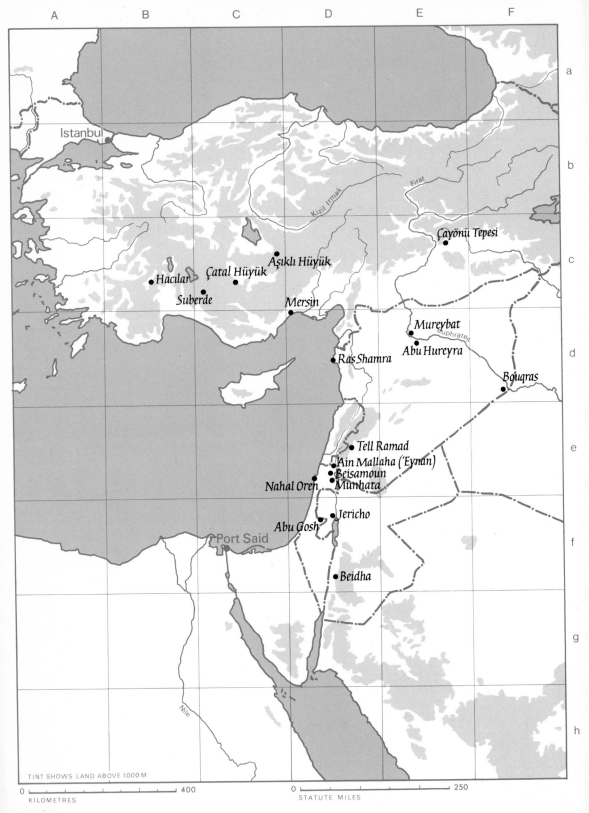

A   B   C   D   E   F

a

b

Istanbul

Kızıl Irmak

Fırat

Çayönü Tepesi

Aşıklı Hüyük

c

Hacılar

Çatal Hüyük

Suberde

Mersin

Mureybat

Euphrates

Abu Hureyra

d

Ras Shamra

Bouqras

Tell Ramad

e

Ain Mallaha ('Eynan)

Beisamoun

Nahal Oren

Munhata

Jericho

Abu Gosh

Port Said

f

Beidha

g

Nile

h

TINT SHOWS LAND ABOVE 1000 M

0   400
KILOMETRES

0   250
STATUTE MILES

62   *The earliest agriculture in western Asia*

The earliest agriculture in western Asia

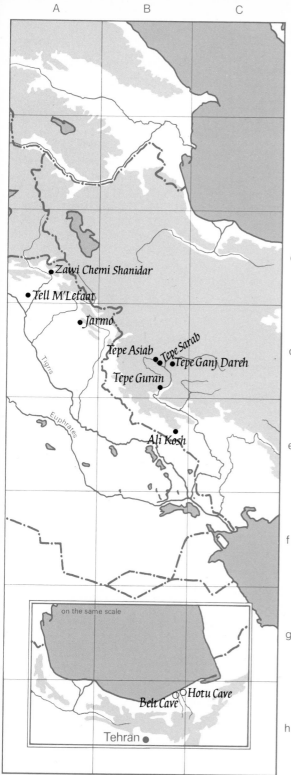

The earliest experiments in food production anywhere in the world took place in western Asia: in an area extending eastwards from the Mediterranean to the Zagros Mountains and northwards from the Red Sea and the Persian Gulf to Anatolia. These experiments may have begun as early as 10,000 bc and by 6000 bc farming communities were widely established. Within this area the development of farming has been examined in three different regions: along the Zagros flanks, in the Levant and in southern Anatolia.

In the Zagros region we find the earliest evidence of domesticated animals, sheep being bred at Zawi Chemi Shanidar by 9000 bc. After this we have no information on farming until the late eighth millennium, when communities at Ali Kosh in Khuzistan and Tepe Ganj Dareh in Luristan were practising agriculture and keeping domesticated goats – at Ali Kosh they also had sheep – although hunting and gathering were still important aspects of the economy. By the seventh millennium bc farming villages probably existed throughout the Zagros region and it appears that the villagers of Jarmo in Iraqi Kurdistan probably herded domesticated swine.

In contrast to the Zagros region, in the Levant and Anatolia the domestication of plants preceded that of animals and in both areas – at Tell Ramad, Pre-Pottery Neolithic A Jericho and at aceramic Hacılar – communities existed in the seventh millennium bc that had no domesticated animals, but lived by agriculture and efficient hunting. Animals probably were domesticated towards the end of the seventh millennium; they may have existed by the Pre-Pottery Neolithic B phase in the Levant and they were certainly present at Çatal Hüyük in southern Anatolia. Despite the advantages of food production over a hunting and gathering economy, non-farming communities survived in all parts of western Asia until c. 6000 bc.

The earliest crops were einkorn and emmer wheat and barley (both naked and hulled, two- and six-row); bread-wheat and some leguminous crops (peas, lentils, vetch, etc.) appeared later.

63

The earliest domesticated animals were dogs, sheep and goat, followed by pig (in northern Iraq) and perhaps cattle (apparently by the seventh millennium in Anatolia). This pioneer agriculture in western Asia provided not only the economic basis of Mesopotamian civilization, but also the ancestors of the first farming communities in Europe.

FURTHER READING

BRAIDWOOD, R. J. and B. HOWE 1960. *Prehistoric Investigations in Iraqi Kurdistan*, Chicago.
HOLE, F. and K. V. FLANNERY 1967. The Prehistory of South-western Iran: A Preliminary Report. *Proceedings of the Prehistoric Society* 33, 147–206.
LAMBERG-KARLOVSY, C. C. (ed.) 1972. Old World Archaeology. *Foundations of Civilization*, San Francisco.
UCKO, P. J. and G. W. DIMBLEBY (eds) 1969. *The Domestication and Exploitation of Plants and Animals*, London and Chicago.

The early civilizations: Mesopotamia, Egypt and the Indus valley

In the course of the fourth millennium BC communities in several different areas of Asia and north Africa evolved urban economies, and by the early third millennium three great urban civilizations had arisen in Mesopotamia, Egypt and the Indus valley. The emergence of an urban economy depended on the production of sufficient food to support not only the section of the community engaged in primary production but also non-food-producing specialists: craftsmen, administrators, etc. This essential increase was achieved by extending the practice of farming from the highland zones (like the Zagros chain) to the alluvial soils of the major river valleys, for these, when irrigated, could be exploited to produce high crop yields. In the past, therefore, irrigation agriculture was considered the prime cause of the rise of urban civilization – Childe's 'Urban Revolution'. Today this seems too simple an explanation and recent studies, such as that of Adams, favour multi-causal explanations, with the emphasis on the social, rather than the economic and technological factors which Childe had emphasized. Nevertheless, irrigation agriculture certainly *was* an important factor, for it was in the river valleys – and *only* in the river valleys – that the earliest urban communities arose. Recent work in eastern Iran has shown that urban, and in certain cases literate, communities existed here as early as they did in Mesopotamia; shortly afterwards, another pocket of urban society arose in Turkmenia. However, although an initial development of urbanism took place in a number of alluvial valleys in western and central Asia, it was only in the three vast flood plains of the Nile, the Tigris–Euphrates valley and the Indus that civilization was maintained; it appears that the smaller valleys could not support indefinitely the high population densities required for urban society. Indeed, even the civilization of the Indus valley collapsed, perhaps after environmental disasters, in the early second millennium BC.

FURTHER READING

ADAMS, R. McC. 1960. 'The Origins of Cities'. In *Scientific American: Old World Archaeology*, 137–43.
ADAMS, R. McC. and C. H. KRAELING (eds) 1960. *City Invincible: a Symposium on Urbanism and Cultural Development in the Ancient Near East*, Chicago.
CHILDE, V. G. 1952. *New Light on the Most Ancient East* (revised edn), London and New York.
MASSON, V. 1968. The Urban Revolution in South Turkmenia. *Antiquity* XLII, 178–87.
UCKO, P. J., R. TRINGHAM and G. W. DIMBLEBY (eds) 1972. *Man, Settlement and Urbanism*, London.

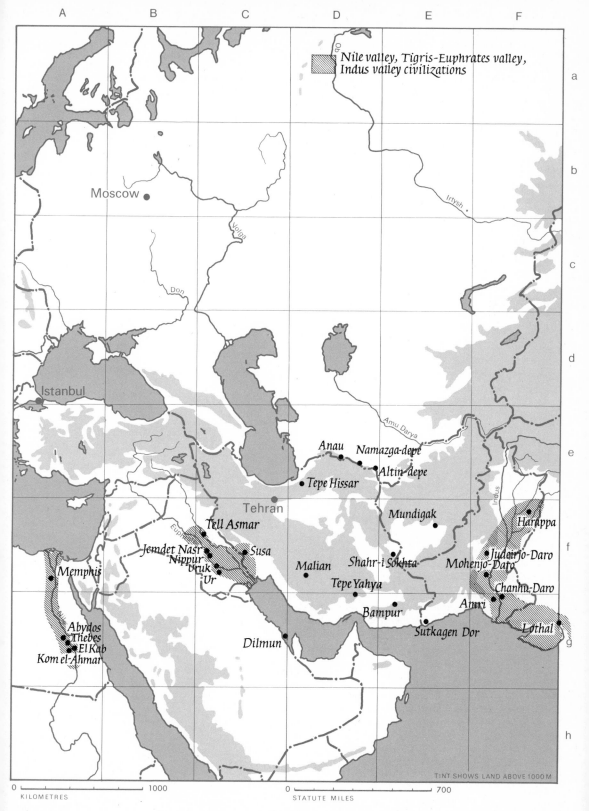

The map contains the following labels:

Column headers: A B C D E F

Row labels: a b c d e f g h

Nile valley, Tigris-Euphrates valley, Indus valley civilizations

Moscow

Volga

Don

Irtysh

Istanbul

Amu Darya

Anau Namazga-depe
Tepe Hissar Altin-depe

Tehran

Mundigak

Indus

Tell Asmar

Harappa

Euph.

Jemdet Nasr Susa
Nippur
Uruk Malian Shahr-i Sokhta Judeirjo-Daro
Ur Mohenjo-Daro

Memphis Tepe Yahya Chanhu-Daro

Bampur Amri

Abydos Lothal
Thebes Sutkagen Dor
El Kab
Kom el-Ahmar

Dilmun

TINT SHOWS LAND ABOVE 1000 M

0 1000 0 700

KILOMETRES STATUTE MILES

The early civilizations: Mesopotamia, Egypt and the Indus valley 65

Neolithic and Copper Age sites in Mesopotamia

The development of farming in the eighth and seventh millennia bc took place in the areas flanking the Mesopotamian plains. Thus, whereas early agricultural sites are known in Khuzistan (at Ali Kosh), on the upper Tigris and its tributaries (Jarmo, Shanidar) and on the upper Euphrates (Çayönü Tepesi, Abu Hureyra), the broad alluvial plains which later supported the civilization of Sumer and its successors were apparently un-inhabited at this stage. The earliest cultures known in this area – the first Mesopotamian cultures dependent on irrigation agriculture – are in fact *late* neolithic cultures, dating from the sixth millennium bc in the north. South Mesopotamia, on the other hand, may not have been settled before *c.* 5000 bc.

Indeed the culture sequences differed considerably as between the north and the south. The earliest phase in the north (named Hassuna-Samarra after two sites with different styles of painted pottery) was succeeded by the Halaf culture, which spread over a large area of northern Mesopotamia in the late sixth and fifth millennia. Both the Hassuna-Samarra and the Halaf cultures had connections with Anatolia in the north-west. The Halafian in particular was a prosperous, well-developed farming culture, in all probability metal-using.

In southern Mesopotamia the earliest occupation belonged to the fifth millennium and was quite different in character from the cultures of the north, showing instead strong connections with those of Susiana and the highlands of Iran. The Eridu and Hajji Muhammad phases were followed by the 'Ubaid culture, the first well known culture of the alluvial lowlands and one which played a leading role in Mesopotamian development. It spread over the whole of Mesopotamia in the mid-fifth millennium bc, bringing the Halafian culture to an apparently abrupt end, and had trading connections over a much wider area, including parts of the Persian Gulf. The 'Ubaid population lived in towns of considerable size, built monumental temples and had a complex social and economic organization. Indeed the 'Ubaid culture was the foundation on which Sumerian civilization developed through the Uruk and Jemdet Nasr (Proto-literate) periods to the Early Dynastic phase.

FURTHER READING

ADAMS, R. McC. 1965. *Land behind Baghdad*, Chicago and London.

BEEK, M. A. 1962. *Atlas of Mesopotamia*, London and Edinburgh.

CHILDE, V. G. 1952. *New Light on the Most Ancient East* (revised edn), London and New York.

MALLOWAN, M. E. L. 1965. *Early Mesopotamia and Iran*, London and New York.

MELLAART, J. 1965. *Earliest Civilizations of the Near East*, London and New York.

ROUX, G. 1965, 1966. *Ancient Iraq*, Cleveland and Harmondsworth.

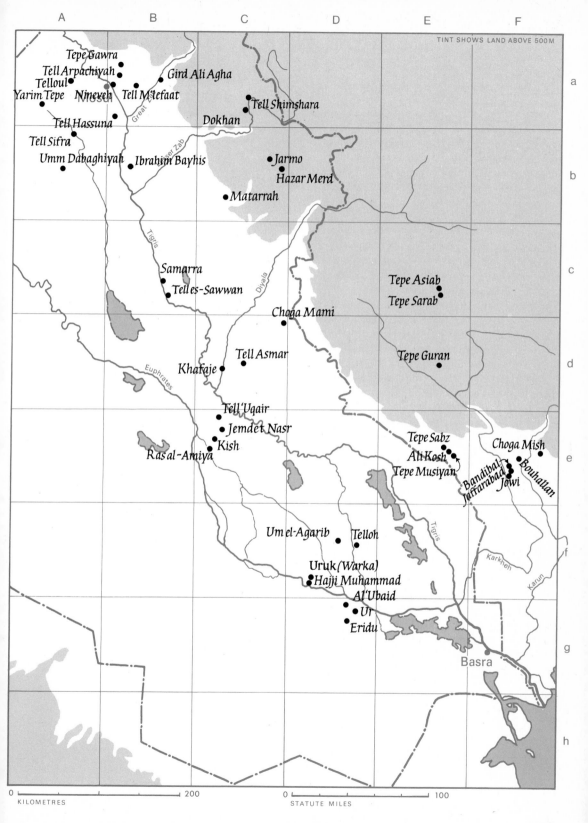

Tepe Gawra
Tell Arpachiyah
Telloul
Nineveh
Yarim Tepe
Tell M'lefaat
Gird Ali Agha
Tell Hassuna
Tell Sifra
Umm Dabaghiyah
Ibrahim Bayhis
Dokhan
Tell Shimshara
Jarmo
Hazar Merd
Matarrah
Samarra
Tell es-Sawwan
Choga Mami
Tepe Asiab
Tepe Sarab
Tell Asmar
Tepe Guran
Khafaje
Tell 'Uqair
Jemdet Nasr
Ras al-Amiya
Kish
Tepe Sabz
Choga Mish
Ali Kosh
Tepe Musiyan
Bandibal
Jaffarabad
Jowi
Bouhallan
Um el-Agarib
Telloh
Uruk (Warka)
Hajji Muhammad
Al'Ubaid
Ur
Eridu
Basra

Niseer
Great Zab
Lesser Zab
Tigris
Diyala
Euphrates
Tigris
Karkheh
Karun

0   200
KILOMETRES

0   100
STATUTE MILES

Neolithic and Copper Age sites in Mesopotamia **67**

Mesopotamia: Sumer, Agade and Elam

The emergence of Sumer – the first urban civilization in Mesopotamia – is well documented in the archaeological record. The earliest settlements of the lower Tigris–Euphrates belong to the 'Ubaid culture of the fifth millennium BC. During the Uruk and Jemdet Nasr phases that followed the 'Ubaid period and preceded the Early Dynastic phase (which began c. 3000 BC), the village societies of the Copper Age developed into the urban civilization of Sumer, in which Erech, Eridu, Ur and Lagash were among the major cities. The most prominent features of the new cities were vast temple complexes, the administrators of which were also in charge of redistribution in the Sumerian economy; their upkeep required large permanent staffs of specialist priests, clerks and artisans, the nature of whose tasks stimulated the invention of writing.

About the same time, civilization emerged in neighbouring Elam. Excavations at Susa in Khuzistan have revealed a sequence of development similar to that in Mesopotamia, but the emerging civilization was not simply an offshoot of Sumer. Indeed, the pictographic Proto-Elamite script, different in kind from Sumerian cuneiform, found at Tepe Yahya and other sites on the Iranian plateau as well as at Susa, suggests the possibility of a non-Mesopotamian basis for Elamite civilization.

The political organization of Sumer was that of independent and often warring city-states, a situation which may have been responsible for the replacement of the temple and priesthood as the centre of authority by the palace and king, who derived his prestige from military success.

A new era – the Akkadian – began with the foundation of Agade, a city in Babylonia, by Sargon in the twenty-fourth century BC. For a while Sargon and his successors unified north and central Mesopotamia and much of Elam. However, their wide authority did not last for long and during the third dynasty of Ur the old Sumerian cities revived. Indeed, the last century of the third millennium saw a late flowering of civilization in Sumer.

FURTHER READING

ADAMS, R. McC. 1960. The Origin of Cities. In *Scientific American: Old World Archaeology*, 137–43.

AMIET, P. 1966. *Elam*, Paris.

CHILDE, V. G. 1964. *What Happened in History* (reprint), Harmondsworth.

HINZ, W. 1972. *The Lost World of Elam*, London.

KRAMER, S. N. 1963. *The Sumerians*, Chicago.

OPPENHEIM, A. L. 1964. *Ancient Mesopotamia*, Chicago.

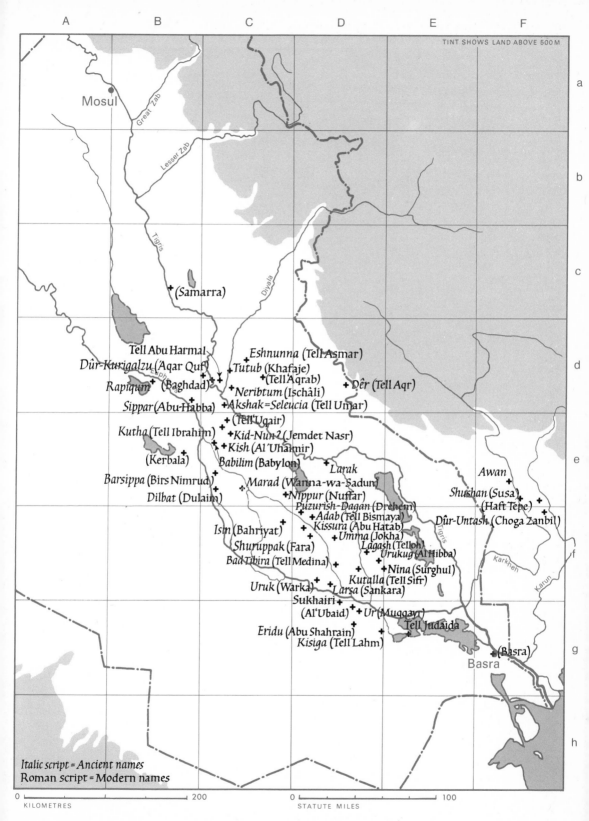

Italic script = Ancient names
Roman script = Modern names

0	200
KILOMETRES	

0	100
STATUTE MILES	

TINT SHOWS LAND ABOVE 500 M

Mesopotamia: Babylon and Assyria

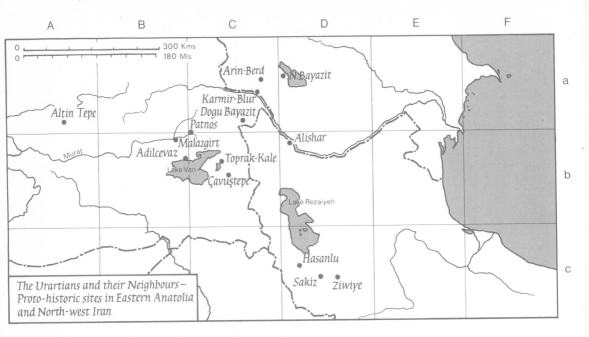

The Urartians and their Neighbours –
Proto-historic sites in Eastern Anatolia
and North-west Iran

Babylonia is the name given to southern Mesopotamia – Sumer and Agade together – after the emergence of a united kingdom ruled by an Amorite dynasty established in Babylon *c.* 1800 BC. Assyria is the name applied to northern Mesopotamia, and its history began when governors of the kings of the third dynasty of Ur were based in Assur before *c.* 2000 BC.

Sumerian civilization finally collapsed *c.* 2000 BC when the empire of the third dynasty at Ur succumbed to internal social pressures and to invasions of Amorites from the west and Elamites from the east. In the following centuries the political focus shifted upstream and settled finally in Babylon, which under Hammurabi and his successors dominated not only Babylonia, but also Assyria, Elam and the Zagros Mountains. By this time the final shift had taken place from the Sumerian to the Akkadian language and the first dynasty of Babylon saw on the one hand the formation of the Old Babylonian literary tradition and on the other the spread of cuneiform writing and the Akkadian language for commerce throughout large areas of south-west Asia. With the conquest of Babylonia by the Hittites *c.* 1600 BC a 'dark age' began and Babylon did not

rise to political power again until well into the first millennium; however, both the literary tradition and the essential structure of Sumerian–Babylonian civilization survived.

The early centuries of Assyrian history are documented largely by information from tablet archives, which show that Assyrian merchants were trading in Anatolia – a practice cut short by the rise of the Hittites. After this Assyria came under the domination of first the Babylonians and later the Hittites, but after *c.* 1300 BC Assyrian kings created a series of empires – individually ephemeral but collectively enduring – which ended only in the seventh century BC. Subsequently Babylonia, too, lost its independence and in 538 BC Cyrus incorporated Mesopotamia into the Persian empire.

FURTHER READING

BEEK, M. A. 1962. *Atlas of Mesopotamia*, London and Edinburgh.
CHILDE, V. G. 1964. *What Happened in History*, chapter 8 (reprint), Harmondsworth.
OPPENHEIM, A. L. 1964. *Ancient Mesopotamia*, Chicago.
ROUX, G. 1965, 1966. *Ancient Iraq*, Cleveland and Harmondsworth.
SAGGS, H. W. F. 1965. *Everyday Life in Babylonia and Assyria*, London and New York.

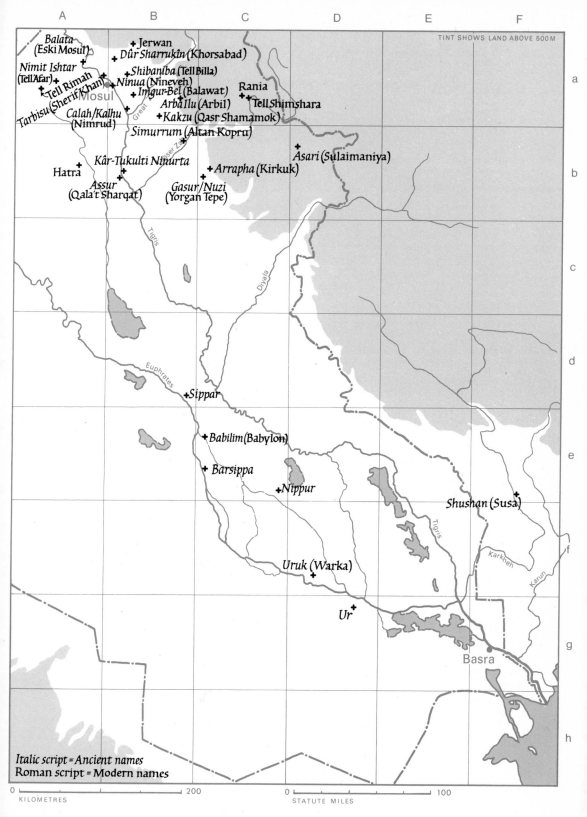

TINT SHOWS LAND ABOVE 500M

Balata
(Eski Mosul)

+ Jerwan

Dûr Sharrukîn (Khorsabad)

Nimit Ishtar
(Tell'Afar)

Shibaniba (Tell Billa)

Tell Rimah

Ninua (Nineveh)

Rania

Tarbisu (Sherif Khan)

Mosul

Imgur-Bel (Balawat)

Arba Ilu (Arbil)

Tell Shimshara

Calah/Kalhu
(Nimrud)

Kakzu (Qasr Shamamok)

Simurrum (Altan Kopru)

Asari (Sulaimaniya)

Kâr-Tukulti Ninurta

Hatra

Arrapha (Kirkuk)

Assur
(Qala't Sharqat)

Gasur/Nuzi
(Yorgan Tepe)

Great Zab

Lesser Zab

Tigris

Diyala

Euphrates

+ *Sippar*

+ *Babilim* (Babylon)

+ *Barsippa*

+ *Nippur*

Shushan (Susa)

Tigris

Karkheh

Karun

Uruk (Warka)

Ur

Basra

Italic script = Ancient names
Roman script = Modern names

0   200
KILOMETRES

0   100
STATUTE MILES

Mesopotamia: Babylon and Assyria   **71**

Neolithic to Bronze Age sites in Anatolia

Anatolia – corresponding roughly to Asiatic Turkey – is a large land mass forming a bridge between the Middle East and Europe; it is not surprising therefore that it contained several distinct cultural zones in later prehistory. Sites in south-east Anatolia, such as Mersin, Tarsus and Sakçagözü, were closely related to Near Eastern settlements (see p. 77), while those in the north-west, notably Troy, belonged to an Aegean culture cycle (see p. 87). This map is concerned in particular with the Anatolian plateau, in which cultures had a distinct regional character.

Research in the last two decades has brought to light a developed early farming culture in south and east Anatolia, lasting from before 7000 to c. 5600 bc. Among the most important sites are Çayönü, Suberde, Hacılar and Çatal Hüyük. The size of the settlement at Çatal Hüyük (13 ha), its elaborately decorated shrines, the abundance and high quality of its artifacts and the precocious development of metallurgy in the region (with smelted copper at Çayönü and Çatal Hüyük) are now well known. This early culture was followed by a number of late neolithic and chalcolithic cultures characterized by different styles of painted pottery, known from Hacılar, Çatal Hüyük West and Can Hasan. They ended c. 5000 bc and the focus of development moved eastwards to north Mesopotamia and the emergent Halafian culture.

Events in the period c. 5000–3000 bc are not well understood, although we do know that there was continuity of settlement in the southeast and that on the plateau Alişar Hüyük, Alaca Hüyük, Büyük Gülücek, Beycesultan and Dündartepe were occupied for at least part of this period.

In the Early Bronze Age (third millennium BC) new developments occurred. In the south-east, communities were in touch with the urban civilizations of Mesopotamia. In the Aegean, civilization emerged (e.g. at Troy). On the plateau, too, we find evidence of a new concentration of wealth and power, demonstrated clearly by the 'royal' tombs of Alaca Hüyük. Shortly after 2000 BC Assyrian merchants settled in

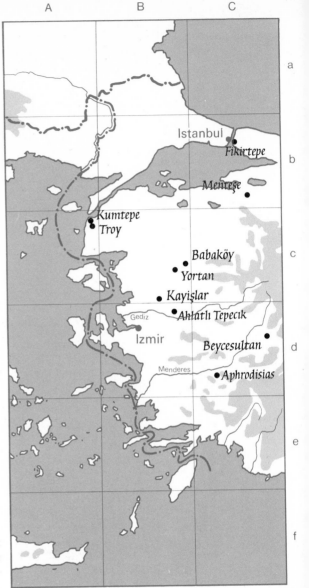

Anatolia (at Kanesh, modern Kültepe, near Kayseri) and continuing Mesopotamian influence on the local Bronze Age eventually gave rise to the civilization of the Hittites.

FURTHER READING

LLOYD, S. 1956. *Early Anatolia*, Harmondsworth.
———— 1967. *The Early Highland Peoples of Anatolia*, London and New York.
MELLAART, J. 1965. *Earliest Civilizations of the Near East*, London and New York.
———— 1967. *Çatal Hüyük. A Neolithic Town in Anatolia*, London and New York.

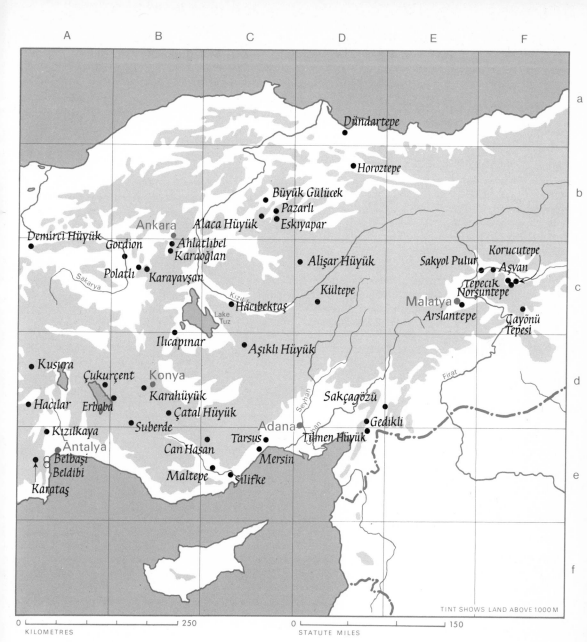

Map labels (grid A–F across top, a–f down right side):

Dündartepe

Horoztepe

Büyük Gülücek
Pazarlı
Alaca Hüyük   Eskıyapar

Demirci Hüyük

Ankara
Ahlatlıbel
Gordion   Karaoğlan

Polatlı   Karayavşan

Alişar Hüyük

Korucutepe
Sakyol Pulur   Aşvan

Malatya   Tepecik
Norşuntepe

Sakarya

Kızıl   Hacıbektaş   Kültepe
Lake
Tuz

Arslantepe

Çayönü
Tepesi

Ilıcapınar

Aşıklı Hüyük

Firat

Kuşura

Çukurçent   Konya

Karahüyük

Sakçagözü

Hacılar   Erbaba

Çatal Hüyük   Seyhan

Gedikli

Kızılkaya   Suberde

Adana   Tümen Hüyük

Antalya   Tarsus
Can Hasan
Belbaşı   Mersin
Beldibi   Maltepe   Silifke
Karataş

TINT SHOWS LAND ABOVE 1000 M

0 ———————————— 250
KILOMETRES

0 ———————————— 150
STATUTE MILES

Neolithic to Bronze Age sites in Anatolia   **73**

The Hittites and their successors

Although as early as the third millennium BC there were in Anatolia societies characterized by considerable wealth, social stratification and advanced technology, true urban civilization did not develop until the beginning of the second millennium BC, through direct contact with north Mesopotamia. This contact began shortly after 2000 BC, when Assyrian merchants established a trading post on the outskirts of the Cappadocian town of Kanesh (modern Kültepe).

The Hittites, creators of this Anatolian civilization, spoke an Indo-European language, and were probably already present in Anatolia early in the second millennium, for Hittite names appear on Assyrian tablets of this date. Hittite history is usually divided into three periods: (1) the Old Kingdom, from the eighteenth to the mid-fifteenth century BC; (2) the Empire, which lasted until the early twelfth century; (3) the Neo-Hittite period, during which Hittite culture survived for almost five hundred years in a few cities in north Syria, established by refugees after the destruction of the main Hittite centres.

The homeland of Hittite civilization was the Anatolian plateau and its capital was Hattusha (modern Boğazköy), which at the time of its greatest development had a circuit of walls more than 6 km long. At its zenith the Hittite empire extended over Syria from the Euphrates to the sea, but in the early twelfth century it collapsed in the upheavals which led also to the fall of Mycenae and the decline of Egypt as a superpower.

The Hittites used the Mesopotamian cuneiform script for all their commercial documents; indeed, for business purposes they used Akkadian, the 'international' language of the day, as well as their native Hittite. A second script, known as Hieroglyphic Hittite, which was used on stone monuments and reliefs, probably represents a native tradition.

Anatolia is rich in ores – indeed it was these which attracted the Mesopotamian merchants – and perhaps the most significant achievement of the Hittites was their mastery of iron-production.

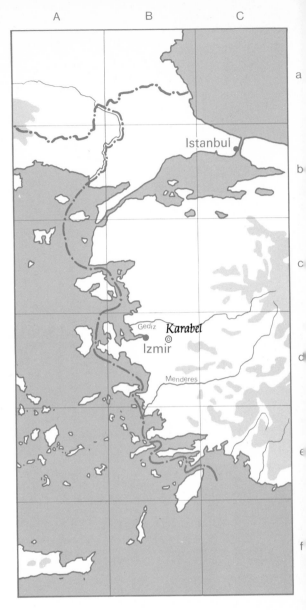

Their rulers seem to have guarded the secret jealously, for iron-working only became widespread in the Near East considerably later, after the fall of the Hittite empire.

FURTHER READING

BITTEL, K. 1970. *Hattusha, the Capital of the Hittites*, New York.
CAVAIGNAC, E. 1950. *Les Hittites*, Paris.
GURNEY, O. R. 1961. *The Hittites*, Harmondsworth.
LLOYD, S. 1956. *Early Anatolia*, Harmondsworth.
——— 1967. *The Early Highland Peoples of Anatolia*, London and New York.

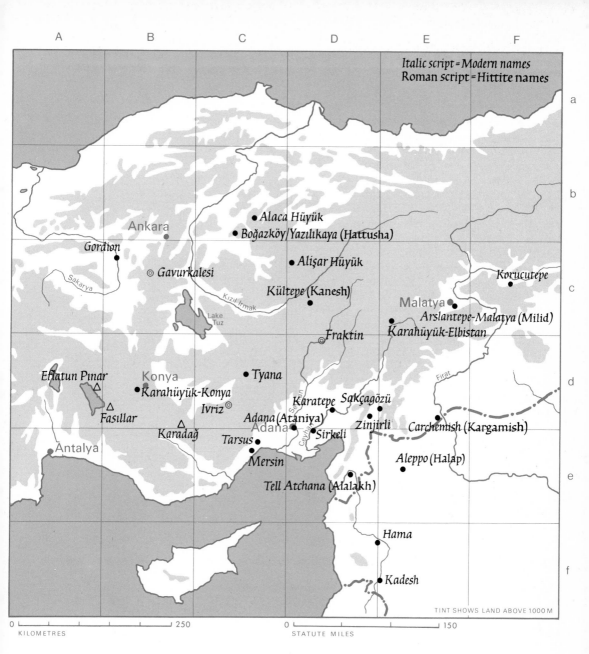

Italic script = Modern names
Roman script = Hittite names

A B C D E F

a

b

Alaca Hüyük
Boğazköy/Yazılıkaya (Hattusha)

Ankara

Gordion

Sakarya

◎ *Gavurkalesi*

Alişar Hüyük

Kızıl Irmak

Kültepe (Kanesh)

Korucutepe

c

Lake
Tuz

◎ *Fraktin*

Malatya

Arslantepe-Malatya (Milid)
Karahüyük-Elbistan

Eflatun Pınar

Tyana

Konya

Firat

d

△

△ *Karahüyük-Konya*

Fasıllar

Ivriz ◎

Karatepe Sakçagözü

Seyhan

Adana (Ataniya)

Zinjirli

Carchemish (Kargamish)

Karadağ

Adana

Sirkeli

Ceyhan

Antalya

Tarsus

Aleppo (Halap)

Mersin

e

Tell Atchana (Alalakh)

Hama

f

Kadesh

TINT SHOWS LAND ABOVE 1000 M

0 _____ 250
KILOMETRES

0 _____ 150
STATUTE MILES

Late prehistoric and proto-historic sites in the Near East

The Mediterranean coast and the hill country west of the Euphrates and south of the Syrian desert formed one of the zones in which the earliest farming developed (see p. 62). But despite this precocious beginning, civilization did not evolve independently in the area. Indeed, literate cultures began relatively late; they were largely derivative in character, owing much to the civilizations of Mesopotamia and Egypt.

Aceramic neolithic sites, datable to the seventh millennium bc, are known from Abu Hureyra on the Euphrates and Ras Shamra on the Mediterranean coast to Beidha, near Petra, in the Jordanian desert. They include, of course, the famous site of Jericho, where stone fortifications enclosed an aceramic settlement of about 4 ha. After *c.* 6000 bc pottery came into use throughout the region.

In the succeeding period, usually known as the chalcolithic and roughly datable to the fifth and fourth millennia BC, many regional cultures and many different influences are recognized. Metal came into use during the fifth millennium and local copper industries developed. Particularly well known is the Ghassulian culture in Palestine, with its buildings of mud-brick on stone foundations adorned with wall paintings.

In the Bronze Age, which began in the late fourth millennium BC, the Levant came under strong influence from the emerging civilizations of Mesopotamia and Egypt. Mesopotamian influence was marked before *c.* 3000 BC, but later, Egyptian influence predominated. Indeed, for long periods in the second millennium BC, most of the region came under direct Egyptian control. From *c.* 2000 BC we know much of its history from Mesopotamian, Egyptian and biblical literary sources, the details of which are beyond the scope of this note. Let it suffice to say that the area was largely urbanized; it supported small semi-independent kingdoms, but did not produce a civilization that exerted influence abroad until the Phoenicians emerged as an international power in the first millennium BC.

The most interesting product of the hybrid influences felt in the Near East was in the sphere of writing. In the Late Bronze Age (after *c.* 1500 BC) numerous different languages and scripts were used. In addition to Akkadian cuneiform and Egyptian hieroglyphic, two local scripts existed: the alphabetic cuneiform of Ugarit and the Phoenician alphabet – ultimately the ancestor of the script we use today.

FURTHER READING

ALBRIGHT, W. F. 1960. *The Archaeology of Palestine* (revised edn), Harmondsworth and Baltimore.
CHILDE, V. G. 1952. *New Light on the Most Ancient East* (revised edn), London and New York.
HALLO, W. W. and W. K. SIMPSON 1971. *The ancient Near East. A history*, New York.
HARDEN, D. B. 1972. *The Phoenicians* (revised edn), Harmondsworth.
MELLAART, J. 1965. *Earliest Civilizations of the Near East*, London and New York.

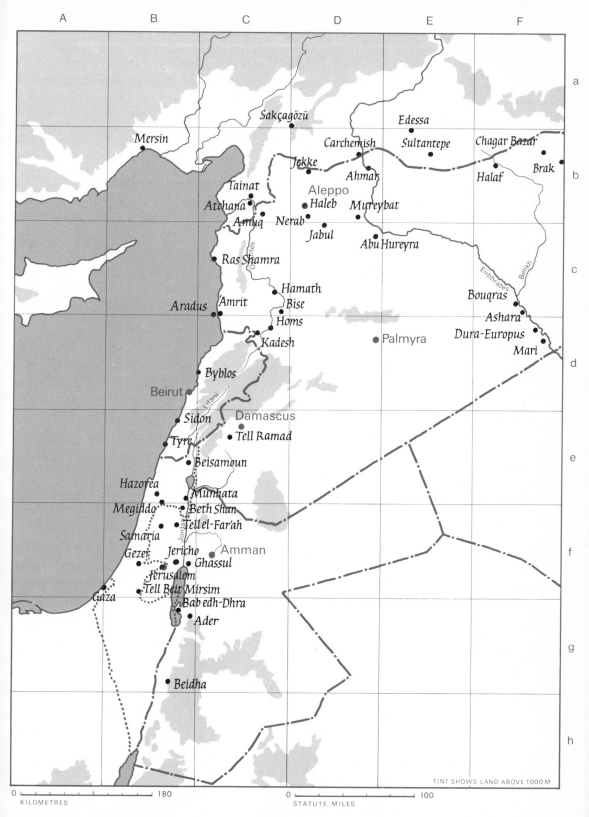

A · · · · · B · · · · · C · · · · · D · · · · · E · · · · · F

a

Mersin

Sakçagözü

Edessa

Carchemish   Sultantepe   Chagar Bazar

Jekke   Ahmar   Halaf   Brak   b

Tainat   Aleppo
Atchana   Haleb   Mureybat
Amuq   Nerab
Jabul
Ras Shamra   Abu Hureyra

c
Aradus   Amrit   Hamath   Bouqras
Bise
Homs   Ashara
Kadesh   Palmyra   Dura-Europus
Mari   d

Byblos

Beirut   Damascus

Sidon   Tell Ramad

Tyre   e
Beisamoun

Hazorea   Munhata
Megiddo   Beth Shan
Samaria   Tell el-Far'ah   f
Gezer   Jericho   Amman
Jerusalem   Ghassul
Tell Beir Mirsim
Gaza   Bab edh-Dhra
Ader

g

Beidha

h

TINT SHOWS LAND ABOVE 1000 M

0 |⌐⊢⊢⊢⊢⊢⊢⊢⊢⊢ 180   0 |⌐⊢⊢⊢⊢⊢⊢ 100
KILOMETRES   STATUTE MILES

Late prehistoric and proto-historic sites in the Near East   **77**

Iran before the Medes and the Persians

Evidence of palaeolithic occupation is still scarce in Iran and the first communities about which we have substantial evidence belong to the Neolithic. In western Iran, on the flanks of the Zagros mountains, is a series of early settlements, including Ali Kosh in Khuzistan and Tepe Sarab and Tepe Ganj Dareh in Luristan. By 7000 bc aceramic communities were partly dependent on cultivated plants and domesticated animals and there were developed farming communities as early as the seventh millennium. According to the slender evidence from Belt Cave and Hotu Cave on the Caspian Sea, farmers may well have occupied this area too at an early date. During the sixth and fifth millennia bc farming communities, characterized by different styles of painted pottery, became established on the Iranian plateau. By 4000 BC smelted copper was in use at sites such as Tal-i Iblis.

In the late fourth millennium BC a process of urbanization took place in south-west Iran, parallel to (and closely connected with) that of Mesopotamia. This process has long been studied in Susiana (the main area of Elamite activity at a later date), but important recent discoveries now show that the late fourth and third millennia saw urban centres established also in south and south-east Iran, at Tepe Yahya and Shahr-i Sokhta. However, hemmed in by mountains and desert, these centres were unable to sustain urban institutions indefinitely and came to an end c. 2000 BC. Only in Khuzistan did civilization continue. Although initially the kings of Elam were dominated by neighbouring Mesopotamian dynasties, after c. 2300 an intermittently independent Elamite state existed for about a millennium, albeit with close cultural connections with Mesopotamia. Elsewhere in Iran, despite the existence of flourishing bronze- and (later) iron-using communities, no urban civilization developed until the emergence of Urartu in north-west Iran and adjacent regions in the early first millennium.

The first Indo-European settlers may have entered Iran shortly after 2000 BC, but in view of the difficulty in equating speakers of particular languages with archaeological cultures, it is only from the fourteenth century BC that archaeologists recognize a distinct 'Iranian' population. However, by the ninth century BC the names of the Medes and the Persians occur in Assyrian documents – in the case of the Persians, the earliest reference to a people who in the sixth century BC established the largest empire to date.

For Bampur and Shahr-i Sokhta, see p. 87.

FURTHER READING

AMIET, P. 1966. *Elam*, Paris.
BURNEY, C. and D. M. LANG 1971. *The People of the Hills*, London and New York.
HINZ, W. 1972. *The Lost World of Elam*, London.
HOLE, F., K. V. FLANNERY and J. A. NEELY 1970. *Excavations in the Deh Luran Plain*, Ann Arbor.
Iran, Journal of the British Institute of Persian Studies.
VANDEN BERGHE, L. 1959. *Archéologie de l'Iran Ancien*, Leiden.

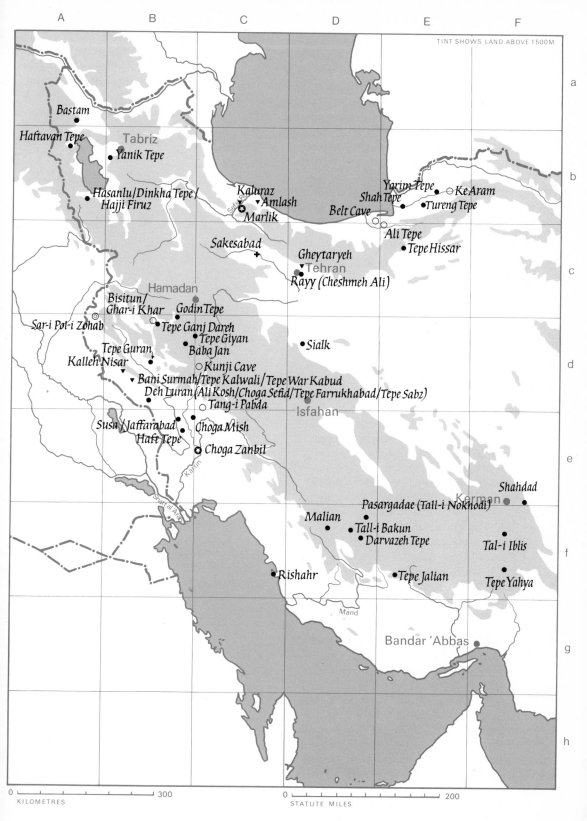

Bastam

Haftavan Tepe

Tabriz

Yanik Tepe

Hasanlu/Dinkha Tepe/
Hajji Firuz

Kaluraz
Amlash
Marlik

Yarim Tepe
Shah Tepe
Ke Aram
Tureng Tepe
Belt Cave

Ali Tepe
Tepe Hissar

Sakesabad

Gheytaryeh
Tehran

Rayy (Cheshmeh Ali)

Hamadan

Bisitun/
Ghar-i Khar
Godin Tepe

Sar-i Pol-i Zohab
Tepe Ganj Dareh

Tepe Giyan

Baba Jan

Tepe Guran
Kalleh Nisar
Kunji Cave

Sialk

Bani Surmah/Tepe Kalwali/Tepe War Kabud
Deh Luran (Ali Kosh/Choga Sefid/Tepe Farrukhabad/Tepe Sabz)

Tang-i Pabda

Isfahan

Susa / Jaffarabad
Haft Tepe
Choga Mish

Choga Zanbil

Shahdad

Kerman

Pasargadae (Tall-i Nokhodi)

Malian
Tall-i Bakun
Darvazeh Tepe

Tal-i Iblis

Rishahr

Tepe Jalian

Tepe Yahya

Mand

Bandar 'Abbas

0 ——————— 300
KILOMETRES

0 ——————— 200
STATUTE MILES

Iran before the Medes and the Persians **79**

Iran: the Medes and the Persians

Both the Medes and the Persians descended from Indo-European groups who settled in Iran not later than the fourteenth century BC. The Medes entered history in the ninth century BC, when according to Assyrian documents they were a powerful force in north-west Iran. Indeed, the collapse of Elam in 640 BC left them the major power in the whole of the Zagros region. With their allies, the Babylonians, the Medes invaded Assyria and captured Nineveh in 612 BC – the first extension of Iranian authority west of the Zagros Mountains.

In Iran, the most important vassals of the Medes were the Persians, who migrated into the mountains north-east of Khuzistan and the modern province of Fars. In 549 BC Cyrus II defeated the Median king Astyages near Pasargadae, thereby becoming ruler of an empire comprising the Median and Persian states. Cyrus (who is often known as 'Cyrus the Great') followed up this victory with an ambitious series of foreign wars. In the west he conquered Lydia and the Greek cities of Asia Minor. In the east he pushed on to the River Jaxartes. Indeed, in ten years, Cyrus enlarged his empire until it stretched from the Aegean to the Oxus. His successors, Cambyses and Darius I, added new territory, including Egypt and Thrace. In 490 BC Darius, and in 480 his son Xerxes unsuccessfully invaded Greece.

By the time of the death of Darius in 486 BC the Achaemenian empire (so called after the dynastic name of the royal family, derived from Achaemenes) had assumed the form it was to retain until Alexander's conquests of 334–325 BC. The empire was divided into satrapies, or governates. In the western satrapies Darius organized a gold and silver currency. A system of roads and posting stations ensured efficient communication between the outer provinces and the royal centres at Hamadan (the old Median capital), Susa, Persepolis and Babylon.

FURTHER READING

CAMERON, G. G. 1936. *History of Early Iran*, Chicago.
CULICAN, W. 1965. *The Medes and Persians*, London and New York.
——— 1970. *Imperial Cities of Persia. Persepolis, Susa and Pasargadae*, London.
NYLANDER, C. 1970. *Ionians in Pasargadae*, Uppsala.
OLMSTEAD, A. T. 1948. *History of the Persian Empire*, Chicago.

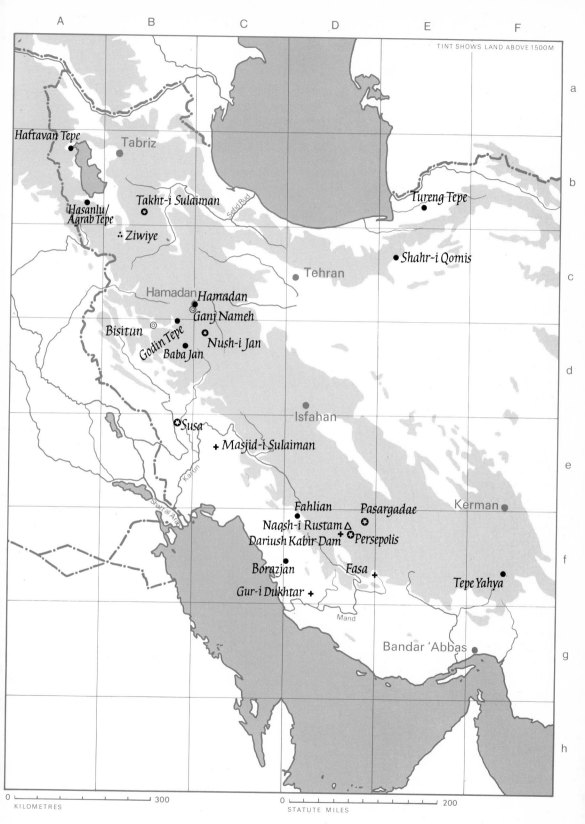

Haftavan Tepe

Tabriz

Takht-i Sulaiman

Hasanlu/
Agrab Tepe

Ziwiye

Tureng Tepe

Shahr-i Qomis

Tehran

Hamadan
Hamadan
Ganj Nameh

Bisitun

Godin Tepe
Baba Jan

Nush-i Jan

Susa

Masjid-i Sulaiman

Isfahan

Fahlian

Pasargadae

Kerman

Naqsh-i Rustam △
Dariush Kabir Dam ✛ ☉ Persepolis

Borazjan

Fasa ✛

Tepe Yahya

Gur-i Dukhtar ✛

Mand

Bandar 'Abbas

Karun

Shatt al 'Arab

Safid Rud

0   300
KILOMETRES

0   200
STATUTE MILES

Iran : the Medes and the Persians   **81**

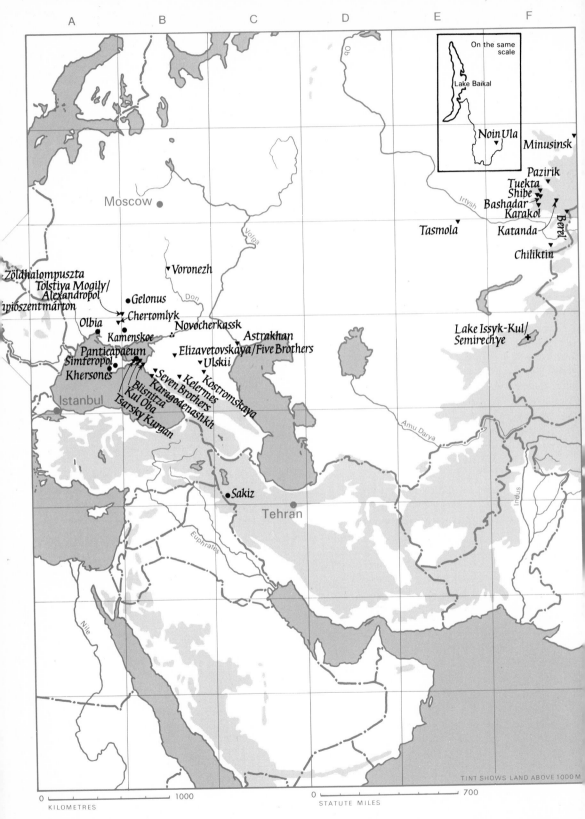

On the same scale

Lake Baikal

Noin Ula

Minusinsk

Pazirik
Tuekta
Shibe
Bashadar
Karakol
Katanda

Tasmola

Berel

Chiliktin

Moscow

Ob

Irtysh

Volga

Voronezh

Don

Zöldhalompuszta
Tolstiya Mogily/
Alexandropol
ipioszentmárton

Gelonus

Chertomlyk

Olbia

Novocherkassk

Kamenskoe

Astrakhan

Lake Issyk-Kul/
Semirech'ye

Panticapaeum
Simferopol
Khersones

Elizavetovskaya/Five Brothers

Ulskii

Kelermes

Kostromskaya

Seven Brothers
Karagodenashkh
Blisnitza
Kul Oba
Tsarsky Kurgan

Istanbul

Amu Darya

Indus

Sakiz

Tehran

Euphrates

Nile

TINT SHOWS LAND ABOVE 1000 M

0   1000
KILOMETRES

0   700
STATUTE MILES

82 *The Scythians*

The Scythians

The name 'Scythian' is loosely applied to a group of nomadic and semi-nomadic tribes who inhabited the Russian steppes in the first millennium BC. The steppes extend from the Danube to the borders of China. They are interrupted by mountain ranges – the Pamir, Tien Shan and Altai massifs – but broad 'corridors' provide natural routes from one region of grassland to the next. It is hardly surprising therefore that many features of Scythian culture, notably the 'animal style' of ornament, are common to Siberia, central Asia and the Black Sea coast.

The Scythians and their neighbours the Cimmerians appear first in written records in the eighth century BC, when they are mentioned in Assyrian and Urartian documents. During the eighth and seventh centuries the Scythians and related groups were recorded in Anatolia and Iran. The Greek historian Herodotus (c. 484–425 BC) wrote a long account of Scythian ethnography. Beyond the borders of the classical world, Urartu, Assyria and Iran, Scythian movements are difficult to follow, for the nomads themselves were illiterate.

Most of the steppe-dwellers were stock-breeders who migrated between summer and winter pastures. They were horsemen who carried their belongings in carts. Several groups, however, maintained permanent settlements and leading Scythians lived in the Greek cities of the Black Sea, such as Olbia and Panticapaeum.

Scythian art comprises many regional styles, linked by a common love of stylized animal motifs, applied not only to objects of gold and other metals – vessels, horse-trappings, personal ornaments, etc. – but also to woodwork, textiles and even (by tattooing) the human body. Much of our knowledge of perishable objects comes from the grave goods deposited in barrows at Pazirik, where freak conditions caused the contents of the wooden burial chambers to become waterlogged and then frozen. The 'frozen' barrows of the Altai were discovered in 1865; they were revisited in the 1920s and again in 1947–49, when Rudenko and his colleagues made a detailed study of the tombs and their contents.

FURTHER READING

ARTAMANOV, M. I. 1969. *Treasures from Scythian Tombs*, London and New York.
BUNKER, E. C., C. B. CHATWIN and A. R. FARKAS 1970. *'Animal Style' Art from East to West*, New York.
MINNS, E. H. 1913. *Scythians and Greeks*, Cambridge.
ROSTOVTZEFF, M. 1922. *Iranians and Greeks in South Russia*, Oxford.
RUDENKO, S. I. 1970. *Frozen Tombs of Siberia*, London and Berkeley.
TALBOT RICE, T. 1958. *The Scythians*, London and New York.

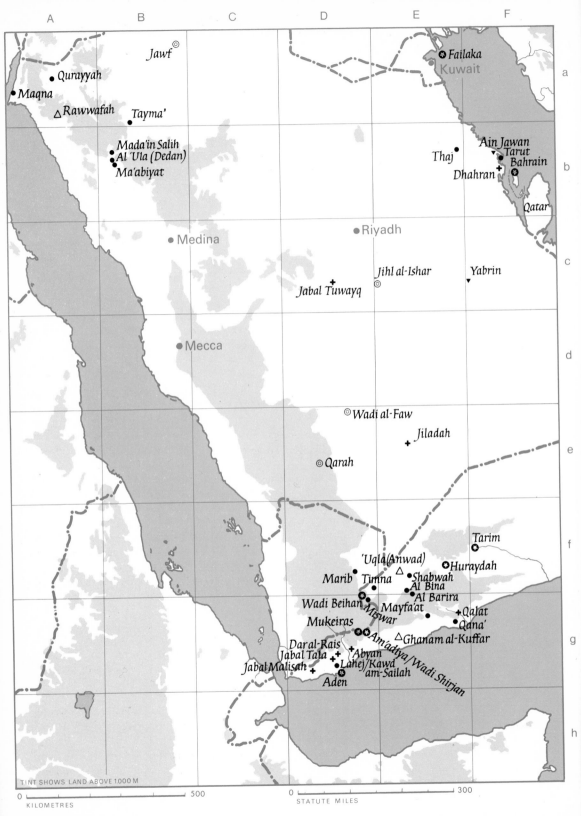

A B C D E F

Jawf ◎

Qurayyah ●

● Maqna

△ Rawwafah

Tayma' ●

Mada'in Salih ●
Al 'Ula (Dedan) ●
Ma'abiyat ●

Failaka ✪ ● Failaka
Kuwait

Thaj ● Ain Jawan
▼ Tarut
Dhahran Bahrain
+ ✪
Qatar

● Medina ● Riyadh

Jihl al-Ishar Yabrin
◎ ▼

Jabal Tuwayq +

● Mecca

◎ Wadi al-Faw
Jiladah
+

Qarah ◎

Tarim ✪

'Uqla (Anwad)
△ Huraydah
Marib ● Timna ● Shabwah ✪
Al Bina
Al Barira ●
Wadi Beihan Mayfa'at
Miswar
Mukeiras + Qalat
Am'adiya / Wadi Shirjan Qana'
Dar al-Rais △ Ghanam al-Kuffar
Jabal Tala + Abyan
Jabal Malisah + Lahej/Kawd
am-Sailah
Aden

a

b

c

d

e

f

g

h

TINT SHOWS LAND ABOVE 1,000 M

0 ————————— 500
KILOMETRES

0 ———————— 300
STATUTE MILES

The Arabian peninsula

The map shows labelled locations: Dibba, Umm an-Nar, Buraimi, Habarut.

The vast desert peninsula of Arabia has been little explored by archaeologists and even today large areas are virtually unknown. The regions best known to the archaeologist are southern Arabia, from Aden to the Oman peninsula, and the north-east coast, from Kuwait to the mouth of the Gulf.

On the Gulf coast, the Danish Archaeological Expedition, which began work in 1953, has discovered and investigated sites ranging in date from the Palaeolithic (notably in Qatar) to the Portuguese period. In Oman, at Umm an-Nar and in the Buraimi oasis, settlements and cemeteries of the third millennium BC yield material comparable with finds at Bampur (phases V and VI), Shahr-i Sokhta and other sites in Iran. Some scholars place *Magan*, the source of copper mentioned in Akkadian documents, in Oman, although this is by no means certain. At Qala'at al-Bahrain the Danish Expedition were able to establish a long sequence of occupation, at the beginning of which they found typical Umm an-Nar pottery. Following the Umm an-Nar phase at Bahrain the Danes discovered a walled city, also of the third millennium BC, which they identify with the state of *Dilmun*, another place-name in Akkadian documents. At Barbar (Bahrain), near Qala'at al-Bahrain, they excavated a temple and on the island of Failaka they found a settlement of the 'early Dilmun' period. The merchants of Dilmun were middlemen in the network of maritime trade which linked Mesopotamia, the Gulf and ports farther east. Indeed, detailed study of the Bahrain material may help to resolve the discrepancy between the chronologies proposed for third-millennium sites in Mesopotamia and those in Iran.

In southern Arabia, the most prominent sites belong to the first millennium BC and the early centuries AD, when several kingdoms derived considerable wealth from commerce: caravan trade with the cities of the Mediterranean world, via Petra, and maritime trade in the Indian Ocean and the Red Sea. These Himyaritic kingdoms included the Sabaeans, Qatabanians (with their capital at Timna), the Minaeans and the

Ausanians (capital: Miswar). The mainstay of south Arabian trade was incense: myrrh from the Hadhramaut and frankincense from Dhofar. Cities contained monumental temples, other civic buildings and dwellings. In the countryside, elaborate irrigation systems made efficient cultivation possible. Among the distinctive features of south Arabian culture were its script, alabaster stelae and large-scale bronzes executed in Mediterranean style.

FURTHER READING

ANATI, E. 1968–72. *Rock Art in Central Arabia.* 3 vols, Louvain.
VAN BEEK, G. W. 1969. The Rise and Fall of Arabia Felix. *Scientific American*, December issue.
BIBBY, G. 1970. *Looking for Dilmun*, London and New York.
BOWEN, R. LE B. and F. P. ALBRIGHT 1958. *Archaeological Discoveries in South Arabia*, Baltimore.
DANISH ARCHAEOLOGICAL EXPEDITION, 1954– . Interim reports in the journal *Kuml*.
DOE, D. B. 1971. *Southern Arabia*, London and New York.
HARDING, G. L. 1964. *Archaeology in the Aden Protectorates*, London.

Afghanistan

Afghanistan, in the highlands of central Asia, has been little studied by the archaeologist. Much of what has been achieved was carried out by members of the Délégation Archéologique Française en Afghanistan (DAFA), which was founded in 1922. Before the arrival of the French, archaeology was, in the words of Louis Dupree, 'at best haphazard, at worst, butchery'.

The earliest sites in Afghanistan belong to the late Pleistocene. Dara-i Kur cave, for example, yielded a 'Mousterian' industry containing blades, which anticipates the industries of the Leptolithic. At Kara Kamar, Coon recovered an 'Aurignacian' blade industry with a C^{14} date of *c.* 32,000 bc – one of the earliest dated leptolithic assemblages. Aq Kupruk yielded a different industry, comprising 'Aurignacian' elements and microliths, but no burins, dated *c.* 18,000–13,000 bc. Several caves, including Kara Kamar (which has a C^{14} date of *c.* 8500 bc), also contain micro-lithic industries, apparently of Kuprukian origin. Similar assemblages, especially on open sites, may represent the earliest, aceramic neolithic. Indeed aceramic levels at Aq Kupruk contain the bones of domesticated sheep and goat.

Our knowledge of the Neolithic in Afghanistan is largely restricted to caves, the occupants of which probably had atypical economies. At Aq Kupruk the earliest pottery, soft ware with zigzag incisions, is dated *c.* 5000–4500 bc. At Dara-i Kur the Late Neolithic is associated with ritual deposits containing goats. For the Copper and Bronze Ages we have the key site of Mundigak, where Casal recognized four main phases of occupation. These range from Mundigak I, the pottery of which recalls Jemdet Nasr and Sialk III, to Mundigak IV, the beginning of which Casal (1961) dated *c.* 2750–2500 BC on analogy with Iranian and Mesopotamian sites, now dated rather earlier. Mundigak IV was an urban settlement containing a palace, temple and other buildings. The third millennium bc also saw the growth of trade in lapis lazuli from Badakhshan. The Fullol hoard indicates that considerable wealth was gained from this long-distance trade.

With the expansion of the Achaemenian empire, Afghanistan came into the orbit of historical civilizations. After Alexander's conquest and a phase of Seleucid rule, an independent dynasty held Bactria and to the Hellenistic period belong the sites of Ai Khanum on the Oxus, and Kandahar. Under the Kushans, who ruled in Afghanistan, Pakistan and northern India from AD 50 to 220, the Buddhist art of Gandhara flourished.

FURTHER READING

AGRESTI, H. 1970. *Rock Drawings in Afghanistan*, Miami. (Field Research Projects, occasional paper no. 14.)
ALLCHIN, F. R. 1957. The culture sequence of Bactria. *Antiquity* XXXI, 131–41.
CASAL, J.-M. 1961. *Fouilles de Mundigak*, (MDAFA vol. XVII), Paris.
DUPREE, L. 1972. Prehistoric Research in Afghanistan (1959–1966). *Trans. American Philosophical Soc.* N.S. 62, pt. 4, Philadelphia.
Mémoires de la Délégation Archéologique Française en Afghanistan. Many vols. 1928– , Paris.
TARN, W. W. 1951. *The Greeks in Bactria and India*[2], Cambridge.

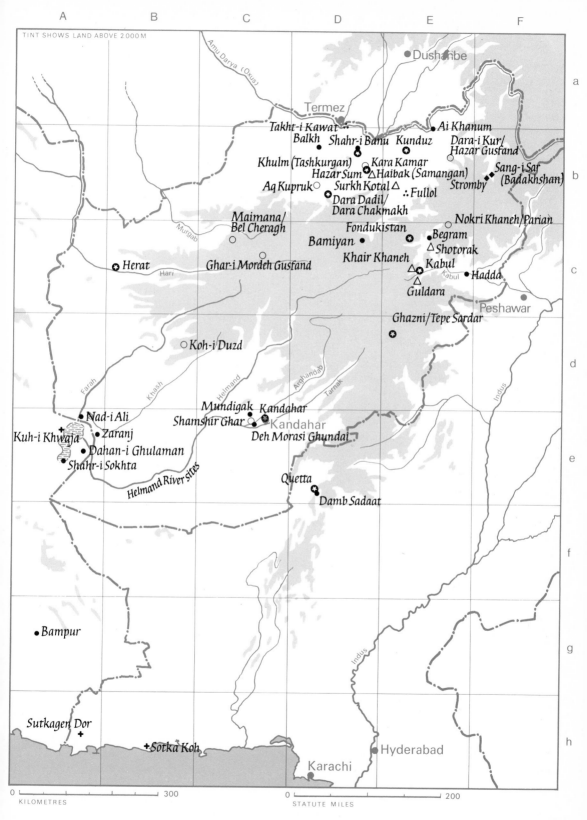

TINT SHOWS LAND ABOVE 2,000M

A   B   C   D   E   F

Amu Darya (Oxus)

Dushanbe

a

Termez

Takht-i Kawat

Balkh   Shahr-i Banu   Kunduz   Ai Khanum

Khulm (Tashkurgan)   Kara Kamar   Dara-i Kur/
                                                Hazar Gusfand

Hazar Sum △ Haibak (Samangan)   Sang-i Sar
                                           (Badakhshan)
Aq Kupruk ○   Surkh Kotal △   Stromby
                                    ∴ Fullol
                 Dara Dadil/
                 Dara Chakmakh   b

Maimana/   Fondukistan   Nokri Khaneh/Parian
Bel Cheragh
                   Bamiyan ●   Begram
              ○   △ Shotorak
Ghar-i Mordeh Gusfand   Khair Khaneh Kabul
○   △   c
Herat   △   Hadda
Hari   Guldara
                                      Kabul
                                                      Peshawar

                                        Ghazni/Tepe Sardar

Koh-i Duzd ○

Farah   Khash   Helmand   Arghandab   Tarnak   d

                                                   Indus

Mundigak Kandahar
Shamshir Ghar ●
                   Kandahar
Nad-i Ali   Deh Morasi Ghundai

Kuh-i Khwaja + Zaranj
                                                                 e
         Dahan-i Ghulaman
Shahr-i Sokhta

Helmand River sites   Quetta

                         Damb Sadaat

                                                                 f

Bampur   g

                         Indus

Sutkagen Dor   h
         +
              +Sotka Koh   Hyderabad

                              Karachi

0 _____ 300
KILOMETRES

0 _____ 200
STATUTE MILES

Afghanistan **87**

The Mediterranean basin

Throughout the later prehistoric period the easily navigable Mediterranean Sea united rather than divided the lands around it, and the region always formed a distinct cultural zone. Even during the Leptolithic a number of coastal settlements existed, and in the Neolithic period and later the Mediterranean basin was densely occupied. No fewer than five civilizations flourished there. Excluding the Egyptians, whose Mediterranean outlet was incidental to their development, we have the Minoan-Mycenaeans in the Aegean during the second millennium BC, the Phoenicians on the Levantine coast beginning in the late second millennium, and in the first millennium BC the Classical Greeks, the Etruscans and finally the Romans, who introduced urban civilization to Europe north of the Alps.

The Neolithic in the Mediterranean began in the seventh millennium bc when the first farmers, probably from Anatolia, settled in Greece. Further movements brought farming to Italy and the west Mediterranean basin in the sixth and fifth millennia bc. The westward spread of a farming economy along the northern and southern shores of the Mediterranean was approximately concurrent, and domesticated animals were known in Cyrenaica – due south of Greece – by *c.* 4800 bc. Most of the early farmers were primarily agriculturists, who preferred to settle on good arable land, such as the plains of Macedonia and Thessaly in Greece and the Foggia plain in southeast Italy. Characteristically, they cultivated wheat and barley, often accompanied by a leguminous crop; they bred sheep, goat, cattle and swine, with a strong emphasis on sheep and goat. In the Aegean the villages were permanent and consequently tells, or mounds of superimposed settlements, occur; in the west, settlements may have been of a more temporary nature. Although the neolithic communities were basically self-sufficient, they traded in raw materials used for tools: hard volcanic rocks suitable for axes, and obsidian or flint for knives. However, neolithic trade was limited in both range and scope; obsidian from Melos, for example, was traded within the Aegean, but not to Italy or the west Mediter-

ranean, where traders exploited local sources on the islands of Sardinia, Lipari, Palmarola and Pantelleria. Clearly, the neolithic cultures of the Mediterranean were successful adaptations to local conditions. The stone temples of the Maltese islands and the megalithic tombs of the west Mediterranean were large, impressive monuments, which betoken flourishing and well-organized communities.

The introduction of copper metallurgy in the late fourth millennium BC (early third millennium bc), whether invented locally or imported from outside, upset the equilibrium of the neolithic communities. As in other areas, the practice of metallurgy led to economic specialization and the abandonment of the self-sufficiency of the community; it led also to a considerable expansion of trade. Early centres of metallurgy existed in the Aegean, in north and central Italy and in southern Spain, all based initially on local ores. In each area the new metal-using societies were economically (and perhaps socially) more developed than their neolithic predecessors, but only in the Aegean did the development continue until a true civilization, that of the Minoans and Mycenaeans, emerged. A vital factor in this development, in addition to the invention of metallurgy, was the emergence of Mediterranean 'poly-culture', in which cultivation of olive and vine accompanied cereal production. This more efficient economy was able to support an increased population, which in turn provided the large labour force required by the developing urban economy. The Minoan-Mycenaean civilization, first recognizable in Crete *c.* 2000 BC was a highly organized bureaucracy with the palace officials and, ultimately, the ruler as the central authority. The palaces, therefore, were more than just residences; they were economic and administrative complexes, supporting specialist craftsmen, merchants and civil servants. The civilization was both literate and artistic. It survived on the mainland until shortly after *c.* 1200 BC, when for reasons which are still in dispute it collapsed completely, to survive only as a memory in the Homeric epics.

IV

In the central and west Mediterranean no comparable civilization emerged, but everywhere there were flourishing Bronze Age communities, with smiths and often other specialist craftsmen. After *c*. 2000 BC seaborne trade in the Mediterranean increased in range, and in their last three centuries of power Mycenaean boats sailed regularly south-east to the Levant and west to southern Italy and Sicily. Indeed, actual colonies of Mycenaean merchants may have existed in these far-flung regions.

On the Levantine coast urban communities had flourished since the third millennium BC, deriving their wealth from trade with the civilizations of Egypt and Mesopotamia. However, it was only in the twelfth century BC, when Mycenaean and Hittite power collapsed and Egypt was in decline, that the Phoenicians emerged as an independent power. Indeed, the Phoenicians were to become the first truly *colonial* power in the Mediterranean, establishing colonies along the north African coast, in western Sicily, Sardinia and Spain, and exploring far outside the Mediterranean, along the Atlantic coast of Africa. According to tradition their colonial activities began in the second millennium BC, but convincing archaeological evidence of settlements in the central and west Mediterranean does not begin until the ninth or even the eighth century. The Phoenicians used iron and were literate, and they diffused through much of the Mediterranean both iron metallurgy and an alphabetic script which later became the basis of both the Arabic and Latin alphabets in use today.

Meanwhile, civilized life was gradually recreated in Greece, and in the eighth and seventh centuries BC the Greeks founded their first colonies in the west Mediterranean and the Black Sea, concentrating on areas where the Phoenicians were not already established: Cyrenaica, most of Sicily, southern Italy, southern France and north-east Spain. In central Italy the Etruscans emerged as a distinct entity by *c*. 700 BC, probably after evolving locally under the stimulus of extensive commercial contacts with both Phoenicians and Greeks. In the succeeding two centuries they expanded to gain control over much of north and central Italy. By this date, urban Iron Age cultures existed throughout Italy, as elsewhere in the Mediterranean, and it was one such culture, the Latian Iron Age, with Rome as its chief city, that finally acquired not only Etruscan, but also Greek and Phoenician possessions and went on to become the first imperial power in Europe: the civilization of Rome.

FURTHER READING

BANTI, L. 1960. *Il Mondo degli Etruschi*, Rome.
CLARK, G. and S. PIGGOTT 1965. *Prehistoric Societies*, London and New York.
HARDEN, D. B. 1972. *The Phoenicians* (revised edn), Harmondsworth.
PIGGOTT, S. 1965, 1966. *Ancient Europe*, Edinburgh and Chicago.
RENFREW, C. 1972. *The Emergence of Civilisation. The Cyclades and the Aegean in the Third Millennium BC*, London.
TAYLOUR, LORD W. 1964. *The Mycenaeans*, London and New York.

Neolithic to Bronze Age sites in western Anatolia and the Cyclades

We are dealing here with two geographical regions: western Anatolia with the offshore islands, and the Cyclades. In both areas settlement was sparse during the Neolithic period, which lasted from *c*. 6000 to 3200 BC. In the east the only known early neolithic site is the Aghio Gala cave on Chios, while in the Cyclades no sites are known, though Melos was exploited for its obsidian, which was traded to many neolithic sites in mainland Greece. Several middle neolithic sites exist in the east, including an early phase at Emborio on Chios and a number of late and final neolithic sites, including Kumtepe in the Troad and the earliest occupation at Poliochni on Lemnos. In the Cyclades the earliest settlements occur in the later Middle Neolithic and belong to a distinctive culture named after the site of Saliagos. The Saliagos culture survived into the Late Neolithic and was succeeded by two cultures, one named after Kephala on Kea and the other known as the Grotta-Pelos culture, which survived into the Bronze Age.

The Early Bronze Age (*c*. 3200–2000 BC, *c*. 2500–1700 bc) saw the apogee of Cycladic and Anatolian developments. Proto-urban communities developed in two distinct centres: north-west Anatolia, represented by the famous site of Troy and by other important sites such as Thermi (Lesbos), Poliochni (Lemnos) and Emborio (Chios); and the Cyclades, where many cemeteries are known and some important settlements such as Chalandriani (Syros) and Phylakopi (Melos). It is often maintained that the Bronze Age of the Cyclades and mainland Greece was introduced by invaders from Anatolia, but Renfrew recently argued for local (but related) developments in all three areas, and also in Crete, based on intensive exploitation of the olive and the vine and the growth of a local metallurgical industry. Metallurgy first became really common in the second phase of the Early Bronze Age and to this phase also belong other important developments in technology, economy and social life.

In the succeeding Middle Bronze Age the Cyclades lost their cultural independence and afterwards came under influence from either Crete or the Greek mainland. Western Anatolia remained independent and Troy itself continued as a leading urban centre. However, the region was overshadowed by the spectacular civilizations of Crete and (later) the mainland of Greece.

FURTHER READING

BLEGEN, C. W. 1963. *Troy and the Trojans*, London and New York.

BREA, L. BERNABÒ 1964. *Poliochni. Città Preistorica nell Isola di Lemnos*, Rome.

EVANS, J. D. and C. RENFREW 1968. *Excavations at Saliagos near Antiparos*, London.

RENFREW, C. 1972. *The Emergence of Civilisation. The Cyclades and the Aegean in the Third Millennium BC*, London.

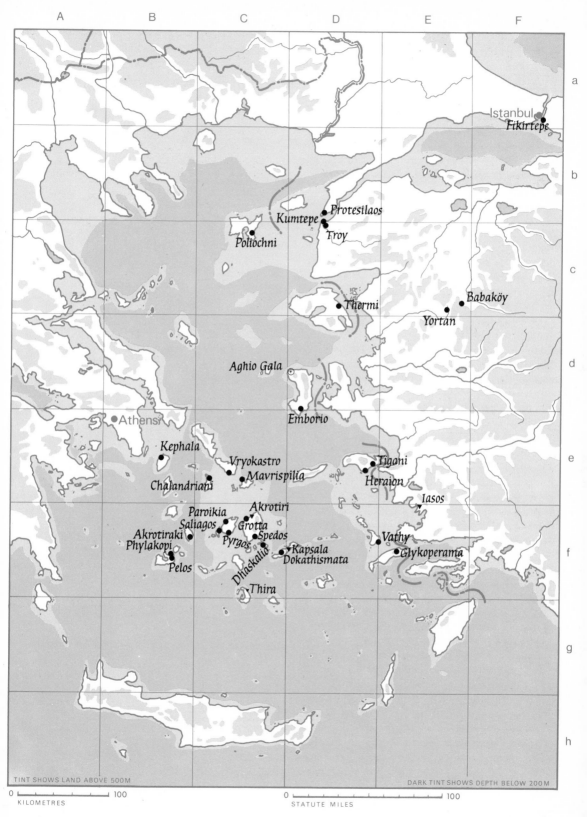

Neolithic to Bronze Age sites in western Anatolia and the Cyclades **91**

Neolithic sites in Greece

The first farmers in Greece arrived before *c.* 6500 bc, probably from Anatolia, bringing with them the domesticated plants and animals which were to remain the basis of the economy throughout the Neolithic: sheep, goats, cattle and swine, einkorn and emmer wheat, barley and several leguminous crops. Even the earliest neolithic sites were usually permanent settlements and in areas where mud brick was used (most commonly in the north) mounds like the tells of western Asia accumulated. Obsidian from Melos was traded over long distances, but apart from this the economy was that of subsistence farming. The earliest neolithic cultures known – that is to say, the cultures of Thessaly (e.g. from Argissa, Soufli, etc.), the Argolid (Franchthi Cave) and Crete (Knossos) – were aceramic. However, by the early sixth millennium bc pottery was in general use. In Thessaly and Macedonia impressed and painted wares occur from an early date, but in the south both plain wares and other decorative traditions are found.

During the Middle Neolithic (*c.* 5000–4000 bc) a greater variety of regional cultures emerged. Best known of these is the Sesklo culture of Thessaly, but different groups existed in Macedonia (represented at Sitagroi), central Greece (Elateia), the Peloponnese (Lerna) and Crete (Knossos), while the Cyclades were now settled for the first time (Saliagos). In the succeeding Late Neolithic (*c.* 4800–4100 BC, *c.* 4000–3300 bc) a number of significant developments occurred: the vine and possibly also the olive were first cultivated, copper-working began on a small scale and at least one site – Dimini in Thessaly – was fortified. Elaborate painted and other decorated pottery characterizes the period.

The final Neolithic (*c.* 4100–3200 BC, *c.* 3300–2500 bc) is less well understood than the earlier phases, although several sites and assemblages are known. Changes in economy and society laid the foundations of the flourishing cultures of the Bronze Age in Greece. Painted pottery became less common and, generally speaking, plain and pattern burnished wares predominated.

FURTHER READING

MILOJČIĆ, V. 1949. *Chronologie der jüngeren Steinzeit Mittel- und Südosteuropas*, Berlin.

RENFREW, C. 1972. *The Emergence of Civilisation. The Cyclades and the Aegean in the Third Millennium BC*, London.

WACE, A. J. B. and M. S. THOMPSON 1912. *Prehistoric Thessaly*, Cambridge.

WEINBERG, S. S. 1965. The Stone Age in the Aegean. *Cambridge Ancient History* I, Chapter 10.

TINT SHOWS LAND ABOVE 500M

• Vršnik

Sitagroi •
Dikilitash •

Nea Nikomedia •

Thessalonika

Sidari •

Asfaka •
Ioannina

Argissa • Rachmani
Trikkala • • Ghediki
Otzaki • • Mesiane-Magoula
Magoula • • Soufli
Magoulitza • Visvikis • • Dimini
Tsani • • Sesklo
Achilleion • • Pyrasos
• Tsangli • Zerelia

Lianokladi •

Cherospelia ○

Elateia (Drachmani) •
Chaeronea • • Orchomenos

Eutresis •

Corinth •   Athens

Gonia •
Hagiorgitika •
Lerna •   Navplion
○ Franchthi Cave

Kalamai

Saliagos •

□
Melos

Knossos •

0 ⊢—————⊣ 200
KILOMETRES

0 ⊢—————⊣ 120
STATUTE MILES

Neolithic sites in Greece **93**

Cyprus

No palaeolithic or mesolithic site has yet been found in Cyprus and the archaeological record begins with an aceramic neolithic culture. This is best known from the village of round stone houses at Khirokitia, which is dated by C¹⁴ to $c.$ 5700 bc. This early neolithic culture apparently came to an abrupt end and the next well documented phase is a Late Neolithic with painted pottery, also represented at Khirokitia. It was succeeded in the early fourth millennium BC (late fourth millennium bc) by the chalcolithic culture named after the site of Erimi.

The Bronze Age, which began $c.$ 3000 BC ($c.$ 2400 bc) was a prosperous period, for Cyprus possesses copper in abundance. The period is known mainly from cemeteries of rock-cut tombs, though settlements are known too, especially in the later phases. Initially the island had little contact with other areas, but in the second millennium BC intense trade was conducted with Minoan Crete and by $c.$ 1500 BC Cyprus became an important commercial centre, exporting pottery (and doubtless copper) to Syria, Egypt and even Nubia. After the take-over of Knossos by Mycenae $c.$ 1400 BC, Mycenaean trade dominated the scene. Indeed, so abundant is Mycenaean pottery in Cyprus that some scholars have suggested that actual Mycenaean colonies were established. However, pottery apart, Mycenaean features are lacking and it seems more likely that the Mycenaean presence consisted simply of merchants lodging in Cypriot settlements.

With the fall of Mycenae $c.$ 1200 BC the situation changed. It seems clear that refugees from the Greek mainland arrived in Cyprus and inaugurated a new dynamic phase in the island's history. Now we find strong evidence for colonies: for example, the town of Enkomi was rebuilt in Mycenaean style. For a century or more civilization of Aegean character survived on the island and Cyprus was a considerable force in the east Mediterranean. During this period iron-working was introduced, probably from Anatolia. After the emergence of the Phoenicians as an effective maritime power, Cypriot influence declined and the island relapsed into a somewhat inward-looking Iron Age, which none the less demonstrated frequent contact with both the Phoenician Levant and the Greek Aegean.

FURTHER READING

CATLING, H. W. 1966. Cyprus in the Neolithic and Bronze Age Periods², *Cambridge Ancient History*, fasc. 43, Cambridge.
KARAGEORGHIS, V. 1968. *Cyprus*, Geneva.
———— 1969. *Salamis in Cyprus*, London and New York.
———— 1969. Chypre. *Archéologie vivante*, Paris.

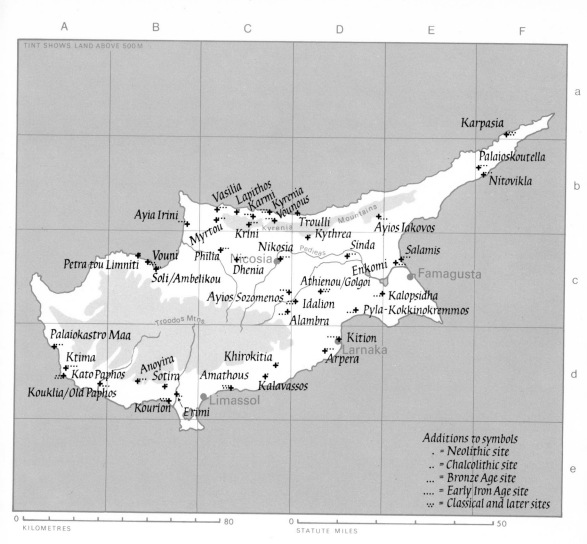

TINT SHOWS LAND ABOVE 500 M

A   B   C   D   E   F

a

Karpasia

Palaioskoutella

Nitovikla

b

Vasilia *Lapithos*
Karmi *Kyrenia*
Ayia Irini *Vounous*
Troulli Kyrenia Mountains
Myrtou *Krini* *Kythrea* *Ayios Iakovos*
Philia *Nikosia* Pedieas *Sinda* *Salamis*
Vouni Nicosia *Enkomi*
Petra tou Limniti *Dhenia* *Athienou/Golgoi* Famagusta
Soli/Ambelikou *Kalopsidha*
Ayios Sozomenos *Idalion* *Pyla-Kokkinokremmos*
Troodos Mtns. *Alambra*

c

Palaiokastro Maa *Kition*
Ktima *Khirokitia* *Arpera* Larnaka
Anoyira *Sotira* *Amathous*
Kato Paphos *Kalavassos*
Kouklia/Old Paphos *Kourion* *Erimi*
Limassol

d

Additions to symbols
. = *Neolithic site*
.. = *Chalcolithic site*
... = *Bronze Age site*
.... = *Early Iron Age site*
∴ = *Classical and later sites*

e

0   80
KILOMETRES

0   50
STATUTE MILES

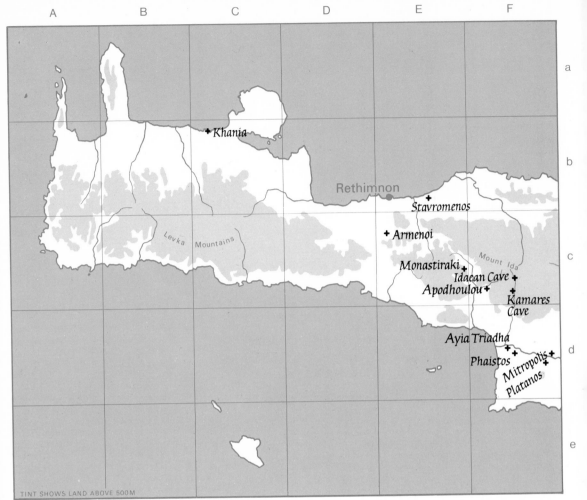

Map labels: Khania, Rethimnon, Stavromenos, Armenoi, Levka Mountains, Monastiraki, Mount Ida, Idaean Cave, Apodhoulou, Kamares Cave, Ayia Triadha, Phaistos, Mitropolis, Platanos

TINT SHOWS LAND ABOVE 500M

Crete

Crete, like most of the smaller Mediterranean islands, apparently was uninhabited during the Palaeolithic. It was settled first some time before 6000 bc by groups of farmers, among whom pottery was unknown. The most informative settlement of this 'aceramic' Early Neolithic phase is Knossos, a site occupied continuously from the Neolithic to the Late Bronze Age, developing from a village of only 2500 square metres to a palace-town covering about 50 hectares. During the Late Neolithic, which lasted from *c*. 4000–3000 BC (*c*. 3300–2500 bc), the traditional cereal crops were supplemented by cultivated figs, vines and perhaps also olives. At the same time, copper metallurgy came into use. These developments in agriculture and tech-

nology provided the economic foundation on which the proto-urban communities of the Early Bronze Age (i.e. the Early Minoan period) developed. By the beginning of the Middle Minoan period (*c*. 2000 BC), Crete supported a civilization; the proto-urban settlements had grown into towns, with a palace at their centre. The palace officials organized the collection and redistribution of food, raw materials and manufactured goods; they supported numerous craftsmen and were literate. The towns were rich and Cretan products reached a high level of technological and artistic achievement. Among the most important palace-towns were Knossos, Phaistos, Mallia, Gournia and Zakro. The Minoans were the first civilization to arise in the Mediterranean and,

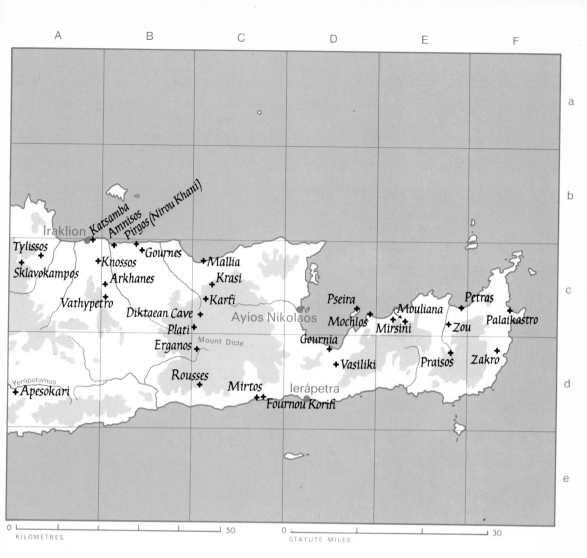

although Crete was in touch with those of Egypt and the Near East, recent research suggests that it was largely a local development. After *c.* 1450 BC, Minoan civilization was overwhelmed by the closely related one of the Mycenaeans of mainland Greece, perhaps in the wake of a natural disaster following the eruption of the volcano on Thera. The non-Indo-European language of the Minoans (written at this stage in the script known as 'Linear A') was replaced by the Greek used by the Mycenaeans (written in 'Linear B'). The hybrid Minoan–Mycenaean civilization survived on the island, as on the mainland, for two and a half centuries, after which, for reasons still in dispute, it collapsed completely and urban life and literacy disappeared.

FURTHER READING

EVANS, J. D. 1971. Neolithic Knossos: the growth of a settlement. *Proceedings of the Prehistoric Society* 37, 95–117.
HOOD, S. 1971. *The Minoans*, London and New York.
HUTCHINSON, R. W. 1962. *Prehistoric Crete*, London and Baltimore.
RENFREW, C. 1972. *The Emergence of Civilisation. The Cyclades and the Aegean in the Third Millennium BC*, London.
WARREN, P. 1972. *Myrtos. An Early Bronze Age Settlement in Crete*, London.

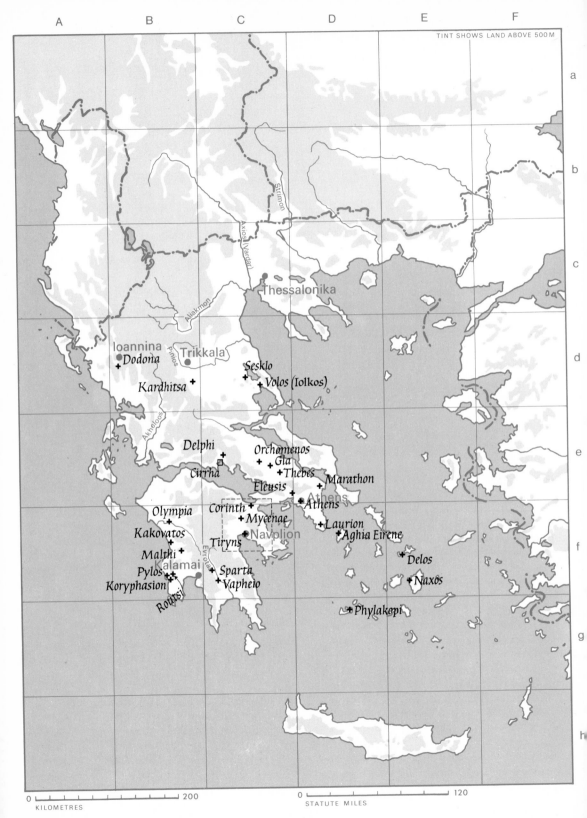

A   B   C   D   E   F

a

b

c

Thessalonika

Ioannina
Dodona   Trikkala

Sesklo
Kardhitsa   Volos (Iolkos)

d

Delphi   Orchomenos
Cirrha   Gla
Thebes   Marathon
Eleusis
Olympia   Corinth   Athens
Mycenae
Kakovatos   Laurion
Tiryns   Navplion   Aghia Eirene
Malthi   Delos
Kalamai   Sparta   Naxos
Pylos   Vapheio
Koryphasion
Roursi   Phylakopi

e

f

g

h

0 ⊢————————⊣ 200
KILOMETRES

0 ⊢————————⊣ 120
STATUTE MILES

98   *Mycenaean and other Bronze Age sites in Greece*

Mycenaean and other Bronze Age sites in Greece

The Bronze Age in Greece, which began *c.* 3200 BC (*c.* 2500 bc), saw the transformation from village to urban economy, culminating in the civilizations of Knossos (see p. 95) and Mycenae.

During the Early Bronze Age (*c.* 3200–2000 BC, *c.* 2500–1700 bc) proto-urban settlements of growing complexity emerged in four regions of the Aegean: southern and east central Greece, Crete, the Cyclades, and north-west Anatolia. Many scholars maintain that a population movement from Anatolia to mainland Greece and the islands took place at the beginning of the Bronze Age; this is disputed by Renfrew, who believes that civilization evolved locally on an indigenous basis. He suggests that many factors contributed to this process, two of the most significant being the intensified exploitation of the vine and olive and the development of a metal industry which stimulated trade and communications.

Minoan civilization developed in Crete *c.* 2000 BC and Mycenaean civilization on the Greek mainland emerged *c.* 1600 BC. The islands of the Aegean came under the influence first of Crete and later of Mycenae. Both civilizations were characterized by palace-based redistributive economies, stratified societies, the use of writing, monumental stone architecture and skilled technology and arts. The decipherment of the Linear B script demonstrated that the Mycenaeans, unlike the Minoans, spoke Greek.

In the fifteenth century BC many Mycenaean features, including the Greek language, were adopted in Crete and for two centuries the two civilizations were effectively one. It is not clear whether Mycenaean domination followed military campaigns or more peaceful contact. The period which ensued witnessed a massive expansion of trade in the Mediterranean basin.

Mycenaean civilization collapsed in the period *c.* 1200–1150 BC. Several explanations have been offered – internal dissent, environmental disaster, invasion from the north – and scholars agree only about the scale of the decline: settlements were abandoned, the literate palace-based aristocracy vanished and the wide network of trade collapsed. Indeed, Greece now entered a 'Dark Age'.

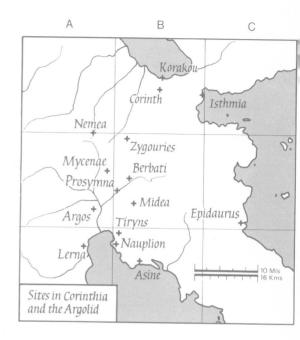

Sites in Corinthia and the Argolid

FURTHER READING

CHADWICK, J. 1963. The prehistory of the Greek language. *Cambridge Ancient History* II, Chapter 39.
DESBOROUGH, V. R. D'A. 1964. *The Last Mycenaeans and their successors*, Oxford.
PALMER, L. R. 1965. *Mycenaeans and Minoans*, London and New York.
RENFREW, C. 1972. *The Emergence of Civilisation. The Cyclades and the Aegean in the Third Millennium BC*, London.
SIMPSON, R. HOPE 1965. *A Gazetteer and Atlas of Mycenaean Sites*, London.
TAYLOUR, LORD W. 1964. *The Mycenaeans*, London and New York.

The Mycenaeans abroad

see map pp. 100/101

The Mycenaean civilization of Greece flourished for just over four centuries, beginning *c.* 1600 BC. At the height of their power the Mycenaeans were involved in a network of trade stretching from Italy to the Levant and southwards into Egypt. We have evidence of commercial contact

Map labels:

A B C

- Luni sul Mignone
- Castiglione
- Naples
- San Silvestro (Giovinazzo)
- Santa Sabina
- Scoglio del Tonno
- Porto Perone (Leporano)
- Punta delle Terrare
- Torre Castelluccia
- Filicudi
- Lipari/Panarea
- Agrigento
- Buscemi
- Thapsos
- Matrensa/Cozzo del Pantano
- Borg in Nadur

a b c d e f g h

between Greece and other Mediterranean areas from the early Mycenaean period (indeed, long-range commerce began in the preceding Middle Helladic phase), but it appears that before *c.* 1400 BC trade was of little importance, while after this date, in the Mycenaean IIIA, IIIB and early IIIC phases, it was organized on a large and profitable scale. The trade is documented by large quantities of Mycenaean pottery and other goods (metal objects and possibly faience) in non-Mycenaean regions. The merchandise imported to Greece in exchange probably consisted mainly of raw materials, especially metal.

Despite their far-reaching contacts, the Mycenaeans established few colonies outside Greece. On Rhodes, Mycenaean settlements did exist; at Trianda, Mycenaeans settled in a Minoan community and the two groups seem to have co-existed peacefully. Colonies may have been planted on other Ionian islands. Cyprus probably was not colonized until late Mycenaean times (i.e. the twelfth century BC), but it then became an important Mycenaean centre. Elsewhere we have no evidence of actual colonies, although in some areas Mycenaean quarters may have been established in native settlements. One suspects, for example, that Tell Abu Hawam in the east and Scoglio del Tonno (Taranto) in the west contained Mycenaean communities.

Following the fall of Mycenae just after *c.* 1200 BC, trade with the West declined dramatically. In the East commerce continued, but the initiative passed to Cypriot and Levantine merchants. Indeed, it was a Levantine group, the Phoenicians, who several centuries later reopened the shipping lanes to the West.

FURTHER READING

MELLAART, J. 1968. Anatolian Trade with Europe and Anatolian Geography and Culture Provinces in the Late Bronze Age. *Anatolian Studies* 18, 187–202.

SIMPSON, R. HOPE 1965. *A Gazetteer and Atlas of Mycenaean Sites*, London.

STUBBINGS, F. H. 1951. *Mycenaean Pottery from the Levant*, Cambridge.

TAYLOUR, LORD W. 1958. *Mycenaean Pottery from Italy and Adjacent Areas*, Cambridge.

—— 1964. *The Mycenaeans*, London and New York.

A   B   C   D   E   F

a

Istanbul

b

Troy

Mytilene

Pitane

Smyrna   Sardis

c

Colophon
Ephesus

Miletus
Müsgebi

Tarsus

Mersin

Eleona
Paliochora

Trianda /
Ialysos
Lartos

d

Tell Atchana

Khan Sheikhoun

Ras Shamra

Hama

H.Iakovos

Pyla Enkomi

Kourion   Maroni   Kadesh   Katna

Byblos

Gharifeh

e

Sarepta

Tell Abu Hawam Jat Tell Achari

Megiddo   Beth Shan

Shechem

'Ain Shems Jericho

Askalon   Tell Beit Mirsim

Port Said   Gaza Lachish

El Arish Tell Fara

f

Mostai

Abusir Heliopolis
Saqqara

Abu Ghurob Lahun

g

Zawyet al-Amwat

El Amarna

Nile

Rifeh

h

Abydos Naqada
Thebes / Gournah

Kizil Irmak   Firat   Euphrates

TINT SHOWS LAND ABOVE 1000 M

0   400
KILOMETRES

0   250
STATUTE MILES

The Mycenaeans abroad   **101**

The Phoenicians at home

The Phoenicians' homeland lay in the central part of the Levantine coast, between Tartus and the area south of Mount Carmel. From the early third millennium BC this region had been drawn into the orbits of Mesopotamian and Egyptian civilization, but it is only after c. 1500 BC that a distinctive Phoenician civilization can be distinguished from that of the Canaanites, who occupied a much larger area comprising the entire coast of the Levant together with parts of the hinterland.

The Phoenicians reached the zenith of their power in the early first millennium BC when the major colonies of the central and west Mediterranean were founded. Phoenician independence ended in their homeland in 574 BC when Tyre fell to the Babylonian king Nebuchadnezzar. In the west, the Phoenicians survived until 146 BC when Carthage was sacked by Rome.

The physical geography of the Levant was largely responsible for the maritime character of Phoenician civilization in which the most prosperous cities were ports, notably Tyre, Sidon, Byblos and Aradus (Ruad). In the twelfth century BC the Mycenaean and Hittite empires collapsed and Egypt suffered a political decline; the Phoenicians siezed this opportunity for expansion and emerged as a leading maritime power.

Our knowledge of the Phoenicians comes from both archaeological and historical sources. The documents, however, are almost entirely the work of other peoples, most of whom wrote in unflattering or downright hostile terms. Among all the ancient civilizations of the Mediterranean, the Phoenicians were pre-eminent in their mastery of the sea. They tackled with confidence voyages not only in the Mediterranean itself, but also in the tidal waters of the Atlantic, where they explored the coastline of Africa. Archaeology reveals them as efficient in commerce and industry, but tells us relatively little about their art and literature. Indeed it is ironic that we know so little of the literature of a people whose most enduring legacy was their alphabetic script, from which developed the Greek, Latin, Arabic and Hebrew alphabets.

FURTHER READING

CONTENAU, G. 1949. *La Civilisation phénicienne*², Paris.
CULICAN, W. 1966. *The First Merchant Venturers*, London and New York.
DIRINGER, D. 1962. *Writing*, London and New York.
HARDEN, D. B. 1972. *The Phoenicians* (revised edn), Harmondsworth.
MOSCATI, S. 1968. *The World of the Phoenicians*, London and New York.

Tarsus ·Adana

Antioch
Aleppo
·Aleppo
Alalakh (Atchana)

Minet el-Beida
Ugarit

Nikosia Enkomi
Salamis

Hamath

Kourion

Aradus/Antaradus
Marathus
Simyra Kadesh
Al Mina
Palmyra
Tripolis
Byblos

Beirut ·Berytus

Sidon
Damascus
Sarepta ·Damascus
Tyre
Hazor

Atlit
Megiddo
·Beth Shan
Samaria
·Tell el-Far'ah
Shechem
Jaffa
Amman
Askalon Jericho
Jerusalem
·Hebron
Gaza Tell Beit Mirsim
Beersheba

TINT SHOWS LAND ABOVE 1000 M

0 ———————— 180
KILOMETRES

0 ———————— 100
STATUTE MILES

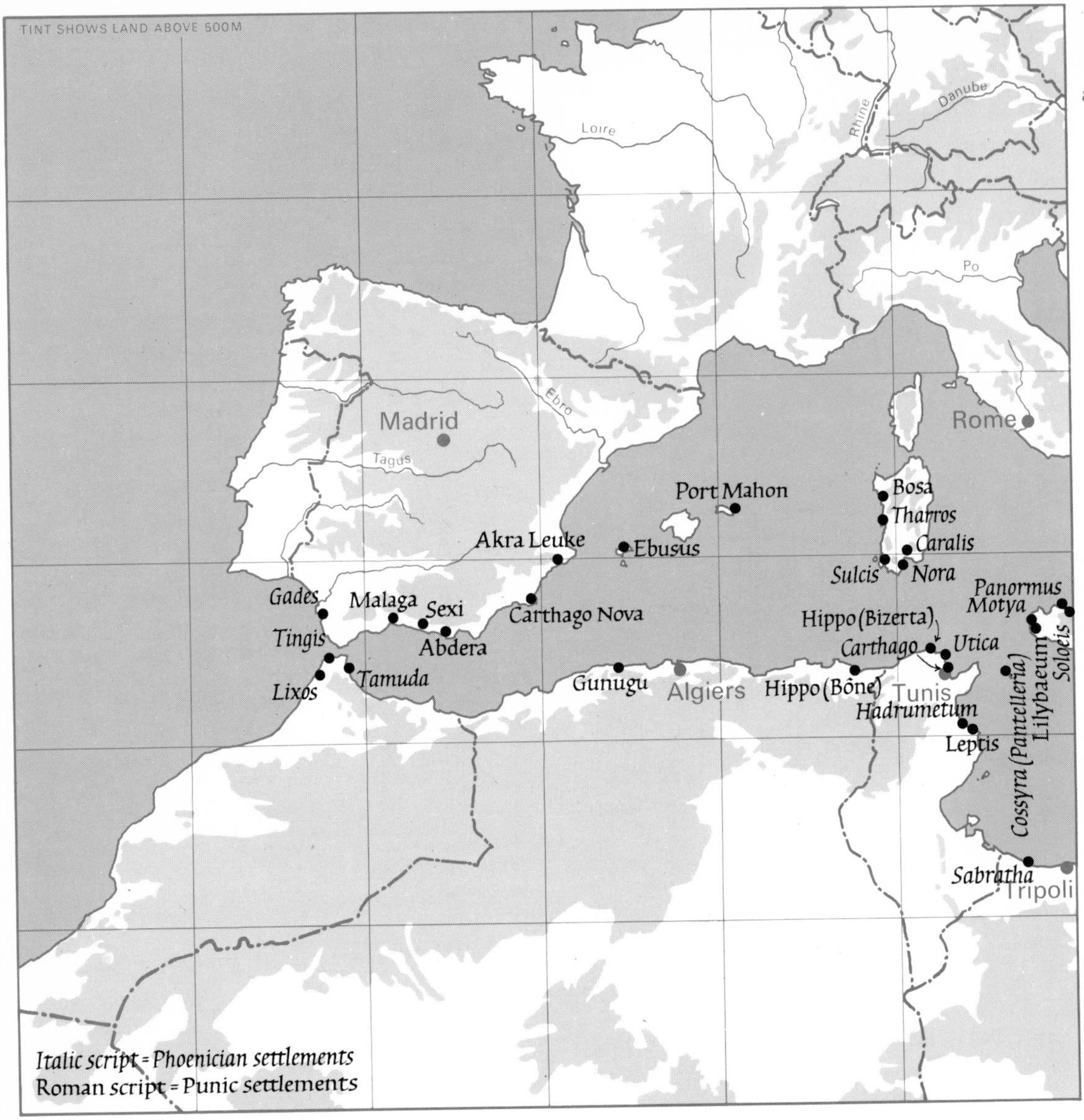

A
B
C
D
E
F
a
b
c
d
e
f
TINT SHOWS LAND ABOVE 500M
Loire
Rhine
Danube
Po
Ebro
Tagus
Madrid
Rome
Port Mahon
Bosa
Tharros
Caralis
Sulcis
Nora
Akra Leuke
Ebusus
Gades
Malaga
Sexi
Abdera
Carthago Nova
Tingis
Lixos
Tamuda
Gunugu
Algiers
Hippo (Bizerta)
Carthago
Utica
Hippo (Bône)
Tunis
Hadrumetum
Leptis
Panormus
Motya
Solоeis
Lilybaeum
Cossyra (Pantelleria)
Sabratha
Tripoli
Italic script = Phoenician settlements
Roman script = Punic settlements

The Phoenicians abroad

The Phoenicians emerged as a significant maritime trading power after the collapse of the Mycenaeans in the twelfth century BC, although by this date they had long been involved in trade between Mesopotamia and Egypt. In the civilized east Mediterranean they established extensive commercial contacts, but no colonies, with the possible exception of Kition (Larnaka) in Cyprus. Indeed, it was only in the central and west Mediterranean, outside the areas directly controlled by the Greeks, that the Phoenicians founded a network of colonies. Ancient traditions claimed that some of these colonies were founded in the second millennium BC, but archaeology has yielded nothing earlier than the ninth or eighth centuries. Among the earliest Phoenician settlements in the West are Carthage, Utica, Hadrumetum and Lepcis Magna in north Africa; Motya in Sicily; a town on Malta; Nora, Tharros, Sulcis and Caralis in Sardinia; Gades in Spain;

Gaulos (Gozo)
Malta

Lepcis Magna

Medina Sultan

Danube

Bucharest

Sofia

Istanbul

Kızıl Irmak

Athens

Kition

Nile

Homeland of the Phoenicians
(see 102–3)

0 ———————— 500
KILOMETRES

0 ———————— 300
STATUTE MILES

probably also a town on Menorca; and possibly other towns in Morocco. The most powerful western colony was Carthage. Traditionally founded in 814 BC, Carthage soon became the leading Phoenician city in the central Mediterranean. By the mid-seventh century it was founding colonies of its own: Ebusus (Ibiza) was established in 654/3. In the sixth and early fifth centuries Carthage came into conflict with the Greeks. Although victorious in the Tyrrhenian

Sea, the Carthaginians were defeated in Sicily and subsequently concentrated on expansion farther west, founding new colonies or reinforcing existing settlements in Sardinia, Spain and north Africa, even beyond the Straits of Gibraltar. In the fourth century Carthage again fought the Greeks of Sicily and in 264 BC became involved in the first of three wars with Rome (the Punic Wars). She suffered a final crushing defeat in 146.

The Phoenicians were the most adventurous

merchants and explorers of the ancient world. This map shows their settlements in the Mediterranean basin, but apparently expeditions were sent even farther afield. In the early sixth century a Phoenician fleet reputedly circumnavigated Africa; in the late fifth century Hanno of Carthage may have sailed down the west coast of Africa as far as 'Cerne', probably at the mouth of the Senegal River; Himilco sailed northwards round Spain, perhaps reaching Brittany and southern Britain.

FURTHER READING

CARPENTER, R. 1958. The Phoenicians in the West. *American Journal of Archaeology* 62, 37–53.
CINTAS, P. 1970. *Manuel d'Archéologie Punique*, Paris.
GUIDO, M. 1963. *Sardinia*, London and New York.
HARDEN, D. B. 1972. *The Phoenicians* (revised edn), Harmondsworth.
MOSCATI, S. 1968. *The World of the Phoenicians*, London and New York.

Archaic and Classical Greece

In the early twelfth century BC Mycenaean civilization collapsed. Greece entered a 'Dark Age' in which the whole machinery of the Mycenaean state, the widespread commerce that supported it and, in many cases, the settlements themselves disappeared. Monumental architecture, literature, painting and sculpture were abandoned and the 'Dark Age' saw the emergence of only one significant advance: the use of iron, which began before *c.* 1000 BC and was rapidly adopted for tools, weapons and ornaments. A crucial event of the period was an invasion of newcomers from the north, the Dorians, although whether they were responsible for the downfall of Mycenaean civilization is still a matter of controversy.

In the succeeding three centuries (*c.* 800–500 BC), known as the Archaic period, prosperity returned. The Greeks gradually re-established urban life, a process accompanied by renewed interest in lands overseas. Many of the characteristics of civilization reappeared in the ninth or eighth centuries: monumental art and architecture, and writing. However, an additional boost and a distinctive aspect was given to the emerging civilization during the 'orientalizing' phase of the seventh century, when renewed commerce in the east Mediterranean brought Greece once more into close contact with the civilizations of Egypt and western Asia.

The fifth and fourth centuries BC formed the Classical period of Greek history. It was the age of independent city-states and is almost universally regarded as the summit of Greek political and cultural development. With the elimination of the Achaemenian threat in the early fifth century, the Greeks became secure in the east Mediterranean and the foundation was laid for the surge of activity in philosophy and the arts, which has contributed so much to the development of 'Western' culture. The complex amalgam of city-states was inherently unstable and the Classical period lasted less than two centuries: destructive rivalry between individual states and alliances made each of them vulnerable. With the emergence of the powerful Macedonian kingdom, the majority of independent city-states disappeared, Greek culture was carried as far east as the Oxus and Indus rivers, and a new, almost imperial, age (the Hellenistic period) began.

FURTHER READING

BURY, J. B. 1951. *A History of Greece to the Death of Alexander the Great*, London and New York.
COOK, R. M. 1961. *The Greeks till Alexander*, London and New York.
FINLEY, M. I. 1963. *The Ancient Greeks*, London and New York.
VAN DER HEYDEN, A. A. M. and H. H. SCULLARD (eds) 1959. *Atlas of the Classical World*, London.

A B C D E F

TINT SHOWS LAND ABOVE 500 M

a

b

+ Apollonia

+ Oricum

Aegae

Crenides +

Amphipolis +

Abdera

Doriscus +

Pella

Methone +

Therma

Eion

Galepsus +

Maronia

Aenus

Alopeconnesus

Cardia +

Priapus

c

Thessalonika

Pydna +

Olynthus +

Potidaea +

Mende +

Hephaestia

Sestus +

Lampsacus +

Abydos +

Scepsis +

Ioannina

Dodona +

Trikkala

Crannon

Larisa +

Scione

Myrina

Sigeum

Cebrene +

d

Ambracia +

Pherae +

Halus +

Antandros +

Assos +

Adramyttium +

Methymna

Antissa +

Pyrrha +

Mytilene +

Pergamum

Pharsalus +

Oreus +

Eresus

Atarneus +

Argos +

Thermum +

Delphi

Opus +

Larymna +

Chalcis +

Elaea +

Cyme +

Phocaea +

e

Pale +

Same +

Calydon +

Naupactus +

Aegium +

Chaeronea

Coronea +

Thebes +

Eretria +

Oropus +

Tanagra +

Delium

Erythrae +

Teos +

Cranii +

Pronni +

Patrae +

Sicyon +

Decelea +

Oenophyta +

Lebedos +

Notium +

Cyllene +

Elis +

Phlius +

Athens

Carystus +

Ephesus +

Olympia

Mantinea +

Argos +

Corinth +

Megara +

Piraeus +

Andros +

Priene +

Miletus +

f

Megalopolis +

Tegea +

Epidaurus +

Troezen +

Hermione +

Naxos

Iasos +

Messene +

Sparta +

Halicarnassus +

Cos +

Gythium +

Cnidus +

Rhodes +

Camirus +

Lindos +

Cydonia +

Knossos +

Gortyna +

h

0 |___|___|___|___|___|___|___| 200
KILOMETRES

0 |___|___|___| 120
STATUTE MILES

Archaic and Classical Greece 107

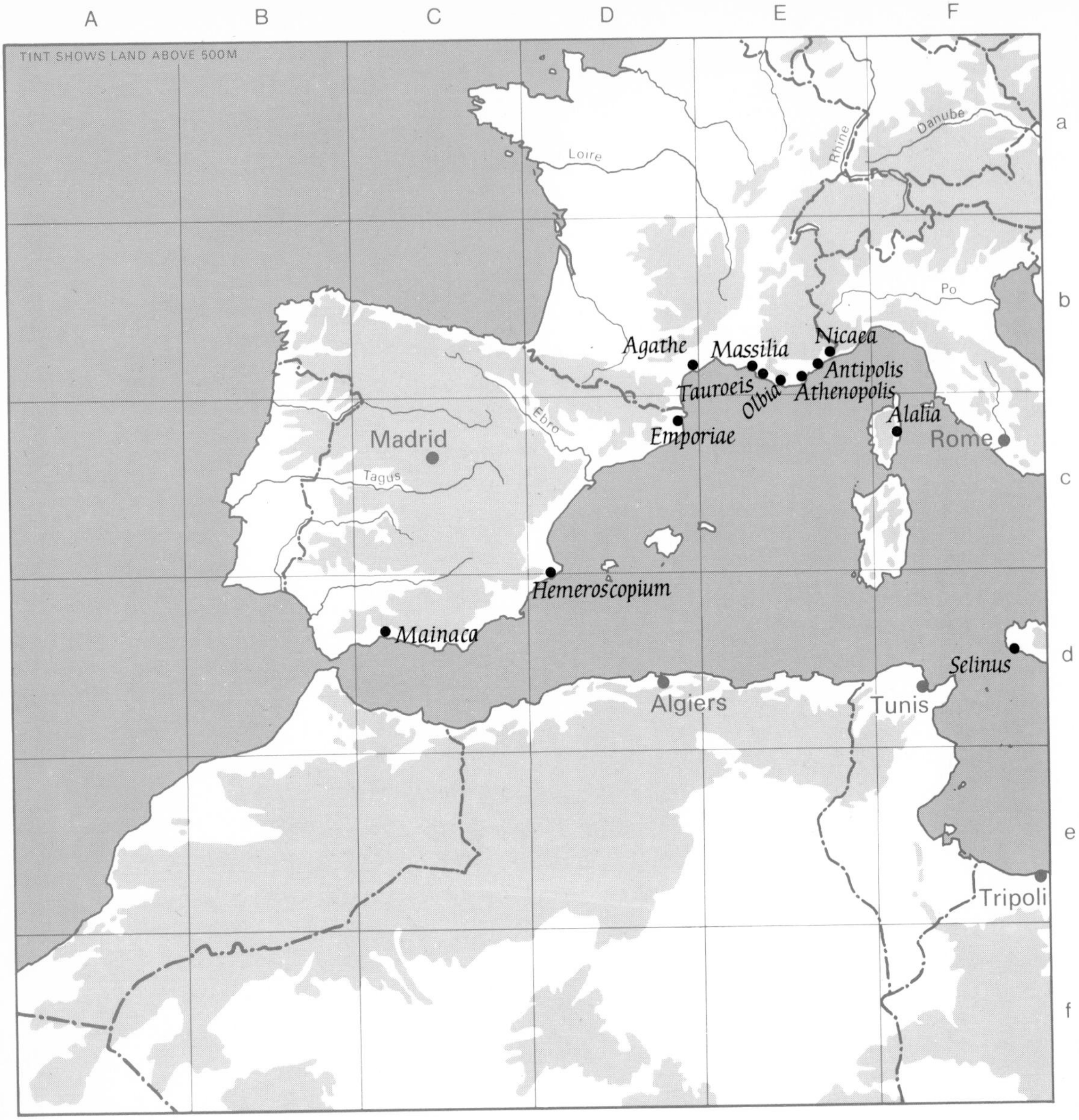

TINT SHOWS LAND ABOVE 500M

Loire

Rhine

Danube

Po

Agathe   *Massilia*   *Nicaea*

Antipolis

Tauroeis   *Olbia*   *Athenopolis*

Emporiae   *Alalia*

Rome

Madrid

Ebro

Tagus

Hemeroscopium

Mainaca

Algiers

Selinus

Tunis

Tripoli

The Greeks overseas

Geographically speaking, Greek expansion overseas before the age of Alexander is divided into three parts: the east Mediterranean, the central and west Mediterranean, and the Black Sea. The period of true colonization, which lasted for about two centuries, *c.* 750–550 BC, followed an earlier phase, also some two centuries long, during which the coast of Anatolia and the neighbouring islands (which had been under strong Greek influence in the Mycenaean period)

were resettled. Thereafter, the history of the Eastern Greeks was closely bound up with that of the Greeks at home; indeed they played a major role in founding colonies farther afield.

In the east Mediterranean, where the Greeks encountered established civilizations, commerce was active, but settlement rare. Important exceptions were the colonies of Al Mina and Naucratis. In Africa the Greeks colonized Cyrenaica, but farther west left the coast to the Phoenicians.

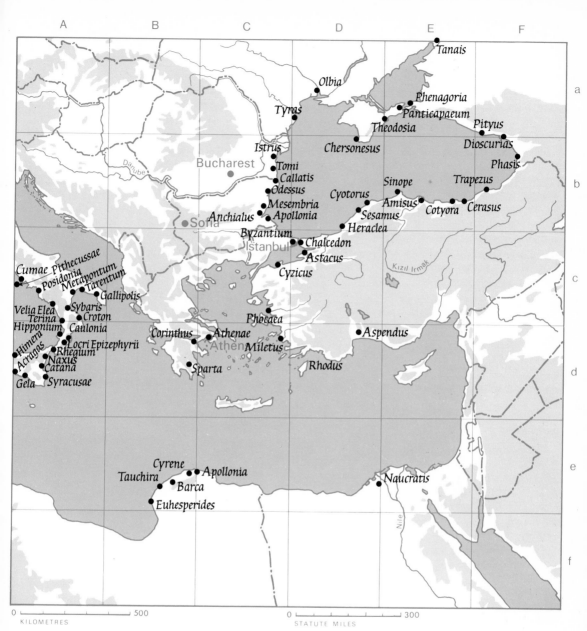

In the central Mediterranean, settlement began *c.* 750 BC with the foundation of Pithecussae on Ischia. In the succeeding two centuries numerous other colonies were founded throughout southern Italy and Sicily. The Greek states of the central Mediterranean influenced the emergent civilization of the Etruscans from the eighth century and at a later date influenced Rome, thereby transmitting much of Greek civilization to the West. Greek colonization advanced farther afield *c.* 600

BC with the foundation of Massalia (Massilia) in southern France; later, it extended to Spain. In the central and west Mediterranean the Greeks were in perpetual competition – and often in open conflict – with the Phoenicians, a role later inherited by Rome.

Greek colonization in the Black Sea may have begun as early as the eighth century BC.

Both in the West and in the Black Sea the Greeks encountered not civilizations, but less developed Iron Age cultures. Not only the Hall-statt and La Tène cultures of Europe, but also Scythian culture show strong Greek influence.

The motives behind Greek activity overseas are not altogether clear. While some scholars believe that land-hunger at home was the primary cause, others stress the role of trade.

On our map we have employed the more familiar Latin forms of ancient names rather than the original Greek forms.

FURTHER READING

BOARDMAN, J. 1964. *The Greeks Overseas*, Harmondsworth and Baltimore.
COOK, J. M. 1962. *The Greeks in Ionia and the East*, London and New York.
DUNBABIN, T. J. 1948. *The Western Greeks*, Oxford and New York.
——— 1957, *The Greeks and their Eastern Neighbours*, London.
WOODHEAD, A. G. 1962. *The Greeks in the West*, London and New York.

Neolithic sites in the central Mediterranean

The Neolithic began in the central Mediterranean before 5000 bc, when the first farmers arrived in south-east Italy, and lasted until *c.* 3500 BC (*c.* 2800 bc), when the first truly metal-using cultures of the Copper Age emerged. Archaeologists recognize three main zones of neolithic settlement: an eastern or Adriatic-Ionian zone, a western or Tyrrhenian zone and a northern or Po Valley zone. Occupation was both earliest and (it seems) most dense in the eastern area, where the characteristic settlement was the *villaggio trincerato*, or village surrounded by one or more ditches. Settlement was exceptionally dense in south-east Italy; on the Foggia plain John Bradford identified from the air more than two hundred *villaggi* and recent work has increased this number considerably. Key sites include Ripoli in central Italy, Passo di Corvo on the Foggia plain, Serra d'Alto and other sites near Matera, and Stentinello and Megara Hyblaea in south-east Sicily. The earliest farmers made Impressed ware and other pottery types; later neolithic communities produced decorative scratched and painted pottery.

Settlement in the Tyrrhenian zone was much less dense and many of the sites were caves, notably Grotta del Santuario della Madonna at Praia a Mare, Grotta delle Felci on Capri and Arene Candide in Liguria. Painted pottery was rare, while Impressed and plain wares were common. Important obsidian sources lay in the region – in Sardinia, and on Palmarola, Lipari and Pantelleria. Indeed, exploitation of the Lipari obsidian almost certainly explains the long-lived neolithic settlement on this otherwise unpromising island.

Neolithic communities in the valleys of the Po and its tributaries differed from those of peninsular Italy and the islands, showing connections with European cultures north of the Alps. The settlements included villages on hills, on lake margins and in caves. Important sites include Quinzano, Rocca di Rivoli, Fiorano Modense, Chiozza di Scandiano, Lagozza and Pescale di Prignano. The earliest culture, Fiorano, is probably of Mediterranean origin, but the next phase, named alternatively after Chiozza or the distinctive 'Square Mouth' pottery, is thought to have affinities in central Europe. The latest neolithic culture of the Po valley, Lagozza, has connections with western neolithic communities in Switzerland and southern France. Lagozza and other late neolithic deposits occasionally yield metal tools, thus heralding the beginning of the local Copper Age.

FURTHER READING

BARFIELD, L. 1971. *Northern Italy before Rome*, London and New York.
BRADFORD, J. S. P. 1966. *Ancient Landscapes* (revised edn), London.
BREA, L. BERNABÒ 1957. *Sicily before the Greeks*, London and New York.
GUIDO, M. 1963. *Sardinia*, London and New York.
RADMILLI, A. M. (ed.) 1967. *Piccola Guida della Preistoria italiana*, Florence.
TRUMP, D. H. 1966. *Central and Southern Italy before Rome*, London and New York.

TINT SHOWS LAND ABOVE 200M

A   B   C   D   E   F

a

• Isolino Virginia   • La Vela
• Isera
• Rocca di Rivoli
Quinzano ✪
• Molino
Casarotto

+ Alba   b

Po

Chiozza di Scandiano
✪ Fiorano Modenese

○ Arene Candide

Grotta all'Onda ○
Riparo la Romita   Grotta del Leone ○
(Asciano)   (Agnano)

+ San Biagio
• Ripabianca di Monterado   c
+ Monte Colombo
Donatelli   • Santa Maria in Selva
Pienza   +
Montalcino +   • Maddalena

Norcia   ✪ Ripoli
• Villaggio Leopardi (Penne di Pescara)
Grotta dei Piccioni
(Bolognano) ○   • Lama dei   d
Peligni
Sasso Furbara +   ✪ Tremiti Islands
Palidoro   Villaggio San Vito
Basi   ○ Grotta la Punta   → ✪ Grotta Scaloria
Filitosa • ○ + Curacchiaghiu   Contrada Guadone • → ✪ Coppa Nevigata
San Vincente   Passo di Corvo •
La Starza   • Canne   ✪ Molfetta
○ Santo Stefano   (Ariano Irpino)   • ✪ • Bari
in Maddalena   La Quercia   Terlizzi + • Polignano a
○ Gaudiano   ✪ Mare   e
Pontine Islands ▫   di Lavello   Altamura ○ Ostuni
○ Grotta Verde (Capo Caccia)   Matera   Francavilla
Grotta delle Felci (Capri) ○   Fontana
Paestum •   Taranto ○ Nardò

▫ Monte Arci   Praia a Mare   Avetrana
○ Grotta S. Angelo 1
• Favella   f

• Carbonia

+ Girifalco

Lipari Acropolis/ ✪
Diana/Castellaro Vecchio
+ Monte Pellegrino   San Basilio   g
+ + Taormina
Termini Imerese   Paternò •
+ Poggio Rosso
Megara Hyblaea
• Stentinello
Calaforno +   Matrensa
Monte Tabuto ◆   ✪
▫ Pantelleria   Grotta Chiusazza ○ Grotta Corruggi   h

0 |————————| 200
KILOMETRES

0 |————————| 120
STATUTE MILES

Neolithic sites in the central Mediterranean   **111**

Copper and Bronze Age sites in Italy

The Italian Copper Age began *c.* 3500 BC (*c.* 2800 bc); sometime between 2500 and 2000 BC it merged into the Bronze Age, which lasted until shortly after 1000 BC. Archaeologists recognize six main Copper Age cultures in Italy: Remedello in the Po valley, a Ligurian culture, Rinaldone in Tuscany and Lazio, Conelle-Ortucchio in the Marche, Gaudo in Campania and Laterza in the south-east. Copper tools appeared first in the Late Neolithic, but they did not come into general use until the full Copper Age. Two centres of metallurgy are known: in the Rinaldone area, using Tuscan ores, and in the Remedello area, using ores from the Alps. Information about the Copper Age comes mostly from graves. In the south, rock-cut tombs were in common use, while in the north trench graves were customary and in central Italy both types occur. The Ligurian group buried their dead in caves.

In the Early Bronze Age true tin bronze replaced copper, and implements, though certainly produced in Italy, show similarities with the products of central Europe. In northern Italy, metal tools have been found in the settlements (often lakeside villages) of the Polada culture, while in peninsular Italy they occur in the hill-top settlements and caves of the Apennine culture, which extended over the entire Bronze Age. In the north, on the other hand, considerable changes took place; in the Middle Bronze Age three distinct areas of settlement emerged in the Veneto, Lombardy and Emilia. All show strong connections with central and eastern Europe, both in bronze typology and in the practice of cremation, which now appeared in Italy. In Emilia the settlements (known as *Terremare*) were urban or proto-urban in structure; sometimes large, they reveal evidence for economic specialization. In the succeeding Proto-Villanovan period, cremation became universal in the north and contacts were maintained with the Urnfield cultures of central Europe. Meanwhile in south-east Italy certain Apennine settlements, notably Scoglio del Tonno at Taranto, developed urban traits, evidently as a result of trade with the Mycenaeans. In the Late Bronze Age, cremation was adopted sporadically in central and southern Italy, but although the cemeteries are usually described as Proto-Villanovan they appear to be an integral part of the local Apennine culture.

FURTHER READING

BARFIELD, L. 1971. *Northern Italy before Rome*, London and New York.

PUGLISI, S. 1959. *La civiltà appenninica. Origine della comunita pastorali in Italia*, Florence.

RADMILLI, A. M. 1963. *La Preistoria d'Italia alla Luce delle ultime Scoperte*, Florence.

RADMILLI, A. M. (ed.) 1967. *Piccola Guida della Preistoria italiana*, Florence.

TRUMP, D. H. 1966. *Central and Southern Italy before Rome*, London and New York.

Ascona

Lagozza

Canegrate

Bor di Pacengo

Val Camonica
Ledro

Cascina Ranza

Polada

Rocca di Rivoli

Le Colombare

Grotta Teresina

Gottolengo

Peschiera

Fimon

Santa Cristina

Villafranca Veronese

Remedello

Barche
di Solferino

Isolone

Fontanella Mantovana

Frattesine

Melara

Castione dei Marchesi

Gorzano

Cumarola

Pescale di Prignano

Grotta del Farneto

Arma di Nasino

Bismantova

Sasso
Marconi

Savignano

Monte Castellaccio

La Panighina

Arma della Gra di Marmo

Grotta all'Onda

Tana Bertrand

Riparola Romita

Grotta del Leone

Colle dei Cappuccini

Conelle

Pianello di Genga

Filottrano

Grotta del Mezzogiorno

Grotta del Orso

Belverde

Ripatransone

Grotta dello Scoglietto

Ponte San Pietro

Rinaldone

Grotta a Male

Luni sul Mignone

Fosso
Conicchio

Grotta dei Piccioni

Allumiere/Coste del Marano

Pian Sultano

Ortucchio

Rome

Grotta Manaccora

Castelluccio dei Sauri

Coppa Nevigata

La Starza

Bisceglie

Giovinazzo

Mirabella Eclano

Terlizzi

Punta
delle Terrare

Casal Sabini

Castiglione

Grotta Pertosa

Timmari

Torre Guaceto

S. Vito
dei Normanni

Gaudo

Matera

Laterza

Cellino

Grotta Latronico

Leucaspide

Scoglio del Tonno

S. Marco

Leporano

Grotta S. Angelo

Torre Castelluccia

Minervino

2/3

Cotronei

0   200
KILOMETRES

0   120
STATUTE MILES

Copper and Bronze Age sites in Italy **113**

Copper and Bronze Age sites in Sicily and the Aeolian Islands

Sicily flourished in the Copper and Bronze Age and, although many traits occur throughout the island, several regional cultures existed. The Copper Age probably began *c.* 3500 BC (*c.* 2800 bc) and the Bronze Age lasted from before 2000 BC until 1000–900 BC. In the Aeolian Islands the Copper Age was a period of decline, for obsidian, which brought prosperity to neolithic Lipari, was rendered obsolete by the new metal implements. The two successive Copper Age cultures of the Aeolian Islands, Piano Conte and Piano Quartara, are characterized by plain pottery. Among the best-known regional cultures of the Copper Age in Sicily are: San Cono, Piano Notaro and Conzo in the south-east, Serraferlicchio in the south, Malpasso and Sant'Ippolito in the interior and Conca d'Oro in the northwest. In south-east Sicily, Grotta Chiusazza near Syracuse has yielded a valuable stratigraphy. The Conzo, Serraferlicchio and Sant'Ippolito cultures produced elaborate painted pottery which is often said to indicate connections with the east Mediterranean, Sicily being the only part of the central Mediterranean to use painted wares in the Copper Age. Among the traits shared by several variants are copper metallurgy and the use of rock-cut tombs – the characteristic tomb type in Sicily throughout the Bronze and Iron Ages.

During the Bronze Age the Aeolian Islands revived, partly because of the expansion of Mediterranean trade. Imported Middle Helladic and Mycenaean pottery occurs in the villages of the Capo Graziano and succeeding Milazzese cultures, demonstrating commercial contacts with the Aegean. Imported pottery occurs in southern Sicily, too, but not until the Early Bronze Age Castelluccio culture. Mycenaean pottery is, however, common in tombs of the later Thapsos culture. In north-west Sicily the Conca d'Oro culture lasted into the Bronze Age, while in the north-east another group developed, known as the Vallelunga culture; neither had Aegean contacts. By the Middle Bronze Age the island was peaceful and prosperous; settlements were permanent and sometimes large, metal was abundant. The Middle Bronze Age ended in the thirteenth century BC. The settlement on Lipari acropolis was destroyed and replaced by the buildings of a totally different culture – the Ausonian – representing an immigration from peninsular Italy, probably the Taranto region. At the same time coastal villages in south-east Sicily were abandoned and replaced by fortified towns in the hinterland. The wealthy Pantalica culture of the inland settlements lasted from the thirteenth century until the arrival of the first Greek colonists in the eighth century BC.

FURTHER READING

BREA, L. BERNABÒ 1957. *Sicily before the Greeks*, London and New York.

BREA, L. BERNABÒ and M. CAVALIER 1956. Civiltà preistoriche delle Isole Eolie e del territorio di Milazzo. *Bullettino di Paletnologia Italiana* 65, 7–99.

CAVALIER, M. 1960–1. Les cultures préhistoriques des iles Eoliennes et leur rapport avec le monde Egéen. *Bulletin de Correspondence Hellénique* 84, 319–46.

RADMILLI, A. M. (ed.) 1967. *Piccola Guida della Preistoria italiana*, Florence.

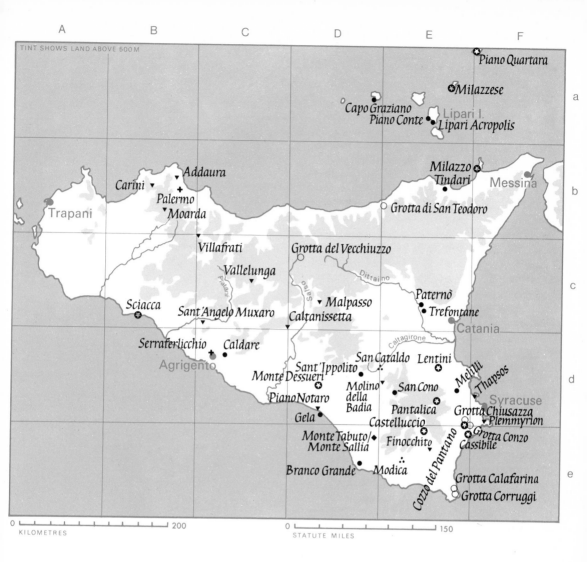

Map labels:

A   **B**   **C**   **D**   **E**   **F**

TINT SHOWS LAND ABOVE 500 M

Piano Quartara

Milazzese

Capo Graziano

Piano Conte   Lipari I.

Lipari Acropolis

a

Milazzo

Tindari   Messina

Carini   Addaura

Palermo

Moarda

Trapani

b

Villafrati   Grotta del Vecchiuzzo

Grotta di San Teodoro

Vallelunga

Paternò

Trefontane

Sciacca   Malpasso

Sant'Angelo Muxaro   Caltanissetta

Catania

c

Serraferlicchio   Caldare

San Cataldo   Lentini

Agrigento   Melilli

Thapsos

Sant'Ippolito

Monte Dessueri   San Cono

Molino   Syracuse

Piano Notaro   della   Pantalica   Grotta Chiusazza

Badia   Plemmyrion

Gela   Castelluccio   Grotta Conzo

Monte Tabuto/   Finocchito   Cassibile

Monte Sallia

Branco Grande   Modica

Cozzo del Pantano

d

Grotta Calafarina

Grotta Corruggi

e

Dittaino

Platani

Salso

Caltagirone

0 ————————— 200
KILOMETRES

0 ————————— 150
STATUTE MILES

Copper and Bronze Age sites in Sicily and the Aeolian Islands   **115**

Copper and Bronze Age sites in Corsica and Sardinia

During the third and second millennia BC the islands of the Tyrrhenian Sea – Corsica and Sardinia – supported flourishing and distinctive cultures. In Sardinia the first metal-using culture is named after the site of Ozieri (the San Michele cave). The Ozieri culture is known chiefly from numerous and frequently elaborate rock-cut tombs, such as Anghelu Ruju, but caves, open settlements and a strange 'ritual' monument at Monte d'Accoddi are also known. During the second millennium BC the Nuraghic culture developed, so-called after the most characteristic class of monuments, the *nuraghi*. These are conical stone towers, often the most prominent features of elaborate stone-walled complexes, more than 6,500 of which exist on the island. The Nuraghic culture survived after the Phoenician and Carthaginian settlement and in some areas *nuraghi* were still being built in the Roman period. As well as the *nuraghi* themselves, the culture is known from megalithic tombs, villages and special monuments, such as temples and sacred wells. The wealth of the Nuraghic culture derived in part from trade in the metal ores in which the island was rich. The bronze figurines of the culture are famous.

The prehistory of Corsica in the Copper and Bronze Ages has much in common with that of Sardinia, but also many differences. The most characteristic monuments are standing stones (menhirs), some plain and others anthropomorphic, sometimes depicted with weapons. In addition there are stone towers known as *torre*, not unlike the Sardinian *nuraghi*. The most famous Corsican site is Filitosa. Grosjean believes that the builders of the *torre* arrived in Corsica in the mid-second millennium BC, perhaps from Sardinia, and that they waged war on the native population – a war symbolized in stone by the weapons shown on the statue-menhirs of the period after their arrival.

The builders of the *nuraghi* and *torre* are sometimes identified with the *Shardana*, recorded in Egyptian documents as one of the 'sea peoples' who raided Egypt between the fourteenth and the twelfth centuries BC.

FURTHER READING

GROSJEAN, R. 1961. Filitosa et son contexte archéologique. *Monuments et Mémoires* (L'Académie des Inscriptions et Belles-Lettres) vol. 52.
——— 1966. *La Corse avant l'Histoire*, Paris.
GUIDO, M. 1963. *Sardinia*, London and New York.
LILLIU, G. 1962. *I Nuraghi*, Cagliari.

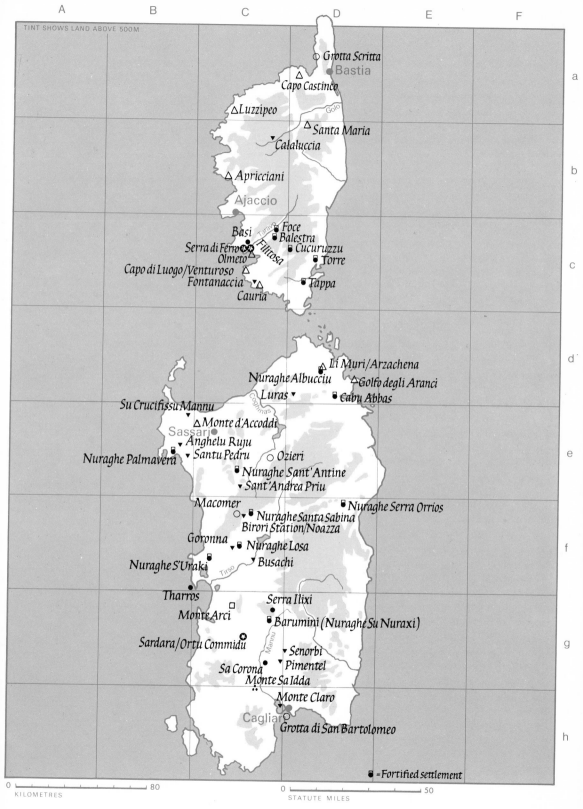

TINT SHOWS LAND ABOVE 500M

○ *Grotta Scritta*

Bastia

△ *Capo Castinco*

△ *Luzzipeo*

△ *Santa Maria*

▼ *Calaluccia*

△ *Apricciani*

Ajaccio

Basi △ *Foce*
□ *Balestra*
Serra di Ferro ⊗⊗ ■ *Cucuruzzu*
Olmeto □ ■ *Torre*
Capo di Luogo/Venturoso △
Fontanaccia ▼ △ ■ *Tappa*
Cauria

■ *Li Muri/Arzachena*

Nuraghe Albucciu ■ △ *Golfo degli Aranci*

Luras ▼ ■ *Cabu Abbas*

Su Crucifissu Mannu
▼
△ *Monte d'Accoddi*
Sassari ●
▼ *Anghelu Ruju*
Nuraghe Palmavera ■ ▼ *Santu Pedru*
○ *Ozieri*
■ *Nuraghe Sant'Antine*
▼ *Sant'Andrea Priu*

Macomer
○ ▼ ■ *Nuraghe Serra Orrios*
■ *Nuraghe Santa Sabina*
Birori Station/Noazza
Goronna
▼ ■ *Nuraghe Losa*
Nuraghe S'Uraki ■ ▼ *Busachi*

Tharros ●
□ *Serra Ilixi*
Monte Arci
■ *Barumini (Nuraghe Su Nuraxi)*
Sardara/Ortu Commidu ✤
▼ *Senorbi*
Pimentel
Sa Corona ●
Monte Sa Idda
▼ *Monte Claro*
Cagliari ●
Grotta di San Bartolomeo

■ = Fortified settlement

0 ┈┈┈┈┈ 80
KILOMETRES

0 ┈┈┈┈┈ 50
STATUTE MILES

Copper and Bronze Age sites in Corsica and Sardinia **117**

Early Iron Age sites in the central Mediterranean

Iron was introduced to the Bronze Age communities of the central Mediterranean, probably through the medium of trade, in the late tenth or early ninth century BC. In many parts of the region Iron Age settlements were organized on an urban basis even before the establishment of Phoenician and Greek colonies in the eighth and seventh centuries and before the emergence of Etruscan civilization *c.* 700 BC. These settlements were larger than in earlier periods, were frequently fortified, and were accompanied by large – sometimes enormous – cemeteries. We have abundant evidence of economic specialization, extensive commercial activity and the accumulation of wealth.

Archaeologists recognize many regional groups, which sometimes may be identified with peoples named by Greek and Roman historians. In mainland Italy, the cultures fall into two broad groups: those who cremated and those who inhumed their dead. Among the most important cremating groups are the Golasecca culture of Lombardy, the Este culture of the Veneto and the Villanovans of Emilia and Etruria, who later developed into the Etruscan civilization, and the Latian Iron Age – the ancestor of Rome. The inhuming groups include the Ligurian Iron Age, the Picene and Iapygian cultures of the Adriatic coast, the Umbrian Iron Age and the Fossa Grave culture of Campania and Calabria.

In Sicily the most prosperous settlements were in the south-east, as in the Bronze Age, and these belong to the later phases of the Pantalica culture. Here, as elsewhere on the island, the dead were mostly buried in rock-cut tombs – the characteristic Sicilian funerary monuments since the Copper Age. However, at a few sites inhumations in trench graves also occur. By comparison with the rest of the central Mediterranean, Sardinia and Corsica remained in relative isolation. The Sardinian Early Iron Age saw the climax of the Nuraghic culture, with impressive fortifications and accomplished metalwork, including distinctive figurines of warriors, deities and animals.

FURTHER READING

BREA, L. BERNABÒ 1957. *Sicily before the Greeks*, London and New York.

BLOCH, R. 1960. *The Origins of Rome*, London and New York.

GUIDO, M. 1963. *Sardinia*, London and New York.

HENCKEN, H. 1968. *Tarquinia and Etruscan Origins*, London and New York.

▼ Meluno
● Vadena
San Zeno ●
● Bellamonte
Bellinzona ▼
Dos Zelòr ●
Ameno ▼ Ca' Morta
Golasecca ▼
● Monte Loffa ▼ Angarano
Sesto Calende
San Bernadino ● Vicenza
di Briona ● Garda ● Padua
● Este

Chiavari ▼
● Villanova
Bologna ● ▼ Imola

▼ Verucchio
● Novilara
● Ancona

Populonia ⊛
⊛ Vetulonia
● Fermo
● Ripatransone

Tarquinia
Luni sul Mignone
⊛ ● Le Accieraie (Terni)
Narce ⊛ ⊕ Veii
⊛ Rome
▼ Alfedena
○ Grotta Manaccora
Rome ▼ Sermoneta
● Coppa Nevigata

▼ Alife

Albucciu ●
Cumae ⊛ Valdisarno
Palmavera ● ● Timmari
Fonte e Mola ● Pithecusa
● ▼ ● (Monte Vico) ⊛ Scoglio del Tonno
Sant'Antine △ Su Tempiesu
Losa ▲ Serra Orios
Pontecagnano ▲ Borgo Nuovo
S'Uraki Torre Saturo
Lugherras ● Torre Castelluccia
△ Esterzili ▼ Torre Mordillo
△ Santa Vittoria
Barumini (Su Nuraxi)
Sant'Anastasia

○ Torre Galli

Lipari Acropolis ⊛
Milazzo ⊛
Erice ● Pozzo di Gotto ⊛ Locri
Segesta ● ▼ Paternò
Polizzello ⊛ Calcarella ▼ Molino della Badia
Sant'Angelo Muxaro ● ⊕ Lentini
Butera ▼ Pantalica
Cannatello ● ⊛ Dessueri ⊕ ⊛ Syracuse
Caltagirone ▼ Cassibile
Finocchito

The central Mediterranean: Carthaginians, Greeks and Etruscans

The first half of the first millennium BC saw the emergence of several maritime powers in the Mediterranean. The most important were the Phoenicians and the Greeks, each of whom dominated large parts of the Mediterranean littoral. The central Mediterranean harboured a third force: the Etruscans, whose authority, although restricted geographically, was absolute along the Tyrrhenian coast of Italy. In the eighth and seventh centuries both Phoenician and Greek colonies were established in the central Mediterranean and at the same time the Etruscan civilization developed locally in central Italy. In the sixth century a struggle for power ensued between the Carthaginians (who led the western Phoenicians), the Greek colonies and the Etruscans. Initially, the three powers controlled completely separate areas. The Phoenicians were supreme along the African coast west of Cyrenaica; they also held Malta and Gozo, Pantelleria, the western tip of Sicily and most of Sardinia. Greek colonies controlled most of Sicily and southern Italy (Magna Graecia) and had a foothold on Corsica and in parts of Spain and France. The Etruscans, whose homeland was the region between the Tiber, the Arno and the sea, expanded both southwards into Campania and northwards into the Po valley.

The Phoenicians were traditional enemies of the Greeks and the Carthaginians inherited this role in the central and west Mediterranean. They were thus drawn into alliances with the Etruscans when, in the sixth century, their territorial ambitions led to open conflict with the cities of Magna Graecia. In 535 a combined Carthaginian and Etruscan fleet defeated a Greek armada off Alalia in Corsica, effectively removing both Corsica and Sardinia from the sphere of Greek control. However, in the late sixth and fifth centuries the Greeks defeated the Etruscans repeatedly in Campania and at the same time gained victories over the Carthaginians in Sicily. The history of the struggle between these powers finally ended with the expansion of Rome. By the second century BC Rome had absorbed the territories of all three into the first European empire.

FURTHER READING

BLOCH, R. 1958. *The Etruscans*, London and New York.
BOARDMAN, J. 1964. *The Greeks Overseas*, Harmondsworth and Baltimore.
GUIDO, M. 1963. *Sardinia*, London and New York.
HARDEN, D. B. 1972. *The Phoenicians* (revised edn), Harmondsworth.
STRONG, D. 1968. *The Early Etruscans*, London and New York.

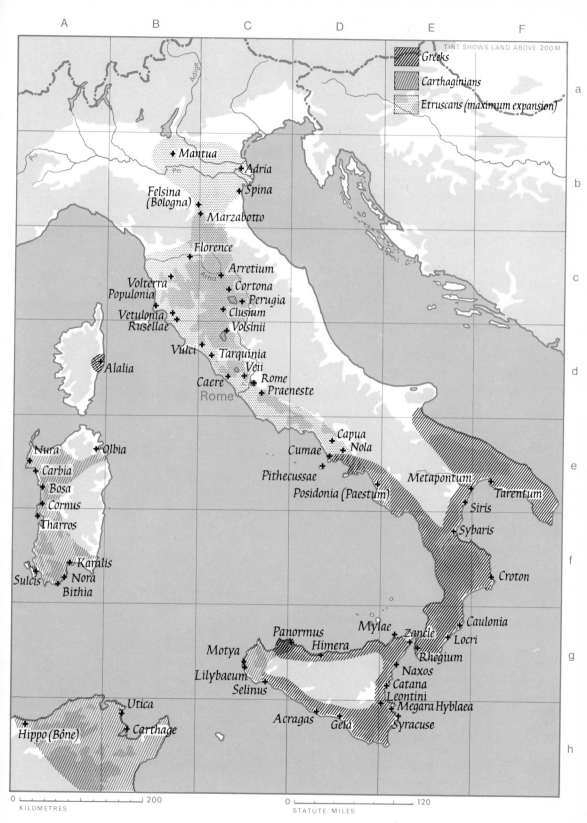

The central Mediterranean: Carthaginians, Greeks and Etruscans 121

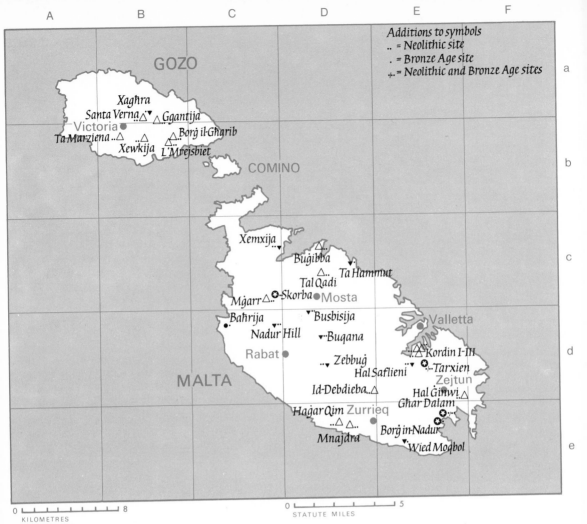

A B C D E F

Additions to symbols
.. = Neolithic site
. = Bronze Age site
⊹ = Neolithic and Bronze Age sites

GOZO

a

Xagħra
Santa Verna ..△ ▽ △ Ggantija
Victoria ● △ △ Borġ il-Għarib
Ta Marżiena ..△ ..△ ..△ ⊙
Xewkija L'Mrejsbiet

COMINO

b

Xemxija ..▽

△.. c

Buġibba
△.. Ta Ħammut
Tal Qadi
Mġarr △ ⊙ Skorba ● Mosta

Baħrija ● ▽ Busbisija
Nadur Hill ▽.. ▽ Buqana

Rabat ● Valletta ●

▽.. Żebbuġ ..△△ Kordin I-III d
Ħal Saflieni ▽. ⊙ Tarxien
Id-Debdieba ..△ Zejtun
Ħal Ġinwi △
Għar Dalam
Ħaġar Qim Żurrieq ●
..△ △.. Borġ in-Nadur ⊙..
Mnajdra ▽ Wied Moqbol e

MALTA

0 └─┴─┴─┴─┴─┴─┴─┴─┘ 8
KILOMETRES

0 └─┴─┴─┴─┴─┘ 5
STATUTE MILES

Malta

The Maltese islands – Malta, Gozo and Comino – were uninhabited during the Palaeolithic period. They were settled first some time before 5000 BC (4200 bc) by farmers who probably came from Sicily or south-east Italy. Like the first farmers elsewhere in the Mediterranean, the settlers made a distinctive type of pottery known as Impressed ware. Although their culture in Malta is named after a cave, Għar Dalam, the majority of the population lived in open villages like that recently excavated by Dr David Trump beneath the temple complex at Skorba. The successors of the first farmers developed a closely-knit society with a flourishing culture. Their most impressive communal activity was the construction of the large and elaborate stone temples for which the islands

are famous. Among the most important temples are Mnajdra, Ħaġar Qim, Mġarr, Skorba and Tarxien on Malta, and Ggantija on Gozo. They buried their dead communally either in small rock-cut tombs or in the enormous carved and painted hypogeum of Ħal Saflieni. The temple builders were in contact with other parts of the Mediterranean, but their culture, with its astonishing architecture, was an indigenous creation. It was brought to an end shortly before 2500 BC (2200 bc), apparently by metal-using invaders, who destroyed the temples. Indeed, the newcomers used the ruined Tarxien temple as a cemetery for cremated remains; accordingly, they are known as the Tarxien Cemetery culture. This was followed by a second Bronze Age culture named after the site of Borġ in-Nadur, which in turn was succeeded by an iron-using culture taking its name from another important site, Baħrija. The Baħrija phase was still in progress when the first Punic colonists arrived in the ninth or eighth century B C.

FURTHER READING

EVANS, J. D. 1959. *Malta*, London and New York.
———— 1971. *The Prehistoric Antiquities of the Maltese Islands*, London.
TRUMP, D. H. 1966. *Skorba*. Research Report of the Society of Antiquities of London, Oxford.
———— 1972. *Malta; An Archaeological Guide*, London.

Neolithic sites in Iberia

see map pp. 124/125

The Neolithic in Iberia began in the sixth millennium bc and lasted until perhaps the mid-fourth millennium. Regrettably, we know less about the Iberian Neolithic than about the same period elsewhere in the Mediterranean. The earliest farming groups belonged to the Impressed ware tradition, which was widely distributed in the Mediterranean from Palestine to the Straits of Gibraltar. In the west, Impressed ware occurs in the coastal regions of Spain and Portugal and at a few sites in north Africa. In all these areas it is found almost exclusively in caves. It is closely comparable with the Impressed ware of southern France, which also occurs mainly in caves and, like the Iberian group, is associated with a flint industry of mesolithic (Tardenoisian) tradition.

Notable sites include Cueva de la Sarsa and Coveta de l'Or, both in Valencia, and El Pany in Catalonia. Impressed ware survived in some areas well into the fourth millennium, by which date other decorated wares, often incised, were in use. Key sites with incised wares are Cueva de la Mujer and Alhama de Granada in Spain and Furninha and Eira Pedrinha in Portugal.

A second element in the Iberian Neolithic had north Italian affinities; square-mouthed pots, paralleled in Italy, occur in caves and pit graves, mostly in Catalonia, but sporadically in other regions, too.

Another important neolithic group in Iberia is the Almeria culture of south-east Spain. Unlike the other neolithic cultures, this group is well represented by open settlements, the most famous of which are El Garcel, Tres Cabezos and Tabernas. The settlements, frequently on hill-tops, have round and oval houses and yield abundant evidence of agriculture. The pottery is plain, and conspicuous among the forms are jars with pointed bases and costrels. In the initial phases, geometric flints were in use, but later bifacial tools became common. Evidence of metal-working occurs at some sites, showing that the Almeria culture played a significant part in the development of the local Copper Age.

The south-west contained groups related to the Almeria culture. These communities buried their dead singly in stone cists, which may have been the forerunners of the megalithic tombs (used for collective burial) of the Copper Age.

FURTHER READING

ÅBERG, N. 1921. *La Civilisation Enéolithique dans la Péninsule Ibérique*, Uppsala.
MUÑOZ, A. M. 1965. *La Cultura Neolitica Catalana*, Barcelona.
SAVORY, H. M. 1968. *Spain and Portugal*, London and New York.
TARRADELL, M. 1959. Problemas Neolíticos. *Primer Symposium de Prehistoria Peninsular*, Pamplona.

TINT SHOWS LAND ABOVE 500M

A   B   C   D   E

a

b

○ Orense

Oporto   Douro   Cachão da Rapa   ✛   Valladolid   c

Cantarranas
Madrid

○ Eira Pedrinha   d

Cabeco dos Mosqueiros
Furninha   ✛ Cabeco da Ministra
○ ○ Rio Maior
Casa da Moura   ✛ Santarem
Olelas ●
Tagus
Lisbon   e

Guadiana

Cueva de los Murciélagos   f
(Zuheros)   Carigüela
de Piñar
Guadalquivir   ○
Lagos   ✛ Montefrío
Seville   Cueva del
Cueva de la Mujer   Agua
Alhama de Granada   ○○
Cueva del Higueron   ○   ○   ○
Cueva Tapada ○
Cueva de Nerja   g
Cueva de los Murciélagos
(Albuñol)

Gar Cahal ○
El'Aliya ○
Caf Taht el Gar   h

Châteauneuf-les-Martigues

Bilbao

Ebro

Montserrat
Cueva Bonica
El Pany

Sant Quirze de Galliners

Barcelona

+Ademuz

Muleta

Valencia

Coveta de l'Or   Cueva del Montgó

Cueva de la Sarsa

Murcia

Cueva Ambrosio

Tres Cabezos

El Garcel

0   200
KILOMETRES

0   120
STATUTE MILES

Neolithic sites in Iberia   125

Cangas de Onís

Río Sil

Padilla de Abajo

Huerta de Arriba

Penha

Valladolid

Oporto   Douro

Madrid

Miguel Ruiz

Ciempozuelos

Pragança

Columbeira   Vila Nova de São Pedro

Zambujal

Praia das Maçãs   Pedra de Oiro

Alapraia   San Pedro de Estoril

Lisbon   Palmela   Anta da Comenda / Tholos da Comenda

Chibannes

Alemtejo Region

Sierra Morena

Fuente Palmera

Atalaia

Guadalquivir
Region   Matarrubilla   Montilla

Alcalá   Carmona   La Sabina
de Gorafe

Dolmen de Soto

Seville   Alcaide

Castro Marim

Cueva de la Menga /
Cueva de Romeral

Mesas de Asta

Gar Cahal

Caf Taht el Gar

Dar es-Soltan

A   B   C   D   E

a

Bilbao

Artajona

Cueva de Toralla

b

Riner   *Puig Roig*

Ebro

Barcelona

c

Es Tudons

San Vicente   *Rafal Rubi*

d

Puntal de Cambra   *Son Marroig (Cave of the Dead)* *Son Mulet* *Cova dels Bous*

Muntanyeta de Cabrera Valencia

Cabezo Redondo   *Más de Menente*

e

Cerro de la Virgen Murcia

Bastida de Totana

Ifre

f

Almizaraque

Tres Cabezos *El Oficio*

Tabernas

El Argar

Los Millares

g

h

0   200
KILOMETRES

0   120
STATUTE MILES

Copper and Bronze Age sites in Iberia   **127**

Copper and Bronze Age sites in Iberia

see map pp. 126/127

The Iberian Copper Age, which lasted from *c.* 3500 to *c.* 2000 BC (*c.* 2800–*c.* 1800 bc), was characterized by an early development of copper metallurgy, proto-urban settlements in the south-east and south-west, long-range trade and the use of monumental collective tombs – corbelled 'tholoi' in the south, rock-cut tombs mostly in the Tagus estuary and megalithic (orthostatic) tombs (cists and passage graves) throughout the south, west and north-east of the peninsula. Controversy surrounds the origins of these phenomena. A diffusionist view holds that some of the settlements (the most famous of which are Los Millares in Almeria, and Vila Nova de São Pedro in the Tagus region) were colonies established by settlers from the east Mediterranean who introduced, *inter alia*, fortified settlements with semicircular bastions, collective burial in built tombs and copper metallurgy. A modified view maintains that these features, although Aegean in origin, were not introduced by 'colonists' but arrived by stimulus diffusion. According to a third view, the Iberian Copper Age developed locally and was independent of eastern influence. This controversy cannot be solved completely until we have a reliable chronology of the local Copper Age, and further research is needed before this can be achieved.

During the third millennium BC the Bell Beaker culture, which some archaeologists believe developed in Iberia, had a wide distribution in the peninsula and in most areas copper metallurgy was practised.

In the succeeding period, which is usually labelled 'Bronze Age' although copper remained in general use, the best-known group is the Argaric culture (after El Argar) of the south-east. This was characterized by fortified hill-top settlements containing rectangular houses, by burial in cists, pits or jars and by a metal industry which included riveted daggers and halberds. Among later developments were the introduction of swords, gold and silver diadems and pottery chalices. Elsewhere in the peninsula Early and Middle Bronze Age groups were either related to the Argaric culture or represented surviving Beaker communities. During the period Iberian metal sources were exploited intensively and, in addition to bronze, gold and silver were widely used. In the early years of the first millennium BC a distinctive north-west Iberian bronze industry emerged with palstaves and sickles of Atlantic Bronze Age type, often found in large hoards like the important cache at Huerta de Arriba (Burgos).

FURTHER READING

BLANCE, B. 1961. Early Bronze Age Colonists in Iberia, *Antiquity* XXXV, 192–202.

LEISNER, G. and V. 1943–65. *Die Megalithgräber der Iberischen Halbinsel: Der Süden* (Berlin, 1943), *Der Westen* (Berlin, 1956–9) and, by V. Leisner, *Der Osten* (Berlin, 1965).

RENFREW, C. 1967. Colonialism and Megalithismus. *Antiquity* XLI, 276–88.

SAVORY, H. M. 1968. *Spain and Portugal*, London and New York.

Early Iron Age sites in Iberia

see map pp. 130/131

During the period *c.* 800–500 BC three developments of particular importance took place in the Iberian peninsula. Firstly there was the spread of Urnfield groups into the north-east. The Urnfield culture of Catalonia, which is an extension of the south-French urnfields, is known from large cemeteries, such as Can Bech de Baix at Agullana and El Molá, and settlements like Cortes de Navarra, with its terraces of rectangular mud-brick houses. The second important development was the emergence in the south-west of the 'carp's-tongue sword' group, plausibly identified with the historical Tartessians (described by Phoenician writers as dwellers in a land rich in metals). This group is known from numerous bronze hoards, including the famous Huelva hoard, a few settlements and burials, and from a remarkable series of carved cist-covers and stelae. The third development was the foundation of Phoenician and Greek colonies along the Mediterranean coast (see pp. 104–5 and 108–9). Elsewhere in the peninsula earlier Bronze Age groups survived with little change.

Out of this amalgam two broad cultural blocs emerged in the Iron Age: the 'Iberian' group along the Mediterranean coast between the Rhône and the Pillars of Hercules, and the 'Celtic' group in the north and west and in the interior of the peninsula. The Iberians and the related Tartessians appear to represent indigenous groups profoundly influenced by the Phoenician and Greek colonies. They spoke a non-Indo-European language or group of languages (not yet deciphered), which they wrote in a script clearly borrowed from the Phoenicians or Greeks. They lived in fortified hill-top settlements which as time passed assumed a progressively more urban aspect. Indeed their whole culture represents local traditions influenced more and more by Punic and Greek civilization.

The Celtic culture in the rest of the peninsula looked towards continental and Atlantic Europe rather than the Mediterranean for its contacts and influences, but in the last few centuries BC it was also influenced by the increasingly urban Iberian culture. Features of particular interest include the stone hill-forts (*castros*) of the north-west and the remarkable gold and silver jewellery produced in the area of the *castros*, which developed out of local Bronze Age traditions.

FURTHER READING

ARRIBAS, A. 1963. *The Iberians*, London and New York.
SAVORY, H. N. 1949. The Atlantic Bronze Age in South-West Europe. *Proceedings of the Prehistoric Society* 15, 128–55.
—— 1968. *Spain and Portugal*, London and New York.
SCHÜLE, W. 1960. Probleme der Eisenzeit auf der Iberischen Halbinsel. *Jahrbuch des Römisch-Germanischen Zentralmuseums Mainz* 7, 59–125.

TINT SHOWS LAND ABOVE 500M

Coaña

Elviña

Rianxo
+ Caldas de Reyes
Cameixa
Hio
S. Ciprián de Lás

Miraveche

Santa Tecla

Chaves

Laundos
Briteiros
Sabrosa
Terroso
Oporto
Douro

Mota del Marqués

Soto de Medinilla

Valladolid

Saldeana

Osera/Mesas de Asta
Las Cogotas

Santa Olaya

+ Penela

Madrid

Penamacor

Cabezo de Araya
La Aliseda
Solana de las Cabañas

Pedra de Oiro

+ Sintra

Medellin

Lisbon

Lapa de Fumo
Alacer do Sal

Mombeja

Monté Salomón

Setefilla
(Lora del Río)

La Guardia

Figueira

Huelva
La Joya

El Carambolo
Carmona
Seville
Osuna

Asta Regia

Toscanos
Torre del Mar

Trayamar
Almuñecar

Guadiana

Tagus

Guadalquivir

- - - - = North-western limit of Iberian culture sites

Europe with Russia

Temperate Europe was not the birthplace of farming; nor was it the home of any of the great ancient civilizations. Nevertheless throughout later prehistory it supported vigorous and successful societies which were responsible for important discoveries. Europe north of the Alps was finally brought into the orbit of urban civilization by the expansion of the Romans in the last century BC and the first century AD.

Europe, already occupied by hunting and gathering communities, was colonized by immigrants from the Asiatic homeland of farming: sites occupied by the first farmers in south-east Europe have C14 dates in the early sixth millennium bc and the farming economy reached the extreme edges of the temperate zone – the British Isles and southern Scandinavia – between c. 4300 and 3500 BC. This extensive spread was stimulated by a combination of an expanding population and the techniques of early farming, which caused soil exhaustion and so required frequent migration to new territory. At this stage Europe was sparsely populated and well provided with fertile soils; it was thus ripe for settlement. The farming economy spread both directly by the arrival of immigrants and indirectly by diffusion of the techniques of farming to indigenous hunting and gathering communities. In the spread of farming three broad 'streams' are recognized: an early movement from eastern Europe along the Danube and its tributaries as far as Belgium and Holland; a second, rather later stream, ultimately of Mediterranean origin, which reached Atlantic Europe from the south; and, later still, a third stream across the plains of northern Europe from the Black Sea to the Baltic.

In most regions of Europe the earliest farming communities apparently had an egalitarian social structure and certainly possessed only simple equipment. They were, however, capable farmers, growing wheat, barley and leguminous crops and breeding cattle, swine, sheep and goat. Later in the period their technology improved and in some cases at least we find evidence of social stratification. Even at an early date farmers in north-west Europe constructed large and impressive stone tombs, which were used for collective burial; we do not know whether these were intended for the whole community or for chieftains' families only.

At a time when farming had not yet reached the farthest parts of Europe, well-established farmers in the south-east were developing copper metallurgy. Already in the fifth millennium BC Balkan metallurgists, exploiting Transylvanian ores, were producing shaft-hole axes and axe-adzes which technologically were the most advanced copper tools in the world. Until c. 3500 BC (c. 2800 bc) European metal-working was restricted to the Balkans and the Mediterranean region, but in the following millennium metallurgy spread almost to the limits of inhabited Europe, partly in the hands of mobile, sometimes warlike, groups whose origin may have been in southern Russia and eastern Europe. These movements carried other technological innovations, such as the wheel, and may indeed have introduced Indo-European languages.

Later in the third millennium BC a more developed metal industry became established in Europe, based on true tin bronze instead of copper. While the old east European homeland of copper metallurgy participated in this later development, the centre of the new industry lay farther west, in south central Europe, where craftsmen obtained Alpine ores. By the mid-second millennium BC bronze industries related to those of central Europe had become established throughout the temperate zone, even in areas without local ores. This bronze industry brought in its wake, to a far greater degree than had the earlier copper industry, a significant increase in trade, the emergence of economic specialization and – for the archaeologist – the first signs of 'wealth'. Indeed, to this period belongs the earliest clear evidence of wealthy chieftains in Europe. The nature and significance of the relationship between the Bronze Age societies of temperate Europe and the contemporary Minoan-Mycenaean civilization of the Aegean is still a matter of controversy. One point, however, seems clear. In the light of the new chronology

(see pp. 9f.) it appears that, although trade with the Aegean may have contributed to the prosperity of the European communities, it began too late to be considered a *prime* cause of the development of the European bronze industry.

In the Late Bronze Age further developments in metallurgy, combined with improvements in the subsistence economy, constituted a minor economic revolution. The communities of the late second and early first millennia were larger, wealthier and supported more specialist craftsmen than those of the Early and Middle Bronze Ages. Through a combination of new population movements and trade this improved economy had spread over large parts of Europe by *c.* 700 B C.

The introduction and spread of iron-working in temperate Europe from the eighth century onwards made metal cheap for the first time. It was now used far more widely than ever before, improving the efficiency of agriculture and of numerous crafts. The additional prosperity achieved in this way was further enhanced by rapidly growing trade with two newly-emerged civilizations of the Mediterranean basin: that of archaic Greece (whence colonies were established in the central and west Mediterranean and on the Black Sea) and that of Etruria. Greek and Etruscan goods occur frequently in the settlements and (more especially) the cemeteries of the European Iron Age, indicating a prosperous trade in luxury goods destined for the chieftains' courts. The profits of trade, combined with the efficient subsistence economy inherited from their Bronze Age ancestors, made more efficient still by the use of iron for agricultural implements, enabled certain later Iron Age communities in central and western Europe to start developing an urban economy. This development was further stimulated by the intensified contacts with the Mediterranean that accompanied the expansion of Rome. By the second century B C the population of France and Germany lived partly in defended towns with high population densities; they had a stratified society with wealthy chieftains and their retinues, specialist craftsmen, peasant farmers and, it seems, a stratum of slaves

acquired through inter-tribal warfare; they had a market economy and minted money, modelled on that of the Mediterranean civilizations. Much of Europe was moving in varying degrees towards an urban economy, but in many areas these first steps in the direction of an indigenous form of urbanism were cut short by the arrival of the armies of Rome and the imposition of a developed urban civilization of Mediterranean origin.

FURTHER READING

CHILDE, V. G. 1957. *The Dawn of European Civilisation*[6], London and New York.
———— 1958. *The Prehistory of European Society*, Harmondsworth.
CLARK, G. 1969. *World Prehistory: a New Outline*, London and New York.
PIGGOTT, S. 1965, 1966. *Ancient Europe*, Edinburgh and Chicago.
RENFREW, C. 1973. *Before Civilization*, London and New York.

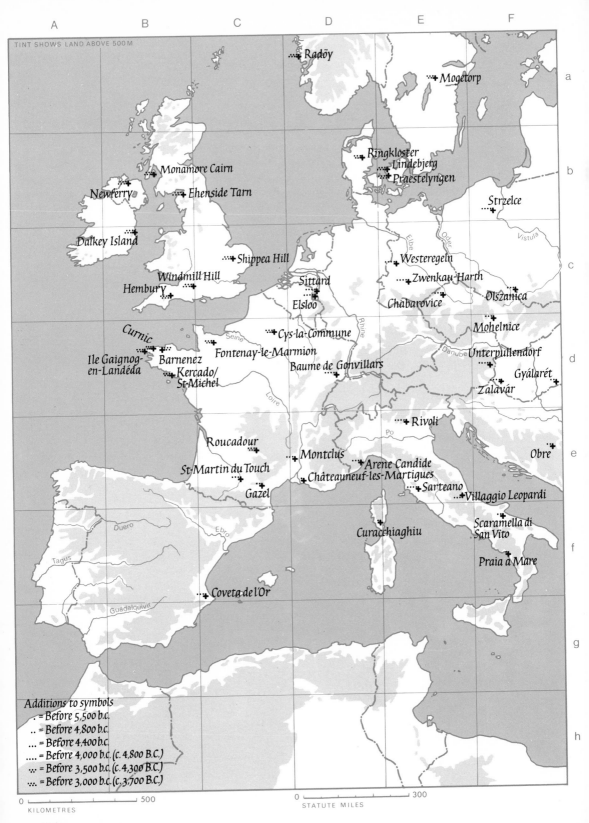

TINT SHOWS LAND ABOVE 500M

Radöy

Mogetorp

Ringkloster
Lindebjerg
Praestelyngen

Monamore Cairn

Newferry
Ehenside Tarn

Strzelce

Dalkey Island

Shippea Hill

Westeregeln

Windmill Hill
Hembury

Sittard
Elsloo

Zwenkau-Harth
Chabarovice

Olszanica

Curnic

Cys-la-Commune

Mohelnice

Ile Gaignog-
en-Landéda
Barnenez
Kercado/
St-Michel

Fontenay-le-Marmion
Baume de Gonvillars

Unterpullendorf

Gyálarét

Zalavár

Rivoli

Obre

Roucadour

Montclus

Arene Candide

St-Martin du Touch
Gazel

Châteauneuf-les-Martigues

Sarteano

Villaggio Leopardi

Curacchiaghiu

Scaramella di
San Vito

Praia a Mare

Coveta de l'Or

Seine
Loire
Rhine
Elbe
Oder
Vistula
Danube
Po
Duero
Ebro
Tagus
Guadalquivir

Additions to symbols
. = Before 5,500 b.c.
.. = Before 4,800 b.c.
... = Before 4,400 b.c.
.... = Before 4,000 b.c. (c. 4,800 B.C.)
..⋮. = Before 3,500 b.c. (c. 4,300 B.C.)
..⋮.. = Before 3,000 b.c. (c. 3,700 B.C.)

0   500
KILOMETRES

0   300
STATUTE MILES

134   *The spread of agriculture into Europe*

The spread of agriculture into Europe

It is highly probable that the farming economy was introduced to Europe from western Asia. Nowhere in Europe, it is thought, did the wild ancestors of *all* the main domesticated plants and animals – emmer wheat, barley, sheep, goats, cattle and swine – occur together; yet every well documented early farming culture of Europe possessed all these crops and animals. Furthermore, the C[14] dates available from many early farming sites show a chronological progression across Europe from the south-east to the north-west, clearly demonstrating the gradual spread from a homeland in Asia.

This progression of C[14] dates was charted initially by Grahame Clark in 1965 and our map is based largely on his original. However, it includes many sites for which dates have only become available since then. Clark used three chronological divisions; we employ six smaller divisions, ranging in length from 400 to 700 'radiocarbon years', chosen for convenience and for the apparently meaningful patterns they produce. The over-all picture demonstrates, as did Clark's map, a general north-westward movement, but also shows anomalies in an otherwise even spread. For example, we have several very early dates (before 5500 bc) in the west Mediterranean basin and a relatively early group (before 3500 bc, i.e. 4300 B C) in Brittany. The significance of these anomalies is not at present clear.

The new economy might have been introduced in its entirety – domesticated plants and animals included – by migrating people, or it might have been spread by stimulus diffusion, that is, by passing on farming techniques from one community to the next without significant movements of people. Both processes probably contributed to the spread of farming into Europe.

FURTHER READING

AMMERMAN, A. J. and L. L. CAVALLI-SFORZA 1973. A population model for the diffusion of early farming in Europe. In C. Renfrew (ed.) *The Explanation of Culture Change. Models in Prehistory*, London, 343–57.

CLARK, G. 1965. Radiocarbon Dating and the Spread of the Farming Economy. *Antiquity* XXXIX, 45–8.

—— 1969. *World Prehistory: a New Outline²*, London and New York.

Radiocarbon, vols 1–13 (1959–73).

Neolithic sites in eastern Europe

Neolithic sites in eastern Europe

The earliest farming settlements in south-east Europe date from the sixth millennium bc. They almost certainly belonged to settlers from Greece or Anatolia, who introduced an economy based on mixed farming and who had no connection with the local hunter-gatherer population. The earliest farmers formed a large cultural group, known as Karanovo I, Starčevo, Körös and Criş, found throughout the Balkans, Romania and Hungary. They lived in small, rectangular, one-room houses made of timber and clay. At this date permanent settlements, which are characterized by tells, existed only in the southern parts of Bulgaria and Jugoslavia. The Near Eastern ancestry of the first farmers is reflected in painted pottery, stamp seals and figurines.

To the east of the Starčevo region, in eastern Romania, the earliest farmers belonged to an off-shoot of the Danubian Linear Pottery culture, which arrived there in the late fifth millennium bc. On the Adriatic coast of Jugoslavia, on the other hand, other communities (which may not have practised farming) used Impressed ware like that of Italy and Greece.

During the Middle Neolithic various regional cultures emerged. The most important of these (e.g. Karanovo II and Veselinovo in Bulgaria and the Vinča-Tordoš (Turdos) culture in Jugoslavia) were formerly thought to represent new intrusions from the south-east. However, it now seems likely that they developed locally out of the early neolithic cultures. The subsistence economy was then sufficiently advanced to permit permanent settlement producing tells in most areas.

The Late Neolithic–Eneolithic (5400–4300 BC, c. 4500–3500 bc) was a period of prosperous development in south-east Europe. The most important cultures were the Boian, Maritsa and Gumelniţa cultures in Bulgaria, the Sălcuţa culture in Bulgaria and Romania, the Cucuteni-Tripolye group in Romania and south Russia and the Vinča-Pločnik culture in Jugoslavia. All probably developed locally, all possessed an efficient farming economy and, except in the Cucuteni-Tripolye area, tell settlement was common. The most significant achievement was the

137

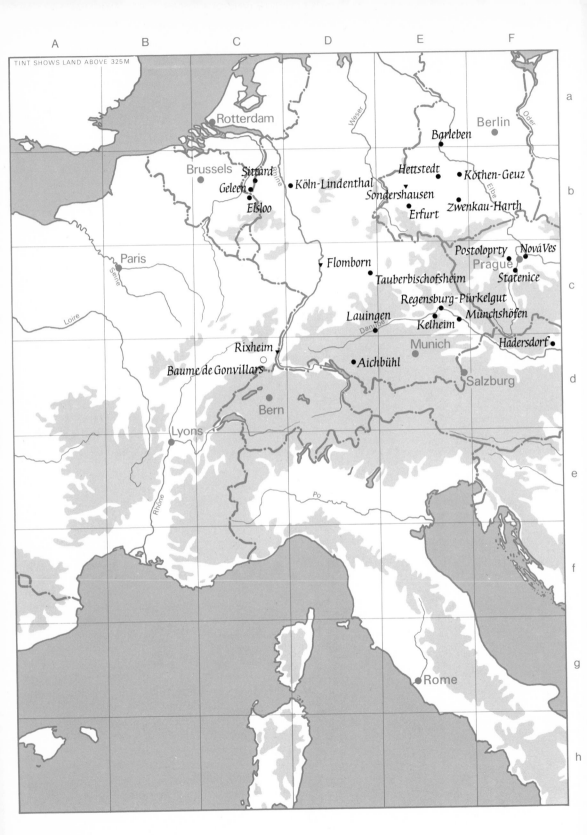

TINT SHOWS LAND ABOVE 325M

A   B   C   D   E   F

Rotterdam

Berlin

Barleben

Brussels

Sittard

Hettstedt   Köthen-Geuz

Geleen   Köln-Lindenthal   Sondershausen

Elsloo   Erfurt   Zwenkau-Harth

Paris

Postoloprty   Nová Ves

Flomborn   Prague

Tauberbischofsheim   Statenice

Regensburg-Pürkelgut

Lauingen   Kelheim   Münchshöfen

Rixheim   Munich   Hadersdorf

Baume de Gonvillars   Aichbühl

Salzburg

Bern

Lyons

Po

Rome

138   *The Danubian cultures*

development of copper metallurgy. Objects of native copper occur even in middle neolithic contexts and by the first half of the fourth millennium bc (before 4500 B C) smiths were producing tools of smelted and cast copper.

FURTHER READING

ALEXANDER, J. 1972. *Jugoslavia before the Roman Conquest*, London and New York.
BERCIU, D. 1967. *Romania*, London and New York.
CHILDE, V. G. 1957. *The Dawn of European Civilisation*[6], London and New York.
GIMBUTAS, M. 1956. *The Prehistory of Eastern Europe*, Cambridge, Mass.
MILOJČIĆ, V. 1949. *Chronologie der jüngeren Steinzeit Mittel- und Südosteuropas*, Berlin.
TRINGHAM, R. 1971. *Hunters, Fishers and Farmers of Eastern Europe, 6000–3000 BC*, London.

The Danubian cultures

see map pp. 138/139

The first farmers to penetrate the temperate forests of central and western Europe belonged to the Linear Pottery or LBK (German: *Linienbandkeramik*) culture, to which Childe gave the name Danubian I. The distribution of the LBK culture extended from Romania and the Ukraine to eastern France, Belgium and Holland and over this vast area it was remarkably uniform. The culture emerged in east central Europe during the sixth millennium B C and had reached Holland by c. 5000 B C (c. 4200 bc). LBK settlements are most common on light soils along the major river systems in central Europe. They appear to have been occupied intermittently, with gaps of perhaps a generation or more, and this suggests that the villagers practised shifting cultivation. LBK communities lived in long rectangular timber houses, probably as extended (rather than nuclear) families. They were mixed farmers, cultivating wheat, barley and other crops and keeping cattle, swine, sheep and goats. In particular, they were skilled cattle-breeders: they domes-

ticated the local wild aurochs and castrated surplus bulls to produce strong, but docile oxen. Their simple equipment included the distinctive incised pottery after which they are named, stone 'shoe-last celts' (which may be hoes or adzes) and household tools of flint. Perhaps the most famous of all LBK sites is Köln-Lindenthal in Germany; other important sites are Sittard and Geleen in Holland, Bylany and Postoloprty in Czechoslovakia, Jurkowice and Zofipole in Poland and Nezwiska in the Ukraine.

After the initial westward spread of LBK farmers across Europe, the cultural unity of the group disintegrated and in the later Neolithic (late fifth and fourth millennia B C) several regional groups emerged, each a local development of the original Danubian I culture. The most important later neolithic groups are the Tisza culture of the Tisza valley in Hungary; the Lengyel culture of the Pannonian plain west of the Danube; the Stroke-Ornamented Ware group in western Czechoslovakia and Poland and parts of Germany; the Rössen culture of Bavaria.

FURTHER READING

CHILDE, V. G. 1929. *The Danube in Prehistory*, Oxford.
——— 1957. *The Dawn of European Civilisation*[6], London and New York.
GIMBUTAS, M. 1956. *The Prehistory of Eastern Europe*, Cambridge, Mass.
MURRAY, J. 1970. *The First European Agriculture*, Edinburgh.
TRINGHAM, R. 1971. *Hunters, Fishers and Farmers of Eastern Europe, 6000–3000 BC*, London.

Neolithic and Copper Age sites in France and Switzerland

The earliest farming communities in France appeared in the south: deposits containing remains of the Impressed Ware culture occur in caves and rock shelters on the Mediterranean coast with C[14] dates from before 6000 to c. 4000 bc (c. 4800

Neolithic and Copper Age sites in France and Switzerland **141**

BC). If the earliest dates are to be trusted, the Early Neolithic was extremely long-lived and during this period restricted to the Mediterranean littoral. In northern Switzerland and north-east France the earliest farmers, who belonged to the Danubian LBK (see p. 140) culture, appeared *c.* 4500 bc and in the following millennium Linear Pottery groups gradually filtered farther west.

Meanwhile in southern France the Chassey culture emerged shortly after *c.* 4800 BC (*c.* 4000 bc) and lasted until *c.* 3200 BC (*c.* 2500 bc); it may have developed out of the local Impressed Ware culture. The Chassey culture is one of a group, often labelled Western Neolithic, to which the approximately contemporary Cortaillod culture of Switzerland also belongs. Whereas the south French Chassey culture is known mainly from caves, the Cortaillod population lived in lakeside villages of wooden houses. Waterlogged conditions have preserved a wealth of material evidence which throws much light on the Cortaillod economy, diet and culture.

The primary Neolithic of Brittany has the same time span as the Chassey culture. Some of the earliest C[14] dates for the Breton Neolithic (*c.* 4700 BC, *c.* 3800 bc) were obtained from megalithic tombs and these are incidentally the earliest dated examples in Europe. It is extremely interesting that impressive megalithic tombs were being constructed by the first farmers in the region.

The third millennium BC saw the fragmentation of the large cultural groups into a variety of regional cultures; it saw moreover the apogee of megalithic tomb building which at one time was practised in many regions of France. In the latter part of the millennium copper metallurgy was introduced, perhaps by diffusion or at the hands of Bell Beaker immigrants, whose characteristic artifacts occur commonly in parts of Switzerland, southern France and Brittany. In Switzerland we find evidence of a second widespread and sometimes metal-using group, the Corded Ware cultures, whose remains occur in late levels in the lakeside villages. Metal, however, did not become common until the Early Bronze Age at least (early second millennium BC).

FURTHER READING

BAILLOUD, G. and P. MIEG DE BOOFZHEIM 1955. *Les Civilisations néolithiques de la France*, Paris.
BENDER, B. and P. PHILLIPS 1972. The early farmers of France. *Antiquity* XLVI, 97–105.
DANIEL, G. 1960. *The Prehistoric Chamber Tombs of France*, London.
GUILAINE, J. 1970. Néolithique ancien de la Méditerranée occidentale et chronologie absolue. *Actas das I Jomadas Arquéologicas*, Lisbon.
GUYAN, W. U. (ed.) 1955. *Das Pfahlbauproblem*, Basel.

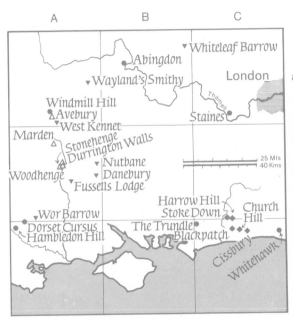

Neolithic sites in the British Isles

The first farmers reached the British Isles *c.* 4300–3700 BC (*c.* 3500–3000 bc). Early C[14] dates come from four different areas: south-west England, East Anglia, Cumberland and north-east Ireland; we also have dates from Scotland which are not much later. It is probable that Britain was settled from both western France and the north European plain, but the evidence is slight and it is hard to document the process in any detail.

TINT SHOWS LAND ABOVE 325M

Åloppe

Stockholm

Kråkerøy

Mogetorp
Brokvarn

Östra Vrå
Säter

Falbygden

Visby
Västerbjers

Ferslev

Ertebølle

Tustrup
Barkaer   Jonstorp

Knebel

Troldhøj   Siretorp

Grønhøj   Kongedyssen
Raevehøj   Jaegerspris
Bundsø   Ellested   Oxie
Blommeskobbel Klekkendehøj
Trolleberg
Hemmelmark
Putlos   Binz   Rzucewo
Futterkamp   Zarrenthin   Danzig   Kaliningrad
Sachsenwaldau   Succase
Himmelspforten Neuenkirchen

Drouwen   Chełmża
Emmerveld   Kleinenknethen Ustowo   Zarębowo   Brześć Kujawski
Havelte   Thuine   Wąsewo   Warsaw
                            Berlin   Sarnowo   Gaj   Janisewek
                Walternienburg Lupow   Szlachcin
Beckum   Ebendorf   Nosocice
Lommel   Drosa   Krzemionki
Ottenbourg Züschen Nietleben   Książnice Wielkie
iennes   Ćmielów
ou de Frontal Urmitz   Hartlieb   Złota
               Mayen   Jordanów

                            Prague

                            Munich

                            Vienna

Bern   Budapest

0   250   0   175
KILOMETRES   STATUTE MILES

144   *Neolithic sites in northern Europe*

Early neolithic settlers in southern England belonged to the Windmill Hill culture. They practised a mixed farming economy, made undecorated pottery with simple forms, used ground stone axes traded from 'factories', such as Great Langdale, and flint from mines, such as Cissbury. The characteristic monuments of their culture include 'causewayed camps' (perhaps community centres used for seasonal meetings), long rectangular enclosures known as 'cursuses' and earthen long barrows with or without wooden chambers. It is possible that the first settlers also built megalithic tombs, for certainly these were in use in the British Isles by *c.* 3700 BC (*c.* 3000 bc). In fact the tradition of building megalithic tombs flourished here in abundant (and confusing!) variety. Particularly important groups are the Severn-Cotswold tombs of south-west England, the Clyde-Carlingford tombs of western Scotland and Ireland and, rather later, the passage graves of the Boyne in Ireland and in the Orkneys. However, there is evidence of many other groups.

Later in the Neolithic new cultures emerged and to this period belong the henge monuments and stone circles described on page 154. During the Late Neolithic, colonists using 'beakers', a distinctive type of pottery vessel, arrived from the continent. In his recent detailed study David Clarke recognized seven groups of immigrants, who came from central Europe and the Low Countries, as well as three major insular traditions. The Beaker colonists arrived between *c.* 2500 and 1800 BC (*c.* 2000–1600 bc). They were metal-users and almost certainly introduced copper metallurgy to the British Isles.

FURTHER READING

CHILDE, V. G. 1947. *Prehistoric Communities of the British Isles²*, London.
CLARKE, D. L. 1970. *Beaker Pottery of Great Britain and Ireland*, Cambridge.
PIGGOTT, S. 1970. *The Neolithic Cultures of the British Isles*, (reprint) Cambridge.
SMITH, I. F. 1965. *Windmill Hill and Avebury. Excavations by Alexander Keiller 1925–1939*, Oxford.

On the north European plain and in southern Scandinavia, north of the area occupied by the Linear Pottery culture, the earliest known farming settlements are dated to the end of the fifth millennium BC (late fourth millennium bc). They belong to the TRB (Trichterbecher or Funnel-neck Beaker) culture, the latest of the primary neolithic groups in Europe, which owed much to indigenous hunting and fishing communities. Although found throughout northern Europe, the TRB culture is known best in Scandinavia. The TRB people were mixed farmers living in villages of timber long houses; they had pottery based on basketry forms; they mined flint and they collected, worked and traded Baltic amber. From an early date they buried their dead singly, either in flat graves or, slightly later, under earthen long mounds with or without internal stone cists. Later still, during the Middle Neolithic, they adopted widely the practice of collective burial in megalithic tombs of west European type, although the custom never spread as far east as Poland. In Scandinavia votive deposits in bogs represent a tradition which continued until the proto-historic period.

In addition to the TRB culture, other groups inhabited northern Europe. In the north, hunting and gathering communities of the Ertebølle culture survived alongside the new farmers. During the Middle Neolithic groups of Single Grave/Battle-axe/Corded Ware and Globular Amphora people spread across northern Europe, probably from the east, and for a while retained their separate identities. Farther north, the Pitted Ware culture, comprising a basically hunting population which also kept domesticated swine, emerged in Norway and Sweden and spread as far as eastern Denmark.

The Late Neolithic was a period of change, in which archaeologists recognize numerous regional cultures. The establishment of bronze industries in the Elbe–Oder and Saale–Warthe regions profoundly affected the population farther north. Copper was already known – if rare – in north Germany and Scandinavia in the Early Neolithic. Now, however, metal was relatively common and local flint workers, in an effort to compete with metal tools, excelled themselves in producing polished and pressure-flaked axes, dagger and arrowheads of outstanding quality.

FURTHER READING

De Laet, S. J. 1958. *The Low Countries*, London and New York.
Gimbutas, M. 1956. *The Prehistory of Eastern Europe*, Cambridge, Mass.
Hagen, A. 1967. *Norway*, London and New York.
Jażdżewski, K. 1965. *Poland*, London and New York.
Klindt-Jensen, O. 1957. *Denmark*, London and New York.
Stenberger, M. 1962. *Sweden*, London and New York.

The Stone Age of arctic Europe

North of the temperate zone and beyond the boundary which demarcates the deciduous from the coniferous forest, hunting and fishing communities survived in Europe throughout the Neolithic and Bronze Ages and into the Iron Age of regions farther south. These communities, sometimes described under the heading of the 'Arctic Stone Age', have often been considered to be part of an immense circumpolar culture, comprising the Eskimos of the New World and the hunting and fishing communities of northern Eurasia. However, it seems most likely that broad cultural similarities between these groups can be explained in terms of adaptation to a similar environment, rather than a shared origin.

Although the arctic zone was unable to support primitive farming, it was rich in wild food resources. Elk, bear and reindeer were hunted on land; water-fowl, seals, halibut and even porpoises were caught on the coast. Early communities in arctic Europe are known from their rock art and from occupied caves and rock shelters, camp sites and occasionally from cemeteries. Tools and weapons were commonly made of slate – so commonly that Scandinavian archaeologists often refer to the 'Slate Culture' – although in some areas quartz and other types of stone were also used. Spearheads, arrowheads and knives are common; the knife handles frequently end in carved animal heads, usually elk. Some communities used pottery, presumably adopted from farming cultures farther south, with which they certainly traded. Of particular note is 'asbestos ware', made from clay mixed with asbestos. On land the arctic hunters used skis and sledges for transport; we have no evidence for domesticated reindeer and the sledges were probably hauled by dogs. At sea they used skin boats, for example when fishing for porpoises.

Like hunting communities in other times and places, the arctic hunters and fishers decorated rock faces with engraved and painted designs in varying degrees of naturalism. Animals predominate, including all those commonly hunted; men, too, appear frequently in hunting scenes. In addition to rock art, mobiliary art occurs: as well as the knife handles already mentioned, we find naturalistic animals, birds and fish and schematic human beings in amber, bone, wood, flint and clay.

FURTHER READING

Clark, J. G. D. 1952. *Prehistoric Europe. The Economic Basis*, London and New York.
Hagen, A. 1967. *Norway*, London and New York.
Hallström, G. 1938. *Monumental Art of Northern Europe from the Stone Age. I. The Norwegian Localities*, Stockholm.
———— 1960. *Monumental Art of Northern Sweden from the Stone Age*, Stockholm.
Kivikoski, E. 1967. *Finland*, London and New York.
Stenberger, M. 1962. *Sweden*, London and New York.

TINT SHOWS LAND ABOVE 500M

Gåshopen
Komsa
Varanger Fjord
(Gråsbakken, Karlebotn, Nordli etc.)
Pechenga
Murmansk/Kola

Narvik
Forselv

Klubba

Marraskoski
Rovaniemi

Rødøy

Zalavrouga

Strand
Bardal
Fosna
Hästskotjärn
Evenhus
Gärde/L.Skärvången
Trondheim
Flatrüet
Nämforsen
Bogge

Bjurselet
Oulu

Kiuruvesi

Grønhelleren
Straume
Ruskenesset
priholmen (Bømlo)
Haukelidsaeter
iste
Nøstvet
Høgnipen/Kalnes
Kråkerøy
Oslo

Suomusjärvi
Porvoo (Askola)
Helsinki
Antrea
Olenii Ostrov
Olonets
Petrozavodsk
Kiukais
Leningrad

Alunda
Jettböle
Åloppe
L.Juusjärvi/Vitträsk
Narva
Kunda

Mogetorp
Östra Vrå
Fagervik/Säter
Stockholm
Tallinn

Pärnu

L.Mjörn
Gothenburg

Siretorp
Copenhagen
Limhamn/Ringsjö/Segebro
Åmose/Bromme/
Maglemose

Danzig

R.Vyg
Petrozavodsk
L.Onega
Olonets
On the same scale

0   400
KILOMETRES

0   250
STATUTE MILES

The Stone Age of arctic Europe **147**

Megalithic monuments in Europe

The term 'megalithic' is properly used to describe monuments built of large stones, but it is often extended to cover structures of otherwise similar type built with drystone walls. Used in this wider sense, megalithic monuments are found throughout western Europe from the Mediterranean to the North Sea, but do not occur east of Italy in the south or Germany in the north. If we exclude from this discussion the Maltese temples (see p. 122), which were built in a different style and may represent an independent tradition, the megalithic monuments fall into three classes: tombs, standing stones (menhirs) and grouped standing stones (enclosures and alignments). Tombs are found throughout the area in which megalithic monuments occur and menhirs are wide-spread except in northern Europe. Enclosures and alignments, on the other hand, are almost entirely restricted to Brittany and the British Isles (see p. 155).

Megalithic tombs were built in a great variety of forms, but three main types may be distinguished: simple closed chambers (stone cists), long chambers (gallery graves) and chambers preceded by an entrance passage (passage graves). However, many intermediate types exist, as well as elaborate forms which almost defy classification. The tombs vary in size from small box-like structures to enormous gallery graves, 15–20 m long, such as Cueva de la Menga in Spain and Bagneux in France. They were frequently covered by mounds of earth and stone. Normally they were used for collective burial and occasionally yield remains of more than 100 bodies.

Material from the earliest megalithic tombs, in Brittany, has given C14 dates in the early fifth millennium BC (early fourth millennium bc) and the earliest British tombs are not much later. We have few C14 dates from other regions, but it appears that megalithic tombs were constructed in most areas in the fourth and third millennia BC and that in some areas simple tombs were still being built c. 1000 BC.

Megalithic monuments have given rise to as much controversy as any aspect of European prehistory, being considered on the one hand the products of a native west European tradition, on the other the type-fossils of a religion carried or diffused from the east Mediterranean. However, C14 dates and the tree-ring calibration have tipped the scales decisively in favour of independent invention; indeed in some areas it appears that megalithic tombs were built by the first local farmers.

FURTHER READING

DANIEL, G. 1960. *The Prehistoric Chamber Tombs of France*, London.
———— 1962. *The Megalith Builders of Western Europe²*, London and New York.
LEISNER, G. and V. 1943, 1956–9, 1965. *Die Megalithgräber der Iberischen Halbinsel*, Berlin.
SPROCKHOFF, E. 1938. *Die nordische Megalithkultur*, Berlin.

TINT SHOWS LAND ABOVE 500M

A   B   C   D   E   F

a

Maes Howe

Tustrup

Grønhøj

b

Lupow

New Grange

Puttos   Liepen

Bryn Celli Ddu

Havelte

West Kennet

Züschen

c

Zennor Quoit

Barnenez

Fontenay-le-Marmion

Ile Longue/
Gavrinis

d

Bagneux

Ors

Montguyon

Cangas de Onis

Arles

e

La Halliade

Antela de Portelagem

Puig Roíg

Filitosa

Giovinazzo

Arzachena

Praia das Maças

Rafal Rubi

Goronna (Paulilatino)

f

Alcalá

Cueva de la Menga (Antequera)

Monteracello

Pantelleria

Los Millares

g

Ta Hammut

h

Vistula

Elbe

Oder

Rhine

Seine

Loire

Danube

Po

Duero

Ebro

Guadalquivir

⫿⫿⫿ Distribution of megaliths

0   500
KILOMETRES

0   300
STATUTE MILES

Megalithic monuments in Europe   **149**

In contrast to the megalithic monuments, which occur widely throughout northern and western Europe, rock-cut tombs have a primarily Mediterranean distribution. Indeed only one group of rock-cut tombs is known in Europe outside the Mediterranean region: a group of more than two hundred in the Marne area of France. In plan and construction the tombs cut into the soft chalk of the Marne region are all very similar: they consist of a large square chamber, often preceded by a small antechamber, both with narrow entrances, connected to the surface by a sloping passage. These tombs have no close Mediterranean parallels and may be unconnected with the Mediterranean ones; probably they were developed locally as rock-cut imitations of the megalithic tombs of the same area: the gallery graves of the Paris Basin.

In the Mediterranean, rock-cut tombs have a wide distribution. In the central Mediterranean they occur in peninsular Italy, Sicily, Malta and Sardinia. They are common in all areas, but the tradition was at its strongest in the larger islands: in Sicily rock-cut tombs were used almost exclusively throughout the Copper and Bronze Ages and continued to be built in the Iron Age until the Greek colonization, while in Sardinia more than 1100 rock-cut tombs are known, mostly belonging to the Copper Age, though continuing in use alongside megalithic graves in the succeeding period. In the east Mediterranean, rock-cut tombs occur in Crete and in mainland Greece but are common only on some of the Cycladic islands and in Cyprus. They belong almost exclusively to the Bronze Age (partly equivalent to the Copper Age in the central Mediterranean). In the west Mediterranean rock-cut tombs occur sporadically throughout southern Iberia, but are common in only two areas: on the island of Mallorca and round the estuary of the River Tagus in Portugal. They belong to the local Copper and Bronze Ages.

The forms of the rock-cut tombs vary considerably, ranging from simple oval or rectangular chambers entered directly from a cliff face, a vertical shaft or a sloping passage to complex monuments with many connected chambers, sometimes decorated in relief or paint or both.

Rock-cut tombs in Europe

see map pp. 152/153

The most elaborate tombs occur on the islands of Mallorca, Sardinia and Malta. The Mallorcan tombs have long rectangular chambers, often with one or more small subsidiary chambers; while they are unlike rock-cut tombs in other areas, their plans are similar to those of the above-ground megalithic tombs found on both Mallorca and Menorca, known as *navetas*. The Sardinian tombs often have complicated plans with numerous chambers and are sometimes decorated in relief or red paint: the most interesting decoration takes the form of skeuomorphic wooden features such as beams and lintels. The most spectacular monument of all is undoubtedly the enormous and labyrinthine hypogeum of Hal Saflieni on Malta, which, like some of the Sardinian tombs, has elaborate decoration in both relief and in paint. All the more complex and unusual rock-cut tombs seem to represent the end-products of specialized insular traditions which exerted little influence on other areas.

Rock-cut tombs were most commonly used for collective burial, especially in the west, but single burial also occurs: in the Cyclades, for instance, single burial was the general rule and in parts of the central Mediterranean it seems as though the earliest tombs contained only single or double inhumations, but that collective burial became the normal rite later on. Where collective burial was practised, the number of inhumations ranged from fewer than ten to, rarely, more than one hundred. In a class of its own is the Maltese hypogeum of Hal Saflieni, mentioned above, which one of the excavators estimated might have housed the remains of some seven thousand individuals. The tombs often show evidence of continuous use over long periods and the Hal Saflieni hypogeum was undoubtedly used for many centuries.

Prehistorians have frequently regarded rock-cut tombs as part of a 'megalithic complex' and until recently it was widely accepted that the whole complex, comprising both rock-cut and megalithic tombs as well as other traits such as statue-menhirs (representing a presumed 'Mother Goddess'), originated in the east Mediterranean and was introduced into western Europe from there. However, just as the calibrated C¹⁴ chronology has indicated decisively that the earliest megalithic tombs occur in north-west Europe, so the admittedly meagre dating evidence suggests that the earliest rock-cut tombs were constructed not in the east but in the central Mediterranean. Several rock-cut tombs of the neolithic period are known in Italy and these should be dated before 3500 BC or even earlier, whereas it is difficult to date tombs in either the east or the west Mediterranean as early as this. Thus it seems that we cannot now believe in an east Mediterranean origin for either megalithic or rock-cut tombs. Indeed there are now no compelling reasons for considering the two tomb forms as parts of a single complex. Rock-cut tombs are essentially Mediterranean while megalithic tombs are north and west European in origin; however, the two traditions overlapped both geographically and chronologically and in some areas influenced each other profoundly.

FURTHER READING

DANIEL, G. 1962. *The Megalith Builders of Western Europe²*, London and New York.

EVANS, J. D. 1959. *Malta*, London and New York.

GUIDO, M. 1963. *Sardinia*, London and New York.

PERICOT GARCIA, L. 1972. *The Balearic Islands*, London and New York.

WHITEHOUSE, R. 1972. The rock-cut tombs of the central Mediterranean. *Antiquity* XLVI, 275–81.

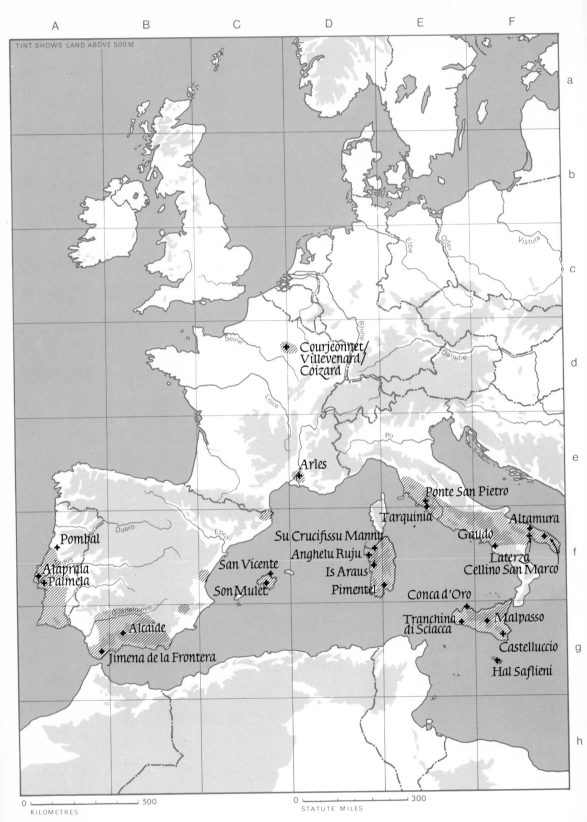

TINT SHOWS LAND ABOVE 500 M

Courjeonnet/
Villevenard/
Coizard

Arles

Ponte San Pietro

Tarquinia

Altamura

Su Crucifissu Mannu
Anghelu Ruju
Is Araus
Pimentel

Gaudo

Laterza
Cellino San Marco

Pombal

Alapraia
Palmela

San Vicente

Son Mulet

Conca d'Oro

Tranchina
di Sciacca

Malpasso

Castelluccio

Alcaide

Jimena de la Frontera

Hal Saflieni

0 |————————| 500
KILOMETRES

0 |————————| 300
STATUTE MILES

152 *Rock-cut tombs in Europe*

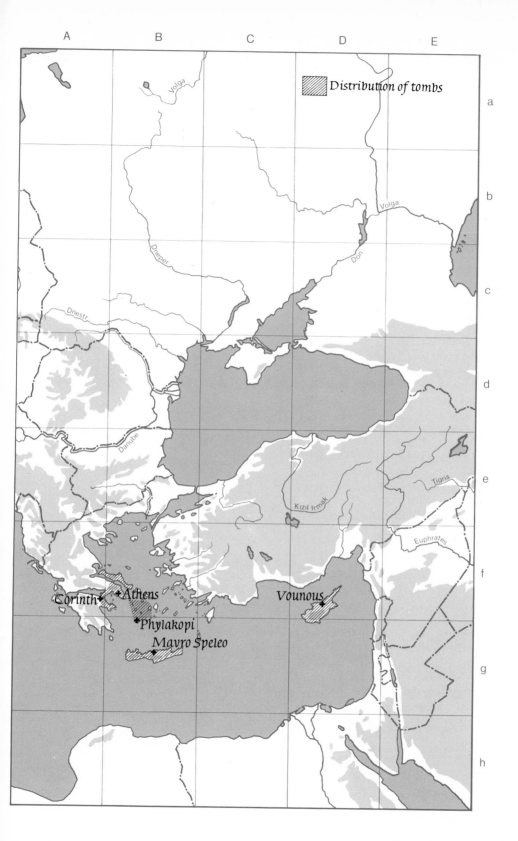

Megalithic enclosures and alignments in the British Isles and Brittany

North-west Europe contains a series of imposing 'ritual' monuments made of large – sometimes very large – stones, in a style of building similar to that of the megalithic chamber tombs. In Brittany we find a number of rectilinear or semicircular enclosures bounded by standing stones. (Only one circular example is known: Er Lannic.) The best known monuments, however, are the alignments of standing stones. In the Carnac region of south Brittany is to be seen a group of alignments, each comprising 10–13 parallel rows several kilometres long and containing nearly 3000 stones in all. Smaller alignments occur throughout Brittany. They often end in rectangular or semicircular enclosures.

The British monuments are different. Although one or two enclosures are approached by avenues, alignments occur only on Dartmoor and are built of very small stones. Almost all the monuments are enclosures and all have a curvilinear plan: circles, 'flattened circles', ellipses and egg-shaped rings. All consist of free-standing stones, except for the last phase of Stonehenge, which includes 'trilithons' (two standing stones supporting a lintel). Outstanding monuments include Stonehenge, Avebury, and Callanish on Lewis in the Outer Hebrides. The British stone circles form part of a group of monuments, not all of which are megalithic, often collectively labelled 'henges'. Henges are embanked enclosures, often surrounding rings of pits or wooden posts rather than stone circles.

We have virtually no dating evidence for the Breton monuments and very little for those in Britain. They probably fall within the period *c*. 3000–1800 BC (*c*. 2400–1500 bc), overlapping the later part of the megalithic tomb tradition.

It has long been maintained that these monuments had an astronomical function. Recently mathematicians and astronomers have investigated the problem anew and, while archaeologists do not accept all their deductions, it does seem clear that many of the British enclosures were laid out with a standard unit of length according to rules of geometry and that the builders used a solar calendar and recorded some of the movements of the moon. The same may be true also of the Breton monuments, currently under review.

FURTHER READING

DANIEL, G. 1962. *The Megalith Builders of Western Europe*[2], London and New York.

GIOT, P. R. 1960. *Brittany*, London and New York.

HAWKINS, G. S. 1966. *Stonehenge Decoded*, London and New York.

THOM, A. 1967. *Megalithic Sites in Britain*, Oxford.

THOM, A. and A. S. 1971. The Astronomical Significance of the Large Carnac Menhirs. *Journal for the History of Astronomy* 2, 147–60.

———— 1972. The Carnac Alignments. The Uses of the Alignments at Le Ménec, Carnac. *Journal for the History of Astronomy* 3, 11–26 and 151–64.

Inset map (upper left): On the same scale

Main map labels (north to south):

A B C D E F
a
b
c
d
e
f
g
h

Broubster
Loch of Yarrows
Learable Hill
Loanhead of Daviot
Tomnaverie
Cullerie
Monzie
Ballymeanoch
Edinburgh
Kingside Hill
Auchagallon
Duddo
Torhousekie
Whitcastles
Glenquicken
Beaghmore
Belfast
Castle Rigg
Long Meg and her Daughters
Drumskinny
Oddendale
Ballynoe
Birkrigg Common
Devil's Arrows
Ilkley Moor
Masonbrook
Dublin
Manchester
Athgreany
Penmaenmawr
Humber
Lough Gur
Ballynamona
Carneddau Hengwm
Lissyviggeen
Mitchell's Fold
Severn
Birmingham
Kealkil
Rollright Stones
Templebryan
Gurranes
Stanton Drew
Avebury
London
Cardiff
Stonehenge
Hampton Down
Merry Maidens
Dartmoor
Rempstone

Upper-right inset (Outer Hebrides):
Steinacleit/
Clach an Trushel
Clach an Tursa
Callanish
Dursainean/Clach Stein
Clach an Teampuill
Clach Mhic Leoid
Cladh Maolrithe
Leacach an Tigh Chloiche
Sornach Coir Fhinn
Gramisdale
Clach Mhor'ā Chè
Rueval
An Carra
Ru Ardvule
Barra
Barra Head

0 ____ 30 Kms
0 ____ 20 Mls

Lower-left inset (Brittany/Carnac area):
Kerzerho
Ste-Barbe
Vieux Moulin
Menec
Kerlescan
Kermario
Kergonan
Le Moulin
Er Lannic
Quiberon
Ile d'Ouessant
Pleslin
Crozon Peninsula
Penmarc'h
Brest
Rennes
Arbourg
Seine
Paris

0 ____ 10 Kms
0 ____ 6 Mls

Legend:
⊕ Enclosure
⌂ Alignment
△ Single stone or group of stones
TINT SHOWS LAND ABOVE 200M

0 |_____| 200
KILOMETRES

0 |_____| 100
STATUTE MILES

Megalithic enclosures and alignments in the British Isles and Brittany   **155**

TINT SHOWS LAND ABOVE 500 M

Madarovce

Ossarn

Jaszladany

Königshöhle (Baden)
Budakalasz
Alsónémedi
Hódmezővásárhely

Vučedol
Gornja Tuzla

Remedello   Villafranca Veronese

Cumarola

Monte Bradoni

Rinaldone

La Starza   Laterza

Anghelu Ruju   Gaudo   Cellino San Marco

Zambujal   Lipari

Vila Nova de São Pedro
Palmela

Alcalá

Mesas de Asta   Almizaraque
Tabernas
Los Millares

0 ————— 500
KILOMETRES

0 ————— 300
STATUTE MILES

156   *Early copper metallurgy in Europe*

Early copper metallurgy in Europe

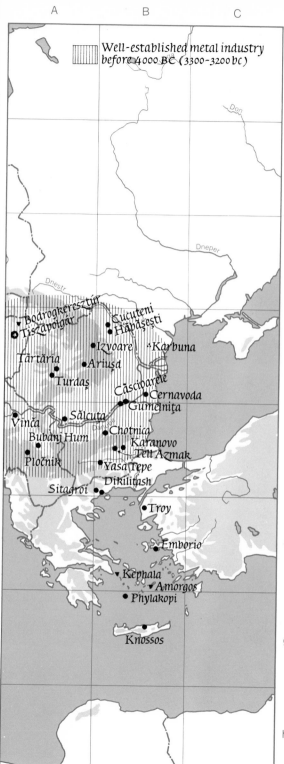

Well-established metal industry before 4000 BC (3300–3200 bc)

Until recently prehistorians believed that metal-working was developed in the Near East and spread thence into Europe, but new studies suggest that metallurgy was also invented independently in eastern Europe. Although the earliest known metal objects in the world come from southern Anatolia, where smelted copper was in use before 6000 bc, prior to 4500 BC (*c.* 3800 bc) a flourishing metal industry existed in the Balkans, although areas between there and southern Anatolia were still without metal. Moreover, the Balkan metal industry was quite unlike that of the Near East, for it was distinguished by the manufacture of core-cast shaft-hole axes and axe-adzes – probably the earliest of all metal shaft-hole tools. It is likely therefore that the Balkan metal industry did develop locally. Indeed the technology required by metal-working could well have developed from the production of graphite-coated pottery, characteristic of several Balkan Copper Age cultures, which like metallurgy needs high kiln temperatures and reducing conditions.

During the period 4500–3000 BC (*c.* 3800–2500 bc) the area of metal-working expanded to cover most of eastern Europe. In the latter part of this period local industries grew up also in parts of the Mediterranean: in the Aegean, Italy and Iberia. The Aegean industry is usually regarded as Anatolian in origin and the Italian and Iberian industries as derivatives of Aegean metallurgy. However, there is no compelling argument against regarding the four industries as independent developments.

The metal objects of this early stage were of pure copper or copper alloyed with arsenic. Bronze, the alloy of copper and tin, was not used in Europe until the late third millennium BC.

FURTHER READING

BARFIELD, L. 1971. *Northern Italy before Rome*, London and New York.

RENFREW, C. 1969. The Autonomy of the South-east European Copper Age. *Proceedings of the Prehistoric Society* 35, 12–47.

―――― 1972. *The Emergence of Civilisation. The Cyclades and the Aegean in the Third Millennium BC*, London.

SAVORY, H. N. 1968. *Spain and Portugal*, London and New York.

TRUMP, D. H. 1966. *Central and Southern Italy before Rome*, London and New York.

157

The Bell Beaker, Battle-axe and Globular Amphora cultures

The millennium *c.* 3500–2500 BC appears in the archaeological record of Europe as a prehistoric 'Migration period', with evidence of numerous, often related, groups spreading across the continent. In a simplified account it is permissible to divide these groups into two main complexes: an eastern complex, comprising the cultures variously labelled the Globular Amphora, Corded Ware, Single Grave, Battle-axe and Boat-axe groups, and a western complex, the Bell Beaker group.

Remains of the eastern complex are found all over east and northern Europe. It may have originated in the Kurgan (Pit Grave) culture of the south Russian steppes. Important traits of this group, which had reached Holland before 3200 BC (2500 bc) are single graves, often under barrows, wheeled vehicles, probably domesticated horses and copper metallurgy. The complex is sometimes said to represent the arrival of the Indo-Europeans.

The Bell Beaker group has a fairly dense but discontinuous distribution in parts of east and central Europe, the Low Countries, the British Isles, Brittany, southern France and parts of Iberia, with sporadic occurrences also in the central Mediterranean. The complex is characterized by a distinctive type of pottery – the Bell Beaker, single graves under barrows (though the latter may not have been an original feature), archers' equipment and copper metallurgy. Two schools of thought exist about the origin of the Bell Beaker group. Many archaeologists favour an Iberian homeland, but the alternative hypothesis of an origin in eastern Europe seems equally plausible. Westward movement from eastern Europe might have resulted from pressure by people farther east, including the Kurgan groups.

Although these mobile groups retained their separate identities, they often mixed freely with indigenous groups and with each other. Though perhaps numerically small, they were probably responsible for important innovations in Europe: the eastern complex introduced wheeled vehicles and perhaps also the domesticated horse to northern Europe, while both groups helped to extend the knowledge of metallurgy from the areas in which it was first practised to virtually the rest of Europe.

FURTHER READING

CHILDE, V. G. 1957. *The Dawn of European Civilisation*[6], London and New York.

CLARK, G. 1969. *World Prehistory: a New Outline*[2], London and New York.

GIMBUTAS, M. 1956. *The Prehistory of Eastern Europe*, Cambridge, Mass.

PIGGOTT, S. 1965, 1966. *Ancient Europe*, Edinburgh and Chicago.

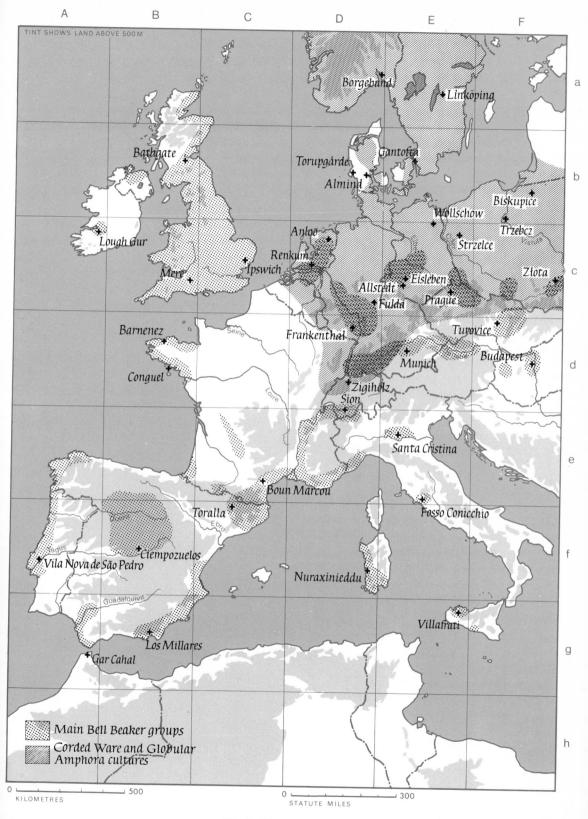

TINT SHOWS LAND ABOVE 500M

A · B · C · D · E · F

a

Borgeband
Linköping

Bathgate

Torupgårde
Gantofta
Almind

b

Biskupice
Wollschow
Trzebcz
Strzelce

Lough Gur

Anloo
Renkum
Złota

Mere
Ipswich
Allstedt
Eisleben
Fulda
Prague

c

Barnenez

Frankenthal
Turovice
Budapest

Conguel

Munich

d

Zigiholz
Sion

Santa Cristina

e

Boun Marcou
Fosso Conicchio

Toralla

Ciempozuelos

Villafrati
Nuraxinieddu

f

Vila Nova de São Pedro

Los Millares

g

Gar Cahal

h

Main Bell Beaker groups
Corded Ware and Globular
Amphora cultures

0 — 500
KILOMETRES

0 — 300
STATUTE MILES

The Bell Beaker, Battle-axe and Globular Amphora cultures   **159**

Late Copper Age to Middle Bronze Age sites in eastern Europe

The rich chalcolithic cultures of eastern Europe (Gumelniţa, Sălcuţa, Vinča-Pločnik, etc.), which developed the earliest metallurgy in Europe (see p. 156) came – perhaps abruptly – to an end and were succeeded by a very different group of cultures: the Cernavoda-Ezero culture in Bulgaria and Romania and the related Baden culture of Hungary, Austria and Jugoslavia. These latter cultures are sometimes thought to be related to groups in Anatolia and sometimes to the Kurgan culture north of the Black Sea. Like their predecessors, they were metal-using and out of them, some time before 2000 BC (but not yet dated by C[14]), developed the full Bronze Age cultures of south-east Europe.

The best known of the Early Bronze Age groups are the Periam (Perjámos) – Pecica culture of southern Hungary and western Romania, the Nagyrév group of eastern Hungary and Slovakia, and the Kisapostag group west of the Danube. In many areas new sites were occupied, often permanent settlements which gradually became tells: good examples are Pecica in Romania and the famous Hungarian site of Tószeg. Cemeteries, often large, are common; inhumation was the usual rite, but cremation was practised in the Nagyrév and Kisapostag groups. Initially metal objects were fairly uncommon. They were closely related to products of the central European Únětice culture and include ingot torques and several types of pin which, like the faience beads that also occur, are often thought to be of east Mediterranean inspiration. Indeed, the Bronze Age of eastern, as of central, Europe is frequently said to have been initiated by metal-workers from the Near East or the Aegean. However, taking into account the calibrated C[14] chronology, a local origin now seems more probable.

The Middle Bronze Age cultures, which developed directly out of the Early Bronze Age groups and which often occur in the upper levels of tells first occupied in the earlier period, were rich in metal. The Füzesabony culture of the Hungarian Plain was especially rich and we have important hoards, such as Hajdusamson and Apa. The late Füzesabony culture contained certain elements of the central European Tumulus culture and it appears that influence from central Europe was exerted on the East.

On the peripheries of the Hungarian/west Romanian area there were other Bronze Age cultures. Notable groups include the Otomani culture of Transylvania and the Monteoru culture of eastern Romania and, in the west, the Vučedol culture of north-west Jugoslavia.

FURTHER READING

ALEXANDER, J. 1972. *Jugoslavia before the Roman Conquest*, London and New York.
BERCIU, D. 1967. *Romania*, London and New York.
CHILDE, V. G. 1929. *The Danube in Prehistory*, Oxford.
——— 1957. *The Dawn of European Civilisation*[6], London and New York.
GIMBUTAS, M. 1965. *Bronze Age Cultures in Central and Eastern Europe*, The Hague.

Late Copper Age to Middle Bronze Age sites in eastern Europe **161**

Early and Middle Bronze Age sites in central Europe

Shortly before 2000 BC a local bronze industry developed in central and eastern Europe. While the metallurgy of the Copper Age came into existence in south-east and southern Europe, the first Bronze Age industries developed round the metal sources of Bohemia and the Alps. The earliest Bronze Age culture in central Europe is named after the site of Únětice (formerly Aunjetitz) in Czechoslovakia. Farther west related groups are named after the cemeteries of Straubing and Adlerberg; to the east, in Hungary and Romania, were the Periam and Nagyrév groups (see p. 161). All these groups are known primarily from cemeteries of single burials, usually in flat graves but occasionally under barrows, from hoards and, less often, from settlements.

In the past the origin of bronze metallurgy in Europe has been explained in terms of immigrant craftsmen from the Near East (probably Syria), where we find close parallels for early European products, such as ingot torques and racquet- and knot-headed pins. However, the recent tree-ring calibration of C^{14} dates shows that the European finds are earlier than their Syrian analogues, strongly suggesting that bronze-working in Europe, like the copper industry, had a local origin, although archaeological research has yet to reveal its development.

The Únětice phase was succeeded about the middle of the second millennium BC by the Tumulus group, in which single burial under barrows was characteristic. Today, the Únětice and Tumulus groups are usually regarded as successive stages of the same basic culture, rather than separate entities, as formerly believed.

The establishment of a flourishing bronze industry and the consequent increase in trade brought prosperity to central Europe and the archaeological record for the period shows the emergence of social and economic stratification in the form of rich, presumably chieftains' burials, like those at Leubingen and Helmsdorf. Metal was now readily available – as it had never been in the Copper Age – and it became customary to bury numerous metal objects with the dead. Hoards, too, are common. The flourishing metallurgy of the Middle Bronze Age formed the basis of the rich Late Bronze Age Urnfield Culture (see p. 170).

FURTHER READING

CHILDE, V. G. 1957. *The Dawn of European Civilisation*[6], London and New York.
DÉCHELETTE, J. 1924–27. *Manuel d'Archéologie préhistorique*[2], vols. I–IV, Paris.
GIMBUTAS, M. 1965. *Bronze Age Cultures in Central and Eastern Europe*, The Hague.
NEUSTUPNÝ, E. and J. 1961. *Czechoslovakia before the Slavs*, London and New York.
RENFREW, C. 1973. *Before Civilization*, London and New York.

A   B   C   D   E   F

a

b

c

Stockholm

Kaliningrad

Danzig

Warsaw

Falkenwalde

Bucholz

Hitzdorf

Wasosz

Kläden

Grobia

Środa

Wahlitz

Granowo

Łęki Małe

Nohra

Beitzsch

Smoszew

Leubingen

Dieskau

Burk

Siedlce

Kruszyniec

Neunheiligen

Schwarza

Helmsdorf

Malnice

Třebivlice

Tachlovice

Slaný

Hradec Králové

Krupá

Houštka

Jaworze Dolne

Hájek

Neuměřely

Kamýk

Unětice

Prague

Záleže

Adlerberg

Hammer

Blučina-Cezavy

Větěrov

Uherský Brod

Bühl

Niederrussbach

Maisbirbaum

Mehrstetten

Straubing

Neudorf

Přitluky

Výcapy-Opatovce

Asenkofen

Gemeinlebarn

Gross Mugl

Matuškovo

Nitrianski Hrádok

Wimsbach

Vienna

Sv.Peter

Aschering

Munich

Winklarn

Regelsbrunn

Singen

Pitten

Sauerbrunn

Budapest

Bern

Elbe

Elbe

Rhine

Danube

Danube

Vistula

Oder

Berlin

0   250
KILOMETRES

0   175
STATUTE MILES

Early and Middle Bronze Age sites in central Europe **163**

Bronze Age sites in France and Belgium

Western continental Europe as a whole did not participate in the earliest phase of the European Bronze Age. Only in two areas did Early Bronze Age industries flourish in the first half of the second millennium BC. The first area was in the Aar and Rhône valleys of Switzerland and France. Here an industry arose based on the exploitation of west Alpine ores. Tools, weapons and ornaments, closely related to those of the central European Únětice industry, occur both as isolated finds and in cemeteries of richly furnished flat graves. The second area was Brittany, where the Armorican Barrow culture flourished. Here burials with rich grave goods were covered with barrows, as in the contemporary and closely related Wessex culture of England. Armorican metal types show connections with both the Únětice culture and Wessex.

Outside these two regions, few metal objects are known, although imported items, sometimes of considerable value, occasionally occur in graves, as at Arlon in Luxembourg.

Elsewhere in France bronze objects appeared in graves first in the Middle Bronze Age (after *c.* 1500 BC) when barrow-building communities like those of central Europe occur in the east; those of the Haguenau forest are widely known. During this period bronze came into general use and hoards of bronze tools, especially axes, are found throughout France.

In the Late Bronze Age (from *c.* 1200 BC) eastern France was affected by the spread of Urnfield people from central Europe, who gradually moved north and west across the country. A later expansion in the eighth century also carried Urnfield ideas and techniques across southern France and into Spain.

In the west different traditions flourished. Unfortunately the evidence is restricted almost exclusively to metal-work, which occurs mostly in large hoards. These metal objects, which differ considerably from those of the Urnfield culture, are sometimes described as the Atlantic Bronze Age or (after one particular metal type) as the carp's-tongue sword complex. The Atlantic Bronze Age was formerly thought to represent a group of invaders ('the sword-bearers'), but today is regarded as a local development out of the industries of the Middle Bronze Age.

FURTHER READING

GIOT, P. R. 1960. *Brittany*, London and New York.

KIMMIG, W. 1954. Zur Urnenfelderkultur in Westeuropa. *Festschrift für Peter Goessler*, 41–98.

SANDARS, N. K. 1957. *Bronze Age Cultures in France*, London and New York.

SAVORY, H. N. 1948. 'The Sword-Bearers': a reinterpretation. *Proceedings of the Prehistoric Society* 14, 155–76.

———— 1949. The Atlantic Bronze Age in South-West Europe. *Proceedings of the Prehistoric Society* 15, 128–55.

A
B
C
D
E
F
a
b
c
d
e
f
g
h
Hamburg
Elbe
Rotterdam
Rhine
London
Brussels
Wijshagen
Bonlez
Hennuyères
Longy
Amiens
Fauvillers
Arlon
Port en Bessin
Graville
Lessay-Manche
Longues
Etrepagny
Heuqueville
Tosson-Maharit
Aulnay-les-Planches
Kernonen
St-Pois
Seine
Fort Harrouard
Paris
Haguenau
Tréboul
Tanwedou
Maure de Bretagne
Villeneuve-St-Georges
Courdemanges
Lingolsheim
St-Fiacre
Lothea
Rolampont
Rixheim
Loire
Cannes-Écluse
Nantes
Chapelle-Heulin
Chaume-les-Baigneux
Les Fontaines-Salées
Dampierre-sur-le-Doubs
Malassis
Pougues
Neyruz
St-Mathurin
Chassey
Sassenay
Bern
Dompierre-sur-Besbre
Les Roseaux
Limoges
Lac du Chalain
Begadan
Cozes
Vilhonneur
Lyons
Cissac
Pauillac
Bordeaux
Alliès
Po
Rhône
Garonne
La Liquisse
Toulouse
Ferrières
Briatexte
Montpellier
Launac
Mailhac
Arbas
Millas
Ebro
Barcelona
TINTS SHOW LAND ABOVE 325 M
0
250
KILOMETRES
0
175
STATUTE MILES

Bronze Age sites in France and Belgium

Bronze Age sites in the British Isles

The practice of metallurgy, first with copper and later with bronze, was probably introduced by different groups of Beaker people from the continent. Subsequently separate local traditions of metal-working flourished in Scotland, Ireland and southern England.

The best known Early Bronze Age group is the Wessex culture of southern England, characterized by single burials, accompanied by rich grave goods, under barrows of specialized forms. As well as bronze tools and weapons and pottery vessels, the grave goods include gold and amber objects and faience beads. Initially inhumation was the normal rite, but later cremation became predominant. The latest period of construction at Stonehenge (phase III) is attributed to the Wessex culture, about which there is continuing controversy, in particular over two points: (1) whether the culture was introduced to Britain by invaders who imposed themselves on the local population as overlords, or whether it arose locally through trade with the continent, and (2) whether or not there was any contact between it and Mycenaean Greece. Neither question has been settled. The second point hinges largely upon chronology and unfortunately we have *no* C^{14} dates for early Wessex material. Related material on the continent yields dates which, if calibrated and transferred to Wessex, are too early to allow such contact. However, it is claimed that the *Pinus aristata* calibration is unreliable for this particular period and that the Wessex culture could at all events be partially contemporary with Mycenae.

Outside Wessex and its extensions into Cornwall and East Anglia, cultures of undoubted local origin flourished. In northern England, Scotland and Ireland, societies practised single burial under barrows, worked metal and made pottery of the type known as Food Vessels, almost certainly of Beaker ancestry. Rich goods, though not as common as in Wessex, occur widely. Of especial interest are the Scottish jet spacer-plate necklaces, similar to Wessex amber necklaces, and the Irish gold lunulae which imitate them.

In the Middle (*c.* 1400–1000 BC) and Late Bronze Ages (*c.* 1000–600 BC) rich grave goods were very rare. Bronze, however, was readily available and new weapons and implements appeared (palstaves, rapiers, sickles, etc. in the MBA, swords and beaten metal shields and vessels in the LBA). The normal burial rite was cremation in urns, either under barrows or in flat urnfields. Bronze hoards became common in the MBA and were more common still in the LBA, when huge founders' hoards of scrap metal occur.

From the MBA onwards settlements are known and these include embanked and palisaded compounds, crannogs and, later, hill-forts. To the MBA belong the earliest 'Celtic' fields, which indicate that the plough was in use.

FURTHER READING

CHILDE, V. G. 1947. *Prehistoric Communities of the British Isles*², London and New York.
EVANS, E. ESTYN 1966. *Prehistoric and Early Christian Ireland*, London.
FEACHEM, R. 1963. *Prehistoric Scotland*, London.
PIGGOTT, S. 1958. *Scotland before History*, London.
RENFREW, C. 1968. Wessex without Mycenae. *Annual of the British School at Athens* 63, 277–85.

On the same scale

A   B   C   D   E   F

Stanydale

Jarlshof

Knowes of Trotty

Cairnpapple

Embo
Migdale   Banff
Orton   Inverkeithny
Loanhead of Daviot

Dalrulzion   Auchnacree

Melfort   Pyotdykes
Badden   Edinburgh
Traprain Law

Drumelzier

Broighter

Glen Trool

Heathery Burn

Boa Island   Topped Mountain   Belfast
Black Lion   Downpatrick   West Tanfield   Folkton
Rathinaun   Butterwick

Tara   Dublin   Manchester
Ballinderry   Knockast   Todmorden
Dowris   Derrinboy   Dinorben   Mold   Stanton Moor
Mooghaun   Bishopsland   Caergwrle
Knocknalappa   Ebnal   Barton Bendish
Guilsfield   Little Cressingham
Cush   Downham Fen   Mildenhall
Ballyvourney   Birmingham   Isleham   Chippenham
Cappeen   Snowshill   Ardleigh

Llyn Fawr   London
Monkton   Manton
Cardiff   Snail Down   Minnis Bay
Taunton Workhouse   Stonehenge   Park Brow   Plumpton Plain
Farway Down   Wilsford   Itford Hill
Harlyn Bay   Deverel   Hove
Treviskey   Rillaton   Arreton Down
Plymstock   Clandon   Shearplace Hill
Pelynt
Gwithian
Knackaboy Cairn

Paris

Brest
Rennes

TINT SHOWS LAND ABOVE 200M

0   200
KILOMETRES

0   100
STATUTE MILES

Bronze Age sites in the British Isles   **167**

TINT SHOWS LAND ABOVE 325M

| | A | B | C | D | E | F |

a
Reyheim
Vigrestad
Vanse
Vesthy
Hassle
Håga
Västerås
Skogstorp
Stockholm

b
Segerstadt
Koparve
Eskelhem
Nackhälle

Bredhøj
Broddenbjerg
Eldsberga
Dömmestorp

c
Muldbjerg
Borum Eshøj
Egtved
Trundholm
Trindhøj
Skrydstrup
Bulltofta
Balkåkra
Kivik
Toppehøj
Grevens Vaenge
Ystad
Madsebakke
Bohnert
Kopaniewo
Rzucewo
Pantau
Kaliningrad

d
Bornhöved
Langen
Bösdorf
Danzig
Borzęcino
Succase
Kończewice
Babięty Małe
Drouwen
Sögel
Tinsdal
Bäk
Trzebiatów
Naclaw
Grünhof-Tesperhude
Rossin
Dötzingen
Friedrichsruhe
Herzsprung
Storkowo
Radoszki
Bleckmar
Heiloo
Exloo-Odoorn
Rethwisch
Neulingen
Biesenbrow
Iwno/Wąsosz
Brześć Kujawski
Margijnen
Bargeroostervelde
Berlin
Biskupin
Enk
Buckow
Warsaw
Wageningen
Bruckhausen-Hünxe
Łęki Małe

e
Bergen-Terblijt
Overloon
Budel
Toterfout-Halve
Mijl
Klewe

f
Prague

g
Munich
Vienna
Bern
Budapest

0 —————— 250
KILOMETRES

0 —————— 175
STATUTE MILES

168 *Bronze Age sites in northern Europe*

Bronze Age sites in northern Europe

The plains of north Europe and south Scandinavia lack metal ores and for this reason they retained a stone-age technology when the more richly endowed areas of central and western Europe had already entered into the full Bronze Age. Indeed objects of imported copper were already reaching north Europe throughout the local Neolithic, and in the northern Late Neolithic, which was contemporary with the Bronze Age farther south, the volume of metal imports increased greatly.

However, when a local bronze industry did develop in Scandinavia, about the mid-second millennium B C, an independent tradition emerged which flourished for roughly a thousand years, characterized by workmanship in both bronze and gold at least equal in skill to that of central Europe. Among the outstanding northern products were vessels, helmets, *lurer* (large wind instruments with a long curving tube) and miniature wheeled vehicles like the famous sun-chariot from Trundholm. Clearly Scandinavia was wealthy in this period, for fine metal goods were abundant despite the need to import the raw materials. The main source of wealth was Baltic amber, which was traded throughout Europe from the Atlantic to the east Mediterranean. The peripheral areas of northern Europe – the Low Countries and north Poland – did not share in this exuberant development of the metal industry although, through the wide-spread network of trade that covered Europe, they did acquire metal goods.

The material culture of the northern Bronze Age is known from hoards, votive deposits in bogs and particularly from burials. Generally speaking inhumation under barrows, sometimes in stone cists, was customary in the earlier Bronze Age. Later, cremation became the normal rite and urnfields – like those of the central European Urnfield culture – occur. Particularly important are the Danish burials in oak coffins, like those found at Egtved and Borum Eshøj, where organic remains, such as woollen clothing and wood, survive in fine condition.

We know only a few Bronze Age settlements in northern Europe; they contain long timber houses (as was the tradition in this area throughout later prehistory). Further clues about life in the northern Bronze Age are provided by scenes depicted on rock-faces, boulders and slabs forming the sides of cists.

FURTHER READING

DE LAET, S. J. 1958. *The Low Countries*, London and New York.
HAGEN, A. 1967. *Norway*, London and New York.
JAŻDŻEWSKI, K. 1965. *Poland*, London and New York.
KERSTEN, K. 1936. *Zur älteren nordischen Bronzezeit*, Neumünster.
KLINDT-JENSEN, O. 1957. *Denmark*, London and New York.
STENBERGER, M. 1962. *Sweden*, London and New York.

The Urnfields of central Europe

During the thirteenth century BC the descendants of the Únětice people in central Europe entered on a period of economic growth. This expansion coincided approximately with the adoption of cremation burial in large cemeteries of urnfields – a practice which has given its name to the Late Bronze Age cultures of the region. Early Urnfield groups are found in Hungary, in eastern Germany (the Lausitz group) and in the north Alpine region (the Knoviz and Hötting groups). In this last area the Urnfield culture developed directly into the culture of the Hallstatt Iron Age, which emerged c. 750–700 BC. The marked prosperity of the Urnfield period was based largely on improvements in bronze technology. Whereas previously copper ore had been collected from the surface or from shallow opencast mines, now true deep mining took place. The excavation of the copper mines of the Mühlbach-Bischofshofen area of Austria has demonstrated that they were organized on an industrial basis, with a large permanent labour force. Metal was produced in abundance, both for home consumption and for export to areas in which ores were unknown, such as the Low Countries and Scandinavia. The Urnfield smiths were not only prolific but skilled; they produced a greatly increased range of goods, which included complicated core-cast tools, as well as sheet-metal armour and utensils.

The size and number of the cemeteries and settlements – even though these are less well known – and the evidence of the bronze industry all point to a larger population in the Urnfield period than existed previously. This increase seems to have been associated with a more efficient subsistence economy, based partly on the introduction and extensive use of the plough.

The Urnfield culture and economy, through a combination of migration and trading activities, ultimately influenced large areas of Europe, laying the foundations on which many of the later Iron Age cultures developed.

FURTHER READING

GIMBUTAS, M. 1965. *Bronze Age Cultures in Central and Eastern Europe*, The Hague.
MÜLLER-KARPE, H. 1959. *Beiträge zur Chronologie der Urnenfelderzeit nördlich und südlich der Alpen*, Berlin.
NEUSTUPNÝ, E. and J. 1961. *Czechoslovakia before the Slavs*, London and New York.
PATEK, E. 1968. *Die Urnenfelderkultur in Transdanubien*, Budapest.

TINT SHOWS LAND ABOVE 325M

Stockholm

Kaliningrad

Danzig

Warsaw

Elbe

Vistula

Berlin
Spindlersfeld
Buch
Elbe
Schweinert
Oberthau
Grossenhain
Weissig
Cosswig
Ode
Miejsce

Žatec
Stredokluký
Prague
Branka

Velatice
Blučina-Cezavy
Komjátna
Rimavská sobota

Pfeffingen
Winklsass
Klentnice
Baierdorf
Vyšný-Sliač
Očkov
Sajó Gömör
Danube
Unterglauheim
Gross Mugl
Čaka
Želiezovce
Aranyós
Unteraching/Kelheim/
Grünwald
Mezőcsat
Mohi
Etting
Vienna
Unter-Radl
Buchau
Munich
Rothengrub
Ilmitz
Piliny
Riegsee
Drassburg
Muzla
Hajdúböszörmény
Volders
Hallstatt
Val
Budapest
Hötting
Mühlbach-Bischofshofen

Poiqoryuuay
Gava

Bern

Rhine

Danube

Ptuj
Kér
Czorvás

0 ———————————— 250
KILOMETRES

0 ———————————— 175
STATUTE MILES

The Urnfields of central Europe **171**

TINT SHOWS LAND ABOVE 500 M

Court St. Etienne
Bad Nauheim
Havré
Flörsheim
Gedinne
Steinheim
Heidesheim
Mannheim
Achenheim
Algolsheim
Rixheim

Bijelo Brdo

Angarano
Blea
Ptuj
Ascona
Fontanella
Dobova
Golasecca
Zencovi
Canegrate
Este
Ripač
Chiavari
Po
Donja Dolina
Bologna
Bismantova
Pianello di Genga

Mailhac
Las Fados
Tarquinia
Cortes de Navarra
Coste del Marano
Agullana
Allumiere
Rome
Can Missert
Timmari
El Molá
Torre Castelluccia

Lipari
Milazzo

Seine
Loire
Rhine
Danube
Elbe
Oder
Vistula
Duero
Ebro
Tagus
Guadalquivir

0   500
KILOMETRES

0   300
STATUTE MILES

172   *The spread of Urnfield cultures in Europe*

The spread of Urnfield cultures in Europe

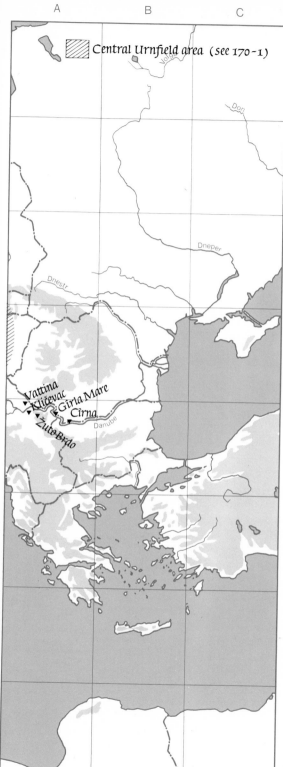

The communities of the Urnfield culture that developed in eastern and central Europe during the thirteenth and twelfth centuries BC practised a more efficient subsistence economy than their predecessors and further increased their prosperity by wide-spread trade in metal and other commodities. These developments were accompanied by a population increase, which led to expansion outside the area of origin and, as Europe was by now well populated, this was followed by displacement of other communities. Hence population movements affected large parts of Europe. In addition, Urnfield ideas and practices spread through the medium of trade and it is not always easy to distinguish between population movements and indirect influence.

The expansion of the Urnfield people was a discontinuous process that occurred over some 600 years, and it took place in several different directions. Urnfield groups moved into northern Italy from the thirteenth century onwards and small numbers pushed on down the coasts, introducing the characteristic funerary rite to south Italy and Sicily. From c. 1000 BC a particularly prosperous version of Urnfield culture, known as the Villanovan, flourished in the Po valley and Etruria, forming the basis from which Etruscan civilization later emerged. Other movements carried Urnfield customs and artifacts south-east into Jugoslavia, perhaps from the twelfth century onwards; the Lausitz group too expanded north-eastwards, extending its territory to the rivers Vistula and Bug. Urnfield groups reached eastern France in the eleventh century and gradually spread both farther west and north into Belgium. Urnfield settlers reached southern France and northern Spain only in the eighth century BC.

FURTHER READING

CLARK, G. 1969. *World Prehistory: a New Outline*², London and New York.

KIMMIG, W. 1954. Zur Urnenfelderkultur in Westeuropa. *Festschrift für Peter Goessler*, 41–98.

MÜLLER-KARPE, H. 1959. *Beiträge zur Chronologie der Urnenfelderzeit nördlich und südlich der Alpen*, Berlin.

PIGGOTT, S. 1965, 1966. *Ancient Europe*, Edinburgh and Chicago.

TINT SHOWS LAND ABOVE 325M

Rotterdam

Berlin

Weser

Rhine

Oder

Elbe

Eigenbilzen

Brussels

Mont Eribus

Court St-Etienne

Laon

Preist

Urmitz

Pfalzfeld

Steinsburg

Montigny

Chassemy

Waldalgesheim

Stradonice

Závist

Paris

Otzenhausen

Prague

Hrazany

Lhotice

Seine

Somme Bionne

Parsberg

Nevězice

Kallmünz

Kelheim

Regensburg

Straubing

Třísov

Loire

Euffigneix

Hirschlanden

Danube

Manching

Passau

Mont Lassois

Ohnenheim

Trichtingen

Heuneburg

Munich

Linz

Avaricum

Wittnauer Horn

Nebringen

Sternberg

Sunzing/Minning

Kuffarn

Alésia

Salzburg-Rainberg

Bibracte

La Tène

Altstetten

Dürrnberg

Salzburg

Hallstatt

Camp de Château

Münsingen

Hölzelsau

Strettweg

Bern

Erstfeld

Lyons

Rhône

Po

Vače

Sv. Skočijan

Magdalenska Gora

Vinica

Nesactium

Jeserine

Mailhac

Glanum

Ripač

Ensérune

Entremont

Nin

Massilia

Rome

174   *The Hallstatt and La Tène Iron Ages*

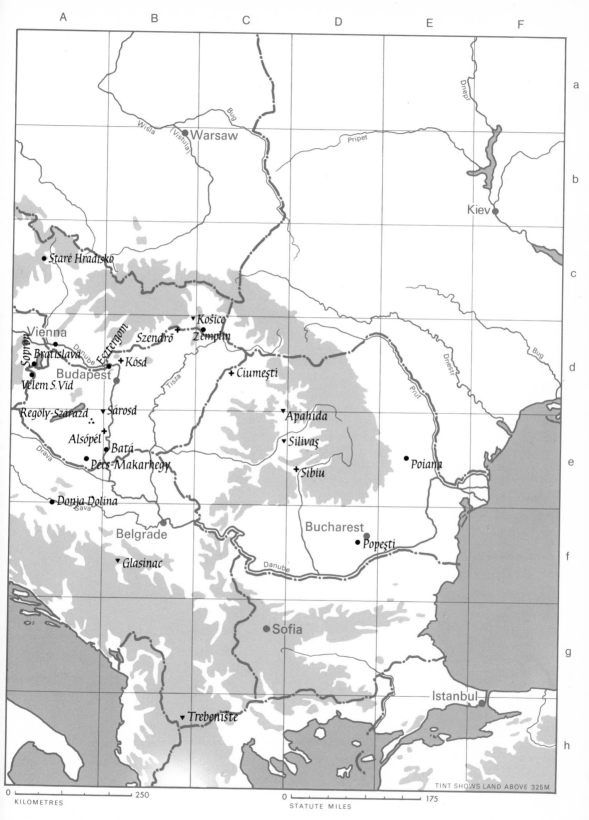

Staré Hradisko

Warsaw

Kiev

Vienna
Sopron
Bratislava
Velem S. Vid
Budapest
Esztergom
Szendrő
Kósd
Košice
Zemplín
Ciumeşti
Regöly-Szarazd
Sárosd
Alsópél
Batá
Pécs-Makarhegy
Apahida
Silivaş
Sibiu
Poiana
Donja Dolina
Belgrade
Bucharest
Popeşti
Glasinac
Sofia
Istanbul
Trebenište

TINT SHOWS LAND ABOVE 325M

0   250
KILOMETRES

0   175
STATUTE MILES

The Hallstatt and La Tène Iron Ages **175**

The Hallstatt and La Tène Iron Ages

see map pp. 174/175

The main Early Iron Age culture in central and western Europe is that named after the Austrian site of Hallstatt. The Hallstatt culture developed directly out of the local Urnfield communities, perhaps stimulated by the arrival of small groups of horse-breeding settlers from the east. The Hallstatt culture, which lasted from *c.* 700 to 500 or 450 BC, comprises the earliest groups that can be securely associated with Celtic-speaking communities. It was based on the mixed farming economy of the Urnfields, made more efficient by the use of implements of iron, which had been introduced in the eighth century. Helped by the exploitation of raw materials such as iron, copper, tin and salt, and by trade, both within Europe and with the civilizations of the Mediterranean, Hallstatt communities prospered: the population increased, settlements became larger and there was more economic specialization. Indeed economic and social disparities were marked and the richest burials, presumably of members of the ruling families, contain four-wheeled wagons, elaborate trappings and many other goods, some imported. Fortified hill-top settlements – first used in Urnfield times – became common in many parts of Europe. They may indicate a state of constant hostility between communities or clans.

In early Hallstatt times the richest centres of Celtic culture had lain in east central Europe. After *c.* 500 BC, however, the focus shifted westwards to the middle Rhine and later still it moved even farther west. The culture which emerged *c.* 500–450 BC is named after the Swiss site of La Tène. In spite of its clear local origins, La Tène culture contains several Mediterranean features, such as its weaponry, the habit of wine-drinking and fashions of personal ornament. The Celtic art styles emerged from this background of indigenous and imported elements (see p. 183).

Throughout the La Tène period economic life, and perhaps social life too, gained in complexity. The *oppida* (fortified settlements) of the second and first centuries BC, such as Manching in West Germany, were true towns with high population densities. Society was highly stratified with wealthy chieftains, specialist craftsmen – workers in metal, glass, pottery, etc. – peasant farmers and almost certainly slaves. This was the culture the Romans encountered when they invaded central and western Europe.

FURTHER READING

CHADWICK, N. 1970. *The Celts*, Harmondsworth.
FILIP, J. 1962. *Celtic Civilization and its Heritage*, Prague.
NEUSTUPNÝ, E. and J. 1961. *Czechoslovakia before the Slavs*, London and New York.
POWELL, T. G. E. 1958. *The Celts*, London and New York.

Iron Age sites in Europe:
Greek and Etruscan imports and princely burials

The Mediterranean civilizations of Greece and Etruria had a considerable influence on the European Iron Age cultures of Hallstatt and La Tène. Europe provided metal ores, amber and other products much in demand in the Mediterranean. In return the Greeks and Etruscans exported luxury goods. Hallstatt and La Tène societies were aristocratic in organization and imported *objets de luxe* were popular at the courts of wealthy chiefs. Although such objects occur on settlement sites, the richest and best-preserved examples come from the tombs in which members of the ruling families were buried, often with four-wheeled wagons or, later, two-wheeled chariots and valuable grave goods.

Before *c.* 600 BC, most of the trade was channelled from the head of the Adriatic along the old amber routes into central Europe. However, after the foundation of the Greek colony of Massalia (Massilia) *c.* 600 BC the emphasis shifted westwards and commerce was conducted along the valleys of the Rhône and Saône, which gave access to the Danube and Rhine.

Many of the imports are metal and pottery vessels connected with the transportation, storage and consumption of wine. Metal vessels occur in both the eastern and western zones of the Hallstatt culture, but pottery is found only in the

Rotterdam

Brussels

Berlin

Königsfeld
Urmitz
Horhausen
Morbach
Waldalgesheim
Somme Tourbe
(La Gorge Meillet)
Weisskirchen
Armsheim
Dürkheim
Grosseibstadt
Lhotka/
Lovosice
Straškov
Hradenín
Paris
Besseringen
Roderbach
Klein Aspergle
Prague
Chlum
Les Jogasses
Somme Bionne
Reinheim
Hatten
Oberwiesenacker-
Parlsberg
Hradiště

Mont Lassois
Vix
Ohnenheim
Pflugfelden
Kappel-am-Rhein
Munich
Sainte-Colombe
(La Garenne)
La Motte St Valentin
Vilsingen
Heuneburg/
Hundersingen
Braunau
Sunzing/
Minning
Mercey
Mantoche
Mont Guérin
Alaise
Grächwil
Uffing
Dürrnberg
Salzburg
Hallstatt
Camp de Château
Bern

Lyons

Voiron

Kleinklein

Le Pègue
Po

Pertuis

Mailhac
Ensérune
Massilia

Rome

Italic script = Sites with imports
Roman script = Sites without imports

0 ⊢⊢⊢⊢⊢⊢⊣ 250
KILOMETRES

0 ⊢⊢⊢⊢⊢⊣ 175
STATUTE MILES

Iron Age sites in Europe: Greek and Etruscan imports and princely burials 177

west. The metal objects include a variety of buckets, bowls, dippers and jugs (*oinochoe*) – and one enormous *krater*, or mixing bowl, from the burial of the 'princess' at Vix.

The princely tombs contained not only drinking-vessels, but also chariots, weaponry and ornaments. The two-wheeled chariot was probably adopted from the Etruscans and weapons and armour imported from the Mediterranean sometimes occur, for example in a grave at Kleinklein in Austria. Imported personal ornaments range from simple brooches to exotic items like the gold diadem from Vix, perhaps made in one of the Greek colonies on the Black Sea.

The influences of Mediterranean styles of ornament on local traditions led to the development of the splendid Celtic art of the La Tène period (see p. 183).

FURTHER READING

DE NAVARRO, J. M. 1928. Massilia and Early Celtic Culture. *Antiquity* II, 423–42.
JOFFROY, R. 1954. *Le trésor de Vix*, Paris.
——— 1958. *Les sépultures à char du premier Age du Fer en France*, Paris.
POWELL, T. G. E. 1958. *The Celts*, London and New York.
RIEK, G. and H. J. HUNDT 1962. *Der Hohmiehele. Ein Fürstengrabhügel der späten Hallstattzeit bei der Heuneburg*, Berlin.

Iron Age sites in the British Isles

The British Iron Age is known chiefly from settlements; burials in large numbers are known only in the latest phase. The absence of abundant grave groups makes it difficult not only to relate British to continental material, but also to build up a detailed chronology.

It is clear that a major component of the British Iron Age was the culture of the local Bronze Age. The principal types of settlement – farmsteads, open villages and hill-forts – all have Bronze Age antecedents. So do characteristic artifacts, such as bone weaving combs and several pottery types, and one of the most common structures – the round post-built dwelling. Hodson (1964) proposed the name Woodbury culture for this native continuum, after the site at Little Woodbury.

At the same time, contact with the continent certainly existed. Continental Hallstatt and La Tène metal objects are fairly common; most were probably introduced by merchants, not settlers. Some iron objects occur as early as *c.* 700 BC (e.g. in the Llyn Fawr hoard), but iron came into general use only after *c.* 500 BC. Hodson, who proposed radical changes to the picture of the Iron Age presented by Hawkes (1959, etc.), recognizes only two actual 'invasions' of settlers from the continent: (1) the bringers of the Arras culture of Yorkshire, with chariot burials and metal types paralleled in early continental La Tène contexts (perhaps beginning *c.* 400 BC); (2) the bearers of the Aylesford culture in south-east England, characterized by cremation cemeteries and artifacts of continental late La Tène type, datable to the first century BC. The Aylesford culture may be correlated with an historical group, the Belgae. Like its continental counterpart, insular Belgic society was urban or at least proto-urban. It was organized on a tribal basis and was socially stratified. Characteristic artifacts include wheel-made pottery and coins, both appearing for the first time in Britain.

The Iron Age cultures of north and west Britain are markedly regional in character. We find, for example, distinctive local settlement types, such as brochs in parts of Scotland and crannogs in Ireland.

FURTHER READING

CUNLIFFE, B. 1974. *Iron Age Communities in Britain*, London and Boston.
HARDING, D. W. 1974. *The Iron Age in Lowland Britain*, London and Boston.
HAWKES, C. 1959. The ABC of the British Iron Age. *Antiquity* XXXIII, 170–82.
HODSON, F. R. 1962. Some Pottery from Eastbourne, the 'Marnians' and the Pre-Roman Iron Age in Southern England. *Proceedings of the Prehistoric Society* N.S. 28, 140–55.
——— 1964. Cultural Grouping within the British Pre-Roman Iron Age. *Proceedings of the Prehistoric Society* N.S. 30, 99–110.
JESSON, M. and D. HILL (eds) 1971. *The Iron Age and its Hill-forts*, Southampton.
ORDNANCE SURVEY 1962. *Map of Southern Britain in the Iron Age*, Chessington.

On the same scale

Clickhimin
Mousa
Jarlshof

Midhowe
Gurness
Keiss
Ben Freiceadain

Dun Carloway
Clettraval
Dun Lagaidh
Burghead
Univai · Dun Fiadhairt
Abernethy
Dunnideer
Glenelg
Barmekin (Echt)
Barra Head
Finavon
Dalruizion
White & Brown Caterthun
Dun Mor Vaul
Craighill / Laws Hill
Traprain Law
Edinshall
Green Knowe
Eildon Hill
Humbleton Hill
Carradale
Yeavering Bell
Hayhope Knowe
Grianan of Ailech
R. Bann
Lisnacrogher
West Brandon
Navan
Staple Howe
Black Pigs' Dyke
Downpatrick
Garton
Dorsey
Arras
Grimthorpe
Danes Graves
Turoe
Tara
Mam Tor
Old Sleaford
Llyn Cerrig
Parciau
Dun Aengus
Dun Aillinne
Dinorben
Snettisham
Tre'r Ceiri
Fengate
Lough Gur
Old Oswestry
West Harling
Cush
Castell Odo
Snailwell
Dingle peninsula
Freestone Hill
Croft Ambrey
Credenhill
Ipswich
Staigue
Hunsbury
Colchester
Midsummer Hill
Birdlip
Barley
Bredon/Danes Camp
Welwyn
Oldbury
Coygan Camp
Bagendon
Wheathampstead
Swarling
Little Woodbury
All Cannings Cross
Aylesford
Glastonbury/Meare
Danebury
Pilsdon Pen
Ows!bury
Gussage All Saints
Hengistbury
Eastbourne
Harlyn Bay
Head
Chysauster
Maiden Castle
Chun

Paris

Brest

Rennes

Seine

TINT SHOWS LAND ABOVE 200 M

0 ⊢⊢⊢⊢⊢⊢⊢ 200
KILOMETRES

0 ⊢⊢⊢⊢⊢⊢⊢ 100
STATUTE MILES

Iron Age sites in the British Isles   **179**

Iron Age sites in northern Europe

Archaeologists working in northern Europe often divide the Iron Age into three periods: pre-Roman, Roman and post-Roman – the last being commonly known as the Migration period. Here we shall concentrate on the first of these, but shall include also some of the most important sites of the Roman Iron Age.

The north European plain and Scandinavia lay outside the Celtic Hallstatt and La Tène cultural areas, and the local cultures of the Bronze Age survived, acquiring the knowledge of iron-working in the second half of the first millennium BC. These cultures are known mainly from cemeteries, usually of flat graves, but sometimes under barrows; cremation was the normal rite. Grave goods are abundant and include many objects imported from the Celtic world. Settlements too are known: the most famous perhaps is the village of rectangular houses at Biskupin in Poland. In the Low Countries the earliest *terpen* (villages built on low artificial mounds to protect them from flooding), like that at Ezinge, belong to this period.

During the first four centuries AD the population of northern Europe was influenced by life in the provinces of the Roman Empire. Roman metal, pottery and glass objects were widely traded. Indeed, trade with the Empire brought great wealth to northern Europe: among the richest imported objects were silver table-ware and other vessels from Hildesheim in Germany and from a grave at Hoby on the island of Lolland.

Among the most interesting finds of the period are objects deposited in bogs. These range from the Celtic silver cauldron from Gundestrup to a boat from Hjortspring whose pieces, when assembled, formed a vessel 17·4 m long. Even more startling are the bodies found in bogs in Denmark and Schleswig-Holstein; well-preserved in the peat, they provide the archaeologist with unique information about the appearance and diet of the dead – and sometimes the violent ways in which they met their death.

FURTHER READING

DE LAET, S. J. 1958. *The Low Countries*, London and New York.

EGGERS, H. J. 1951. *Der Römische Import im Freien Germanien*, Berlin.

HACHMAN, R. 1960. Die Chronologie der jüngeren vorrömischen Eisenzeit. *Bericht der Römisch-Germanischen Kommission* 41, 1–276.

JAŻDŻEWSKI, K. 1965. *Poland*, London and New York.

KLINDT-JENSEN, O. 1957. *Denmark*, London and New York.

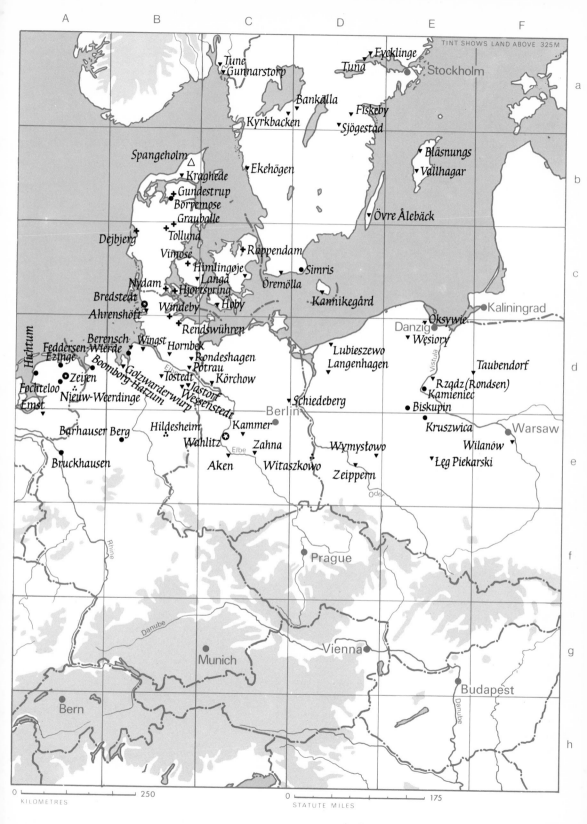

Tune
Gunnarstorp
Eycklinge
Tuna
Stockholm

Bankälla
Kyrkbacken
Fiskeby
Sjögestad

Bläsnungs
Spangeholm
Vallhagar
Kraghede
Ekehögen
Gundestrup
Borremose
Grauballe
Övre Ålebäck
Dejbjerg
Tollund
Vimose
Rappendam
Himlingøje
Simris
Langå
Öremölla
Bredstedt
Nydam
Hjortspring
Ahrenshöft
Windeby
Hoby
Kannikegård

Kaliningrad
Oksywie
Rendswühren
Danzig
Wingst
Hornbek
Węsiory
Berensch
Feddersen-Wierde
Rondeshagen
Lubieszewo
Taubendorf
Ezinge
Potrau
Langenhagen
Zeijen
Boomborg-Hatzum
Golzwarderwurp
Tostedt
Körchow
Rządz (Rondsen)
Fochteloo
Jastorf
Kamieniec
Emst
Nieuw-Weerdinge
Wessenstedt
Schiedeberg
Biskupin
Berlin
Barhauser Berg
Hildesheim
Kammer
Kruszwica
Warsaw
Wahlitz
Zahna
Wilanów
Bruckhausen
Aken
Witaszkowo
Zeippern
Łęg Piekarski
Wymysłowo

Elbe

Rhine

Prague

Danube

Vienna

Munich

Budapest

Bern

Hichtum
Vistula
Oder
Danube

Celtic art

The art style we describe as 'Celtic' or, in its later phases, 'La Tène' emerged in the mid-fifth century BC and the earliest Celtic ornament occurs in the princely tombs of the middle Rhine, the focal point of late Hallstatt and early La Tène culture. The style was probably created by Celtic craftsmen in response to the Greek and Etruscan goods, especially metal objects, exported to areas north of the Alps.

Surviving Celtic art consists primarily of ornament styles used by the metal-worker: weapons and armour, vessels and personal ornaments in bronze, silver and gold were specially favoured by the Celtic craftsmen. In contrast to contemporary art styles in the Mediterranean, Celtic ornament is largely non-naturalistic, portraying people and animals only in highly stylized forms and relying heavily on abstract pattern. Almost all the decorative techniques available to the metal-worker were employed: ornament in relief (cast or repoussé), engraving, filigree, enamel and inlays of coral and other materials.

The great authority on Celtic art, Paul Jacobsthal, recognized four principal sources of inspiration: a native Hallstatt tradition, a classical component from the Mediterranean, an animal-centred nomadic tradition and an oriental element. He postulated four major styles. The Early style, which lasted for about a century, evolved into the Waldalgesheim style, which survived into the third century BC. This developed into two contemporary styles, the Plastic and the Sword styles, which survived until c. 100 BC. After this date few elaborate works were produced on the continent and the most accomplished ateliers were now situated in Britain and Ireland, where they flourished until the Roman conquest (and later in some areas). Indeed, some of the most famous Celtic works of art, such as the bronze mirrors of England, belong to the period c. 50 BC–AD 50.

Although most surviving examples of Celtic art are in metal, typical decoration occurs also on pottery, wooden objects and glass, as well as on monumental stone sculpture, the latter especially in Provence under the influence of Greek communities on the coast.

FURTHER READING

CHADWICK, N. 1970. *The Celts*, Harmondsworth.
JACOBSTHAL, P. 1944 (reprinted, with corrections, 1969). *Early Celtic Art*, Oxford.
MEGAW, J. V. S. 1970. *Art of the European Iron Age. A study of the elusive image*, Bath.
POWELL, T. G. E. 1966. *Prehistoric Art*, London and New York.
SANDARS, N. K. 1968. *Prehistoric Art in Europe*, Harmondsworth and Baltimore.

TINT SHOWS LAND ABOVE 500 M

A   B   C   D   E   F

a

+ Gundestrup
+ Brå
Broighter
+ Rynkeby
+ Torrs
+ Lough na Shade
Keshcarrigan + Stanwick
Turoe
Clonmacnoise Llyn Cerrig Bach
+ Lincoln (R. Witham)
Trawsfynedd + Snettisham
Tal-y-Llyn Desborough
Birdlip + Ipswich
London (Battersea/Wandsworth/Brentford)
+ Aylesford
+ Eigenbilzen
La Courte Pfalzfeld Panenský Týnec
Frasnes-lez-Buissenal Waldalgesheim Hradiště
Courtisols Heidelberg Mšecké Žehrovice
Basse-Yutz Klein Aspergle Brno-Malomĕrice
+ Auvers Rodenbach Parsberg
Amfreville Reinheim
Somme Bionne Hirschlanden Kosd
La Charme Kappel Trichtingen
Kermario Euffigneix Hallein-Dürrnberg
Neuvy-en-Sullias Hölzelsau Hallstatt
Nebringen
Holzgerlingen
Port
La Tène
+ Aurillac

Noves
+ Fenouillet + Entremont
Roquepertuse

b

c

d

e

f

g

Mezek
Istanbul
On the same scale

h

0   500
KILOMETRES

0   300
STATUTE MILES

Celtic art **183**

Bronze Age and Early Iron Age sites in European Russia

Within the area of this map, Bronze Age sites fall into four regional groups: the Caucasus, the north Pontic area, the forest zone of eastern Europe and central Russia, and the Baltic area. Although many settlement sites are known, in the past attention has been concentrated on burials and, as in so much of Europe, Bronze Age archaeology is largely grave archaeology.

The Caucasus, where metal ores occur, was an early centre of metallurgy. To the Copper Age (probably early third millennium BC) belong rich barrow burials, the most famous of which is Maikop, where the grave goods included copper tools and silver vessels. Gold and silver occur frequently in the elaborate Bronze Age (early second millennium BC) barrows at Trialeti, which covered burial shafts containing inhumations sometimes placed in four-wheeled carts and accompanied by numerous objects. Cemeteries of poorer graves and several settlements are also known. The Late Bronze Age and Early Iron Age sites of the Caucasus belong to the Kuban culture. This had a characteristic repertory of bronze objects and survived into the seventh century BC.

The north Pontic area was another early centre of metallurgy and shared with the Caucasus the practice of burial under barrows, sometimes on carts (which in this area were two-wheeled vehicles). The earliest (Pit-grave) stage, with simple burial pits under barrows, was succeeded by the Catacomb stage, characterized by burials placed in niches in the sides of deep shafts. This in turn was succeeded by the Timber Grave culture, which developed in the lower Volga region and later spread westwards. It survived into the first millennium BC and is often regarded as 'Proto-Scythian'.

In the forest zone of central Russia and eastern Europe flourished the Fatyanovo complex, known chiefly from cemeteries of flat graves. The Fatyanovo culture of the upper Volga and the related Balanovo group of the middle Volga form part of the great Corded Ware/Battle-axe complex of northern Europe, with battle-axes forming one of the characteristic grave goods. The Fatyanovo complex was succeeded by the Abashevo culture, in which burial in shafts under barrows was customary. Both groups placed metal tools in the graves. Farther east, in the Urals, existed a culture named after the cemetery at Turbino, although the best known site is the settlement preserved in a peat bog at Gorbunovo.

North of the Fatyanovo area and extending westwards into Poland, the Baltic culture developed without serious interruption from the third millennium BC (with a Baltic Corded Ware phase related to other Corded Ware groups) to the eighth century BC. During the first half of the second millennium intense trade with the Únětice culture of central Europe took place.

FURTHER READING

GIMBUTAS, M. 1965. *Bronze Age Cultures in Central and Eastern Europe*, The Hague.
MONGAIT, A. L. 1961. *Archaeology in the USSR*, Harmondsworth.
SULIMIRSKI, T. 1970. *Prehistoric Russia. An Outline*, London and New York.

Bronze Age and Early Iron Age sites in European Russia **185**

South and east Asia, Australasia and

The maps which follow illustrate the archaeology of an enormous area, in which conditions range from the continental tundra of northern Siberia to the tropical islands of the Pacific. Inevitably, the nature and pace of human development has varied from region to region. China had an accomplished bronze industry in the second millennium BC; Australia lacked metal tools until the arrival of the Europeans. In this short introduction we shall discuss just three phenomena: the peopling of Japan, Australasia and the islands of the Pacific; the origins of food production in China and south-east Asia; and the emergence of the earliest urban societies of eastern Asia, in the valleys of the Indus and the Huang-ho.

By the beginning of the late Pleistocene (*c.* 100,000 years ago) groups of palaeolithic hunters lived in many parts of the Old World, from Europe and southern Africa to the Far East. Nevertheless, large areas of the globe were still uninhabited: the Americas, much of Australasia, Japan and the Pacific. The barrier which prevented expansion into these areas was, of course, the sea. Before the use of rafts or boats, man could cross only narrow stretches of water. However, the lowering of sea level during the glacial maxima, when huge volumes of water were converted to ice, provided an opportunity for movement into areas which were normally inaccessible. Thus, as we shall describe in the introduction to section VII (p. 212), man entered the Americas, perhaps in pursuit of game, by way of the Bering Straits 'land bridge' during the last glaciation, probably *c.* 25,000–10,000 years ago. Similarly, low sea levels created a land bridge between the Asian mainland and Japan, the earliest inhabitants of which arrived, probably by way of Sakhalin, sometime before *c.* 14,000 bc.

In the islands of south-east Asia, progress was halted even in periods of low sea level by the deep-water channels south and east of Borneo that make up 'Wallace's line', the natural barrier which divides the fauna of Australasia into western and eastern groups. Despite this barrier, man certainly reached Australia by *c.* 30,000 bc and comparison of the earliest stone tools from Australia with assemblages in south-east Asia hints that the earliest Australians possibly arrived more than 40,000 years ago.

The colonization of New Zealand and the Pacific, on the other hand, seems to be a recent phenomenon. We have no sites in the Pacific earlier than the second millennium BC and the settlement of New Zealand is usually dated *c.* AD 700.

The development of food production in eastern Asia followed an irregular course. While farming is attested in parts of China in the fifth millennium bc, efficient agriculture based on rice did not reach Japan till the third century BC. Food production in China began on the fertile loess and loess-derived soils of the Huang-Ho and Yangtse valleys. Carbon 14 dates, recently published by the Chinese Academy of Sciences, from Pan P'o Ts'un and other early neolithic sites range from 3944 bc for an un-named site in Shensi to 3788 bc and 3754 bc from Pan P'o Ts'un itself. An unspecified site in Hupei, apparently associated with irrigation agriculture, yielded a date of 4420 bc.

The main food plants associated with early village farming in China are millet, rice and (probably) wheat. At Pan P'o Ts'un we have evidence for domesticated dogs and pig, with small numbers of sheep, cattle and horses. It is just possible that fowl, too, were domesticated.

In south-east Asia, food production may have begun at an earlier date, although village farming was not introduced until the third millennium bc. Instead of permanent settlements, we find caves and coastal middens used by communities of the Hoabinhian culture, which may have supplemented hunting and gathering by the domestication of water chestnuts and other local plants.

Two civilizations emerged in eastern Asia in the second and third millennia BC. Each developed in the flood plain of a major river, where fertile soil and abundant water enabled the state to produce sufficient food for large urban populations. In Pakistan and adjacent areas, the Indus Valley civilization emerged in the third millennium BC; in China, the civilization of the Shang dynasty developed a thousand years later.

The Indus Valley civilization probably developed shortly before 3200 BC (2500 bc) – we have dates of *c*. 2400 bc from Kot Diji – and lasted for more than a millennium. At its greatest extent, the Indus Valley civilization occupied a huge area, from Rupar in the Simla hills to Sutkagen Dor on the coast of the Arabian Sea and from Ukhlina in the Jumna basin to Kathiawad. Its focus, however, was the Indus valley. Here stood the two greatest cities of the Indus Valley civilization: Harappa in the Punjab and Mohenjo-Daro in Sind. Both cities were large; their massive defences each had a circuit of about 5 km. They contained the same main components: a citadel, a rectangular grid of streets and state-controlled granaries. The citadels contained the main ceremonial and public buildings. The streets, which were lined with houses and other buildings, consisted of main arteries 15 m wide and numerous narrow alleys. The granaries had a huge capacity; at Harappa the building occupied an area of 900 sq. m.

The Indus Valley civilization was literate. We possess numerous square seals with short pictographic inscriptions, which have yet to be deciphered. There is evidence for trade with the Persian Gulf and one of the ports of the Indus Valley civilization has been excavated at Lothal.

In China, the civilization of the Shang dynasty (*c*. 1500–1027 BC) developed on the flood plain of the Huang-Ho in northern Honan. For years the Shang dynasty was associated almost exclusively with the site of its later capital at Hsiao Tun near Anyang. It was here, for example, that the famous 'oracle bones' were discovered. However, since 1953 Chinese archaeologists have been investigating earlier Shang sites in the Cheng Chou region, 160 km south of Anyang. It is abundantly clear that the Bronze Age Shang civilization developed out of the local Neolithic. Bronze technology was evolved locally, metal-workers making use of the potters' familiarity with kilns operated at high temperatures. Among the early Shang sites near Cheng Chou are Lo Ta Miao and Erh Li Kang. The 'classic' site of Hsiao Tun (Anyang) was occupied from at least 1300 BC. Most Shang cities had a square or nearly square plan, aligned on the cardinal points, and they were usually walled. Cheng Chou itself was about 2000 m. across and had an area of 350–400 ha.

The 'oracle bones' found at Hsiao Tun were used for divination. They consist of bones and tortoise shells engraved or, less often, inscribed *in Chinese* with questions which were solved by noting how the bones cracked when subjected to heat. The fact that the oracle bones were inscribed in Chinese underlies the long continuity of urban civilization in China where we find, in effect, an unbroken development of city life from *c*. 1500 BC to the present day.

FURTHER READING

ALLCHIN, B. and R. 1968. *The Birth of Indian Civilization*, Harmondsworth and San Francisco.
CHANG, K.-C. 1968. *The Archaeology of Ancient China* (revised and enlarged edn), New Haven and London.
HAMMOND, N. (ed.) 1973. *South Asian Archaeology*, London and Park Ridge.
KIDDER, J. E. JR. 1959. *Japan before Buddhism*, London and New York.
MULVANEY, D. J. 1969. *The Prehistory of Australia*, London and New York.

The Indus Valley civilization

The Indus Valley civilization, sometimes called after the site of Harappa, arose during the third or late fourth millennium BC. Apparently it developed locally in the Indus valley out of cultures allied to contemporary groups in Afghanistan and eastern Iran. The Early Harappan phase had begun by 3500 BC (C^{14} dates between *c.* 2800 and 2200 bc) and the full urban civilization, or Mature Harappan, had emerged by *c.* 2600 BC (*c.* 2300 bc). Geographically, the Mature Harappan is the largest of the ancient civilizations in the Old World, extending for more than 1500 km from north to south. It is characterized by a settlement pattern typical of many later city-based societies in Asia, with huge urban agglomerations surrounded by small settlements; the towns of intermediate size, found in Mesopotamia, do not occur. The two largest cities, Mohenjo-Daro and Harappa, each cover several hundred hectares. They are surrounded by small settlements, rarely larger than 10 hectares. The major cities, as well as some of the smaller towns, have impressive mud-brick defences, a citadel occupied by public buildings (notably granaries) and streets laid out on a grid plan with efficient main drainage. As in the other civilizations of the Old World, the cities of the Indus valley were supported by intensive food production, specialized crafts and external trade. Agriculture was varied and efficient; industry was diverse; commercial contact with Afghanistan, Iran, Mesopotamia and southern India is well attested. Though the Indus Valley civilization was literate, the script has not been deciphered; for this reason, we know far less about it than about the civilizations of Mesopotamia and Egypt. The Indus Valley civilization came to an end in *c.* 1900 BC (*c.* 1600 bc) perhaps as a result of catastrophic floods, such as periodically inundated the southern settlements, or perhaps at the hands of the Aryan intruders, whose invasion of north-western India is recorded in the Vedic hymns.

For Sotka Koh and Sutkagen Dor, see map on p. 87.

FURTHER READING

PIGGOTT, S. 1950. *Prehistoric India*, Harmondsworth.

RAO, S. R. 1973. *Lothal and the Indus Civilization*, Bombay.

THAPAR, B. K. 1973. New traits of the Indus civilization at Kalibangan: an appraisal. In Hammond, N. (ed.), *South Asian Archaeology*, London.

WHEELER, Sir M. 1966. *Civilizations of the Indus Valley and beyond*, London.

———— 1968. *Early India and Pakistan to Ashoka*[2], London and New York.

———— 1968. *The Indus Civilization*[3], London and New York.

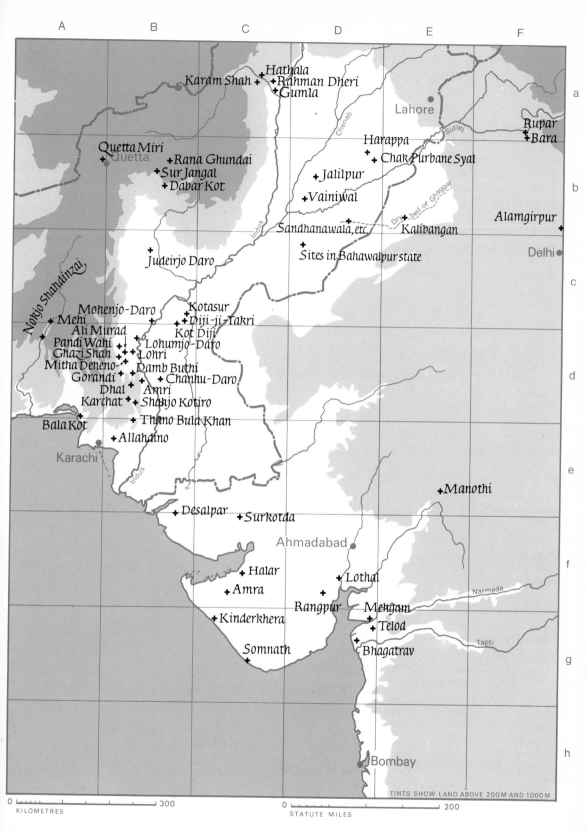

The Indus Valley civilization   **189**

The Indian subcontinent excluding the Indus Valley civilization

The early Neothermal period in the Indian subcontinent is represented by a number of widely distributed microlithic industries. Among the regions in which sites are particularly numerous are Gujarat and central India. The microlithic industries may have developed locally out of the flake tradition of the 'Middle Stone Age', but such a development has yet to be proved. Their chronology, too, is poorly understood, although it is almost certain that they are post-Pleistocene. At Rangpur, a microlithic industry was shown to be pre-Harappan, but in some areas similar industries may have continued until a much later date.

The first farmers in the subcontinent probably arrived as immigrants from Iran some time before c. 4400 BC (c. 3600 bc). Subsequently farming communities became established in much of Pakistan, where they formed the basis of the Harappan, or Indus Valley, civilization (see p. 188).

Outside the region of Harappan civilization, groups of communities using pottery and ground stone axes are still often described as 'neolithic', although the nature of their subsistence economy is not always clear. One such group existed in Kashmir, where the best known site, Burzahom, was occupied from before c. 3000 BC (c. 2400 bc) to c. 1700 BC (c. 1400 bc), or later. A second group occupied the valleys of the Krishna and its tributaries and here communities kept domesticated cattle, sheep and goats. The first phase of this culture is dated c. 2900–2300 BC (c. 2300–1800 bc) at Utnur; in the second phase, c. 2300–1800 BC (c. 1800–1500 bc) copper and bronze came into use; in the third phase, c. 1800–1250 BC (c. 1500–1050 bc) metal became more common and horses may have been bred.

Harappan civilization came to an apparently abrupt end c. 1900 BC (c. 1600 bc), perhaps at the hands of Aryan invaders, possibly for environmental reasons. In the centuries that followed, chalcolithic (copper-using) farming societies persisted in the Indus valley, but at an economic level inferior to that of the city-dwelling Harappans; whether these societies were Aryan-speaking is a matter of dispute. Post-Harappan chalcolithic communities existed in many other parts of the subcontinent: in Malwa and the Deccan, for example, and on the east coast. Perhaps to this period too belongs the first phase of occupation at Hastinapura in the Ganga valley and the 'Copper Hoard culture' of the Ganga basin, Bihar and Bengal.

Iron-working was introduced from the west perhaps as early as c. 1000 BC, by which date speakers of Indo-European languages certainly existed in the Indian subcontinent. Indeed, the Early Iron Age, with its Vedic traditions, belongs to the threshold of history and the later Iron Age, which saw the annexation of Pakistan first by the Persians and later by Alexander the Great, and the life of the Buddha (c. 560–480 BC) is genuinely 'historic'.

FURTHER READING

ALLCHIN, B. and R. 1968. *The Birth of Indian Civilization*, Harmondsworth and San Francisco.

ALLCHIN, F. R. 1973. Problems and Perspectives in South Asian Archaeology. In Hammond, N. (ed.), *South Asian Archaeology*, London and Park Ridge.

MISRA, V. N. and M. S. MATE (eds) 1965. *Indian Prehistory*, Poona.

PIGGOTT, S. 1950. *Prehistoric India*, London.

SANKALIA, H. D. 1962. *Prehistory and Protohistory in India and Pakistan*, Bombay.

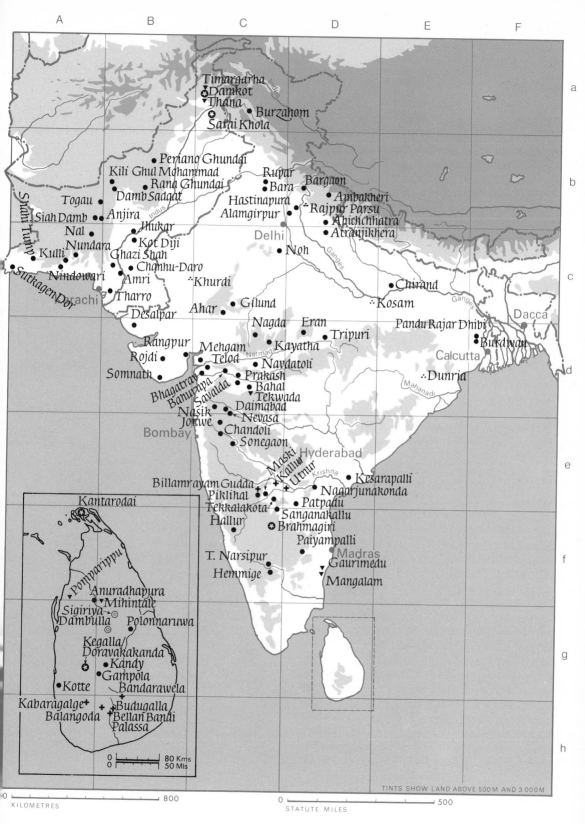

The Indian subcontinent excluding the Indus Valley civilization **191**

Neolithic sites in China

The earliest farming communities in China, known as the Yang-Shao culture, cultivated the fertile loess soils of the Huang-Ho valley in Honan and Shansi, especially near the confluence of the Fen and Wei rivers – K.-C. Chang's 'nuclear area' of neolithic development. Most settlements were compact and self-sufficient, comprising semi-subterranean dwellings built round a communal long-house. Many villages had a regular plan, with evidence of specialist quarters, e.g. for potters. Houses were post-built, with walls of wattle-and-daub and stamped clay floors. Important excavated sites include Yang-Shao itself and Pan P'o Ts'un, which occupied 3 ha. and was defended by a ditch. Yang-Shao farmers cultivated millet and wheat, but probably not rice, as is often claimed. The earliest cultivation was slash-and-burn shifting agriculture, but permanent settlement probably began at an early date. The most common domesticated animals were dogs and pigs, pannage for which was provided by the deciduous woodland of the loess. Cattle and sheep were bred in smaller numbers and at one site, Hsin Ts'un, we have evidence for breeding silkworms. Recent C^{14} dates from Pan P'o Ts'un range from 3944 to 3477 bc.

A second major culture, or group of cultures, exists in the Chinese Neolithic: the Lung-Shan. When first discovered, the Lung-Shan sites were thought to be roughly contemporary with those of the Yang-Shao culture, but we know now that in at least some areas they are later. At its greatest extent, the Lung-Shan culture (many regional variants of which have been recognized) was distributed throughout east and south-east China. Lung-Shan settlements tended to be larger than the villages of the Yang-Shao culture. They were permanent and often had ramparts of beaten earth. Cattle and sheep gradually assumed greater importance and in the east rice became a major crop. It is thought that Lung-Shan society was hierarchic with a part- or even full-time priesthood. Reports of bronze objects from late Lung-Shan sites indicate the beginning of metallurgy.

FURTHER READING

CHANG, K.-C. 1968. *The Archaeology of Ancient China* (revised and enlarged edn), New Haven and London.
CHENG, T.-K. 1959. *Archaeology in China*. Vol. I. *Prehistoric China*, Cambridge.
PEARSON, R. 1973. Radiocarbon dates from China. *Antiquity* XLVII, 141–3.
WATSON, W. 1961. *China before the Han Dynasty*, London and New York.
WHEATLEY, P. 1971. *The Pivot of the Four Quarters*, Edinburgh and Chicago, 22–30.

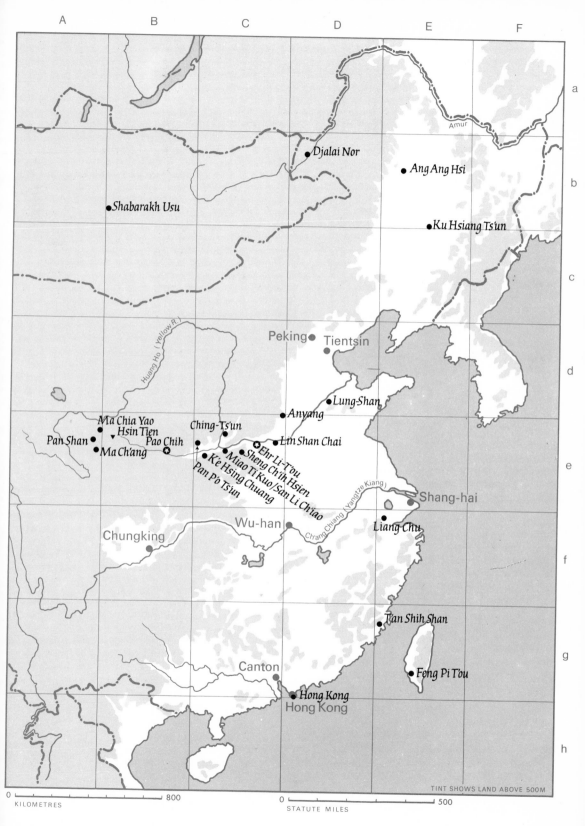

Neolithic sites in China   193

Early civilization in China

The transition in China from a society of more or less autonomous agricultural villages to urban states with a central authority originated in the Huang-Ho valley. The first state was that of the Shang dynasty, which had its later capital at Hsiao Tun (near modern Anyang). Excavation at Anyang revealed a planned city with a walled administrative and ceremonial centre surrounded by extra-mural residential and industrial suburbs. Investigation of the cemeteries, which contain imposing tombs with sacrificial victims, confirmed the existence of a slave-owning aristocracy. The famous 'oracle bones', connected with divination, showed that Shang civilization was literate and we have abundant evidence of a sophisticated bronze technology.

Shang civilization, which developed out of the local Neolithic, was already emerging as a Bronze Age society c. 1850 BC and has a full urban structure some three centuries later. Hsiao Tun itself belongs to the latter part of the Shang period; among earlier sites is Cheng Chou, a walled city aligned – as was customary in China – on the cardinal points.

The Shang state was superseded by that of the Chou, who emerged from the Wei-Shui valley on the borders of Shensi and sacked Hsiao Tun c. 1030 BC. The Chou period is usually divided into two phases: (1) the western phase, during which the capital was in Shensi (at one time it occupied the site of Hao near Sian), and (2) the eastern phase after 771 BC, when the capital was transferred to Loyang in Honan. During the latter phase, the provinces in the west were overrun by nomads from Mongolia and parts of the Great Wall were built as a barrier against further incursions.

Chou society differed markedly from that of the Shang period and many differences are to be seen in the material culture. The whole city, for example, was now brought within the walls; a new type of temple was introduced; the horse was used for riding, and iron technology appeared. The Chou state occupied a far larger area than the compact territory of the Shang rulers. It ended in 249 BC, when the Ch'in dynasty came to power.

FURTHER READING

CHANG, K.-C. 1968. *The Archaeology of Ancient China* (revised and enlarged edn), New Haven and London.
CHENG, T.-K. 1960. *Archaeology in China*. Vol. 2. *Shang China*, Cambridge.
NEEDHAM, J. 1954. *Science and Civilization in China*. Vol. 1. *Introductory Orientations*, Cambridge.
WATSON, W. 1961. *China before the Han Dynasty*, London and New York.
WHEATLEY, P. 1971. *The Pivot of the Four Quarters*, Edinburgh and Chicago.

Roman script = Shang sites (Early Bronze Age)
Italic script = Chou sites (Late Bronze Age)
Roman script underlined = Shang and Chou site

A   B   C   D   E   F

a

Amur

b

c

⊕ T'ang Shan

+ Li Yü   Peking ●   Tientsin

Huang Ho (Yellow R.)

+ Ch'ü Yang
+ Shih Chia Huang
Hsing T'ai   ● Ch'eng Tzŭ Yai
Anyang / Hsiao Tun   ● Lin Tzŭ
Hsin Tsun   ⊕ Han Tan (Chao Wang Ch'eng)
Shang Ts'un Ling   ● Ch'ü Fu
P'u Tu Ts'un   ▼ Hui Hsien
Sian ⊕   ⊕ Loyang   Cheng Chou/Tung Chai
+   ▼   ▼ Hsin Cheng
Tou Chi T'ai   *Hua Hsien*

d

e
Yen Tun Shan
Hsin Yang ▼   Shang-hai ●
⊕ Shou Hsien
Yangtze Kiang

Wu-han ●
Ch'ang Chiang

Chungking ●

⊕ Ch'ang Sha   f

Shih Chai Shan ▼

g
Canton ●
+ Hong Kong
Hong Kong

h

TINT SHOWS LAND ABOVE 500M

0   800
KILOMETRES

0   500
STATUTE MILES

Siberia and adjacent regions

Siberia extends from the Urals to the Pacific. In the north is the tundra, to the south are the steppes and desert of Kazakhstan, Sinkiang and Mongolia; between them lies the temperate zone of forested taiga. Archaeological research in this huge area contains many gaps, but, thanks largely to the work of Okladnikov, we possess detailed information on such regions as the Lena basin, Lake Baikal and Yakutia.

Siberia was first occupied by man in the late Pleistocene, when leptolithic groups moved into the taiga zone. The earliest leptolithic sites were those of big-game hunters, equipped with flint industries of Mousterian tradition, but with blades and burins usually described as 'Gravettian'. The hunters' encampments consisted of semi-subterranean houses with walls and roofs of mammoth bones, presumably covered by skins. They recall the earth houses of recent circumpolar cultures. The best known sites are Mal'ta and Buret'. A different, apparently later, type of settlement is represented by Afontova Gora and other sites where, instead of earth houses, simple tent settings survive. It was from Siberia that the first inhabitants advanced into Japan and the Americas (see pp. 199 and 214).

Hunting and fishing communities survived in Siberia throughout the prehistoric period; indeed, even in the last century farming was restricted to parts of the Yenisei and Angara valleys. Okladnikov (1962: 275) distinguishes six groups of Neothermal hunter-gatherers: (1) sedentary fishers on the Amur river and the east coast, (2) hunters and fishers in the Baikal region, (3) hunters and gatherers in the steppes and deserts of Trans-Baikalia and Mongolia, (4) migratory reindeer-hunters and lake-fishers in the tundra zone, (5) hunters and fishers in Yakutia, and (6) hunters and fishers in western Siberia. Several groups, including communities of the Isakovo phase in the Baikal region, manufactured pottery and polished stone knives. The first metal objects, of unknown origin, appeared in the Glazkovo phase, perhaps in the mid-second millennium bc (Michael 1958).

FURTHER READING

CHARD, C. S. 1959–72. Reports on 'Northeast Asia'. In *Asian Perspectives, passim*.

MICHAEL, H. N. 1958. The Neolithic Age in Eastern Siberia. *Trans. American Philosophical Soc.* N.S. 48, 5–108.

—— 1964. *The Archaeology and Geomorphology of Northern Asia: selected works*. (Arctic Institute of North America: transl. from Russian sources 5), Toronto.

OKLADNIKOV, A. P. 1962. The Temperate Zone of Continental Asia. In Braidwood, R. J. and G. R. Willey (eds), *Courses toward Urban Life*, Edinburgh and Chicago.

—— 1965. *The Soviet Far East in Antiquity*. (Arctic Institute of North America: transl. from Russian sources 6), Toronto.

—— 1970. *Yakutia before its incorporation into the Russian State*. (Arctic Institute of North America: transl. from Russian sources 8), Montreal and London.

Map labels (grid A–F, a–h):

- Uelen
- Chokurovka
- Khairgas
- Karaga
- Kavran/Khayryuzovo
- Volba
- Syalaakh
- Klyuchevskoye/Kamaki
- Ust-Kamchatsk
- Suntar
- Yakutsk
- Ymyyakhtakh
- Ostrovnoye/Petropavlovsk
- Sinsk
- Kullaty
- Okhotsk
- Tarya
- Suruktakh-Khaya
- Churu
- Munku
- Golygino
- Nyuya
- Daban
- Chastinskaya
- Afontova Gora/Krasnoyarsk
- Makarovo/Ponomarevo/Shishkino
- Minusinsk
- Buret'
- Mal'ta
- Irkutsk
- Shilka Cave
- Kitoi
- Ulan Ude
- Khabarovsk
- Djalai Nor
- Ussuriyisk/Chapigou River
- Ulan Bator
- Ang Ang Hsi
- Shinobuchi/Temiya
- Shabarakh-Usu
- Mo River (L.Khanka)
- Tetyukhe
- Senkina Shapka
- Tadushi River
- Ku Hsiang Ts'un
- Vladivostok/Tigrovaya/Cape de Fries
- Poset
- Lin Hsi
- Miyagi Region
- Peking
- Kanto Plain/Tokyo

Rivers/places: Lena, Vilyuy, Angara, Yenisey, Aldan, Amur, Hwang Ho

TINT SHOWS LAND ABOVE 1000 M

0 ————— 1200
KILOMETRES

0 ————— 700
STATUTE MILES

Siberia and adjacent regions **197**

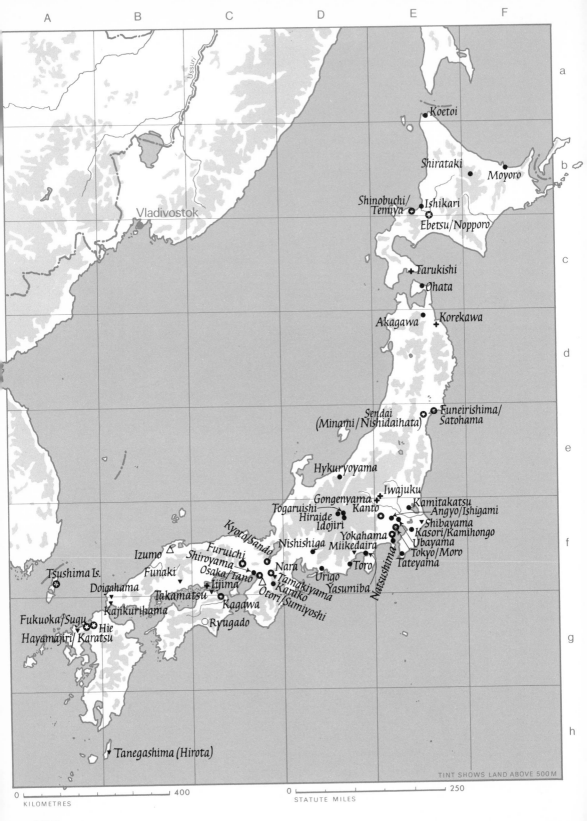

Japan

Despite occasional claims of lower palaeolithic discoveries, the islands of Japan were probably first occupied towards the end of the Pleistocene. At the peak of the last glaciation, when sea level was at its lowest, a land bridge connected Korea, Japan, Sakhalin and the Siberian mainland. The earliest inhabitants were bands of hunters from the mainland, equipped with blade-scrapers, burins and bifacial projectile points. The earliest C^{14} dates so far obtained, from Shirataki (Hokkaido) and Yasumiba (Honshu), are between 13,850 and 12,350 bc.

The first settled communities belong to the Jomon culture, which is best known from numerous middens in the Tokyo region. Typical Jomon settlements were situated near the coast. They contained round or trapezoidal houses with semi-subterranean floors. The contents of the middens indicate a strong dependence on sea-food. Shell-fish occur in huge numbers, but the discovery of fish-hooks and harpoons, together with the bones of shark and tunny, suggest that boats were used for off-shore fishing. On land, Jomon hunters, armed with the bow, preyed on deer, wild pig and other game. The earliest C^{14} date for a Jomon midden (at Natsushima, Honshu) is 7500 bc; this is sometimes rejected, but we have dates from several sites before 5000 bc.

Towards the end of the Jomon period, long after the invention of pottery, some groups began to cultivate millet, buckwheat, beans and hemp. The only domesticated animal was the dog.

However, it was not until the Yayoi period, which began in the third century BC, that rice cultivation was introduced to Japan, providing the subsistence base for substantial settlements. The Yayoi culture was introduced from Korea and it contained many Korean and Chinese traits. Cist burial, for example, found also in Korea, became common. Fine bronze objects, especially weapons and mirrors, were imported from China. Metallurgy itself, in both bronze and iron, was introduced. By the Proto-historic period (c. AD 400–600) a feudal society existed and the monumental tombs of the ruling families occupied large moated compounds of up to 32·4 ha.

Buddhism was introduced in the late sixth century and this event marks the beginning of the medieval period in Japan.

FURTHER READING

ESAKA, T. 1957. [Jomon Culture],* Tokyo.
GROOT, G. S. 1951. The Prehistory of Japan, New York.
KIDDER, J. E., JR. 1959. Japan before Buddhism, London and New York.
SHIMIZU, J. and Y. KURATA 1957. [Yayoi Culture],* Tokyo.

*Title translated from Japanese.

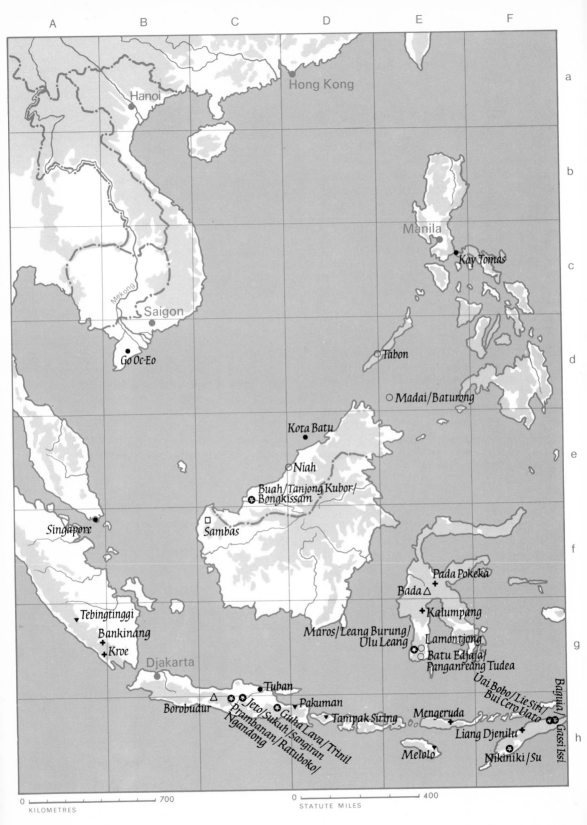

A B C D E F

a

Hanoi

Hong Kong

b

Mekong

Saigon

Manila

c

Kay Tomas

Go Oc-Eo

d

Tabon

Madai/Baturong

Kota Batu

e

Niah

Buah/Tanjong Kubor/
Bongkissam

Singapore

Sambas

f

Pada Pokeka

Bada △

Kalumpang

Tebingtinggi

Maros/Leang Burung/
Ulu Leang

Lamontjong

Bankinang

Batu Edjaja/
Panganreang Tudea

Krve

g

Uai Bobo/Lie Siri/
Bui Cero Uato

Djakarta

Baguia

Tuban

Grassi Issi

Borobudur △

Jeto/Sukuh/Sangiran/Trinil

Pakuman

Mengeruda

Prambanan/Ratuboko/

Guha Lava

Tampak Siring

Liang Djenilu

Ngandong

Melolo

Nikiniki/Su

h

The islands of south-east Asia

The islands of south-east Asia have aroused the interest of archaeologists for several reasons, notably as the 'stepping-stones' by which man first reached Australia and the Pacific from the Asian mainland. In many areas, however, archaeological research has scarcely begun and few syntheses exist.

The earliest stone industry in the region, the Patjitanian, consists mainly of chopping tools and scrapers. It was recognized by von Koenigswald at Patjitan in central Java in 1935 and similar industries are now known over a wide area. The age of the earliest Patjitanian assemblages is still unknown, although we have a C^{14} date of 45,000 bc from Tabon. In Borneo, the enormous cave at Niah yielded artifacts and human remains with a radiocarbon date of 38,000 bc. Despite the absence of confirmatory dates (we have dates of 30,000 bc from Australia and 24,000 bc from Kosipe in Papua), Glover (1973) conjectures on the basis of tool typology that man may not only have crossed 'Wallace's line', a natural barrier of deep water channels between Borneo and Sulawesi, but also reached Australia some 60,000–40,000 years ago.

In early neothermal times, groups of hunters and gatherers comparable with the Hoabinhian communities of the Asian mainland became widely established. Indeed, industries reminiscent of the Hoabinhian are reported from Java, Borneo and Sumatra. They occur in caves and coastal middens and include edge-ground pebble tools, mortars and, at Tuban for example, tools of shell and bone. The duration and economic status of these Hoabinhian-type cultures are still uncertain. By the third millennium bc, if not earlier, new and distinctive tool types had been introduced to the region: quadrangular adzes, apparently derived from mainland China, and round axes from the north, perhaps brought by way of the Philippines. Further evidence of intermittent influence from the north exists in Sulawesi, where the Proto-Toalian culture contains barbed arrowheads comparable with those from the Philippines, Korea and Japan.

The earliest metal objects may have arrived in the western islands of south-east Asia c. 600 BC. They consist of imported bronzes of late Chou

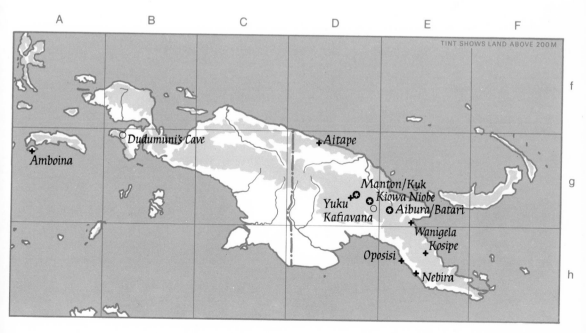

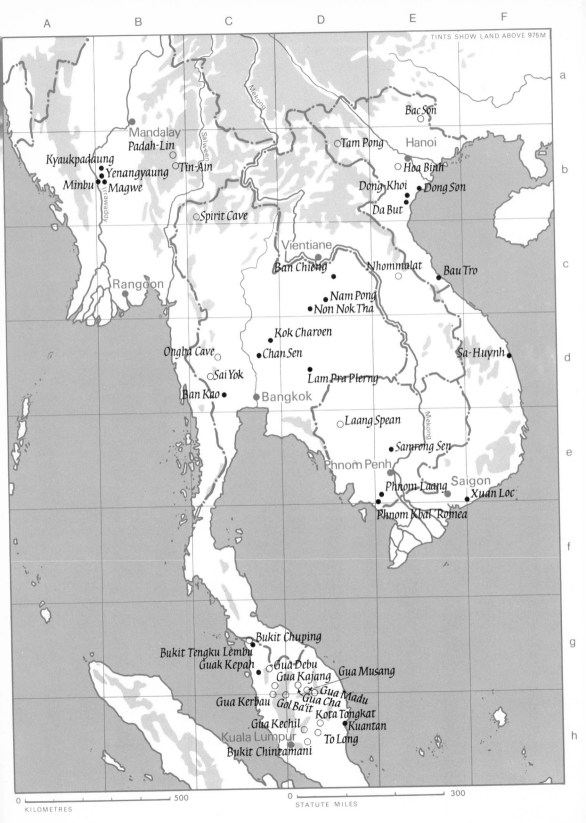

TINTS SHOW LAND ABOVE 975M

A   B   C   D   E   F

a

Bac Son

Mandalay

Padah-Lin   *Tam Pong*   Hanoi

Kyaukpadaung   *Tin-Ain*

Yenangyaung   *Hoa Binh*

Minbu   *Magwe*

Dong Khoi   *Dong Son*

Spirit Cave   *Da But*

b

Vientiane

Ban Chieng   *Nhommalat*   *Bau Tro*

Rangoon

Nam Pong

Non Nok Tha

c

Kok Charoen

Ongba Cave   *Chan Sen*   *Sa-Huynh*

Sai Yok

Ban Kao   Bangkok   *Lam Pra Plerng*

d

Laang Spean

Samrong Sen

Phnom Penh

Phnom Laang   Saigon

Xuan Loc

Phnom Khal 'Romea

e

f

Bukit Chuping

Bukit Tengku Lembu   *Gua Debu*   *Gua Musang*

Guak Kepah   *Gua Kajang*   *Gua Madu*

Gua Kerbau   *Gol Ba'it*   *Gua Cha*

Kota Tongkat

Gua Kechil   *Kuantan*

Kuala Lumpur   *To Lang*

Bukit Chintamani

g

h

0   500

KILOMETRES

0   300

STATUTE MILES

202   *Neolithic sites in south-east Asia*

and Dongson type and socketed axes and drums which, as the discovery of moulds confirms, were locally made. Notable funerary deposits which yielded bronzes are Tebingtinggi (Sumatra) and Melolo (Sumba). Iron arrived in the early centuries A D. However, metal was by no means universal at this date; it arrived in the highlands of New Guinea and in Australia only after contact with Europeans.

FURTHER READING

GLOVER, I. C. 1973. Island Southeast Asia and the settlement of Australia. In Strong, D. E. (ed.), *Archaeological Theory and Practice*, London and New York, 105–30.
HARRISSON, T. 1972. The prehistory of Borneo. *Asian Perspectives* XIII, 17–45.
SOEJONO, R. P. 1971. The history of prehistoric research in Indonesia. *Asian Perspectives* XII, 6—91.
WHITE, J. P. 1972. *Ol Tumbuna* (Terra Australis 2), Canberra.

Neolithic sites in south-east Asia

The date when food production began on the mainland of south-east Asia still presents considerable problems. Today south-east Asia boasts a wide variety of locally domesticated food plants and this has led some researchers to suppose that it was therefore an early centre of domestication. Recent discoveries at Spirit Cave in Thailand appear to support this belief, but more evidence is required before we can be sure.

We do possess, however, a growing amount of information about the hunting and gathering communities which preceded the earliest food-producers. The Hoabinhian culture, named after a site in North Vietnam, has a wide distribution on the mainland of south-east Asia, and variants occur on the western islands (see p. 198). The Hoabinhian stone industry appeared in the late Pleistocene. It had a long local ancestry and consisted mainly of pebble tools, usually worked on one face only, and flakes. At the end of the Pleistocene the first edge-ground implements occur. By c. 6000 bc, if not earlier, pottery had come into use.

Typical Hoabinhian industries are generally found in association with coastal middens or in caves near major rivers. Indeed, it appears that Hoabinhian hunters and gatherers preferred these relatively open conditions to the dense forest into which surviving groups retreated in the face of more advanced societies. Coastal middens often reveal a dependence on shellfish, while riverside groups relied on game, such as wild pig, and vegetable foods.

The finds from Spirit Cave now show that before the middle of the eighth millennium bc Hoabinhian groups were selecting a wide range of wild plants including *Prunus* beans, peas, *Areca*, bottle gourd, water chestnut, etc.; indeed, the excavators suggest that even at this early date several species (e.g. the beans and the peas) were being domesticated. To judge from other sites, however, hunting and gathering continued for millennia in some areas, long after cultivation had begun in others.

In the third millennium bc a break occurred in the cultural continuity. Influence from the north, perhaps brought by immigrants of Mongoloid stock, introduced the first permanent settlements supported on a subsistence economy of cereal cultivation, root crops and fruit.

FURTHER READING

CHANG, K.-C. 1970. The beginnings of agriculture in the Far East. *Antiquity* XLIV, 175–85.
GLOVER, I. C. 1973. Late Stone Age traditions in South-East Asia. In Hammond, N. (ed.), *South Asian Archaeology*, London and Park Ridge.
GORMAN, C. F. 1969. Hoabinhian: a pebble-tool complex with early plant associations in south-east Asia. *Science* 163, 671–3.
—— 1971. The Hoabinhian and after: subsistence patterns in South-East Asia during the late Pleistocene and early Recent periods. *World Archaeology* 2, no. 3, 300–20.

A B C D E F

a

• Tagaung

• Halingyi

Mandalay

• Pagan (Aramaddanapura)

Mekong

Salwin

b

Mrohaung

Hanoi

Irrawaddy

Prome

Sri Ksetra

• Chiengmai
• Lampun

Vientiane

c

Pegu

Rangoon

Sukotai • Sawankalok

Thaton
Martaban

△ • Srideb

Pitsanulok

• Roi Et

Tra Kieu

Mi Son ⊙ Quang Nam

Dong Duang

d

Lop Buri   • Pimai

Korat

Ayudhya   Panom Rung

U-Thong   △

Nakhon Pathom

Dong Si Maha Phot

Bassac

• Vat Phu

Pra Vihara

Koh Ker

Binh Dinh
(Vijaya)

Kanburi Kao

Phong Tuk

Ratburi   Phanat   Vatek   + Banteai Srei

Non Phra   Angkor Wat

Bangkok

Phetchaburi   Banon   Sambor Prei Kuk

Sambor (Sanllupura)   Kauthara

• Mergui   + Kompong Preah   Panduranga

Phnom Penh

Phnom Penh

Ta Keo   Saigon

Angkor Borei

Phnom Da (Vyadhapura)   Oc Eo

Da Noi

f

Takuapa • Jaya

Ligor

⊙ Satingpra

g

⊙ Gunong Jerai

Pengkalan Bujang

h

Kuala Lumpur

• Kampong Sungei Lang

Malacca

0 _____ 500
KILOMETRES

0 _____ 300
STATUTE MILES

204   *Early civilizations in south-east Asia*

Australia, while microlithic industries with backed blades and burins occur mainly in the southeast. Notable sites of the later stone industries in Australia are Devon Downs and Fromm's Landing, both on the Murray River. Most Middle Stone Age communities hunted kangaroo, wallaby, small animals such as lizards, fish and birds. Artistic activity was not uncommon: Kenniff Cave and Toombs Shelter contain stencilled hands and other painted motifs, including spear-throwers, boomerangs and shields.

The first European settlers (Sydney was founded in 1788) reported that the inhabitants of Australia relied entirely on hunting and gathering; they had no horticulture (unlike the natives of New Guinea) and the only domesticated animal was the dingo, a dog similar to the pariah of southern Asia. The total population may have been about half a million. Most groups had industries of the 'Recent Stone Age', although in Tasmania earlier traditions survived, mainly because the islanders were without boats and had lived in complete isolation from the mainland for more than 10,000 years. In the Recent Stone Age of south-eastern Australia microliths and backed blades became rare; spears, we assume, were tipped with wood. Indeed, wood, bone and vegetable fibres were used for most purposes. Although simple stone flakes continued to be used in many areas the only well-made stone tools were edge-ground axes and, in the north, foliate points.

FURTHER READING

BOWLER, J. M., R. JONES, H. ALLEN and A. G. THORNE 1970. Pleistocene human remains from Australia: a living site and human cremation from Lake Mungo, western New South Wales. *World Archaeology* 2, no. 1, 39–60.

JONES, R. M. 1973. Emerging picture of pleistocene Australians. *Nature* 246:5431, 278–81.

LAWRENCE, R. 1968. *Aboriginal habitat and economy*, Canberra.

MULVANEY, D. J. 1969. *The Prehistory of Australia*, London and New York.

MULVANEY, D. J. and J. GOLSON 1971. *Aboriginal Man and Environment in Australia*, ANU, Canberra.

According to legend, the ancestors of the Maori reached New Zealand in a series of canoe-borne migrations from Polynesia, culminating in the arrival of the Fleet *c.* AD 1350. Traditional genealogies indicate that the legendary discoverer of New Zealand, Kupe, reached North Island *c.* AD 950–1150. While it is clear that the first New Zealanders did come from Polynesia, it is equally clear from archaeological evidence that the traditional accounts are – as might be expected – inaccurate.

The earliest sites found in New Zealand so far date from *c.* AD 750. They occur mostly in North Island, the first landfall for settlers from Polynesia and a more attractive environment for immigrants from the tropics than the cooler South Island. The earliest settlers were hunters and gatherers, and coastal sites such as Wairau Bar take the form of middens containing the remains of fish, shellfish, shore birds and moas. Indeed, their concentration on the vulnerable, flightless moa, which was often the size of an ostrich, caused archaeologists to call the earliest settlers 'Moa hunters', although the term 'Archaic' is used now for the phase before the period of the 'Classic' Maori. Archaic groups eventually hunted the moa to extinction, after which they relied more and more on coastal and marine resources: shellfish, snappers, etc.

Before the fourteenth century horticulture was introduced to North Island. The cultivated plants were of Polynesian origin: sweet potato (*kumara*), taro and yams. *Kumara* was stored in pits during the winter and these, indicative of garden cultivation, occur on sites of the fourteenth century and later. *Kumara* was grown only in North Island and in the northern part of South Island; farther south hunting and gathering remained the subsistence base.

The Classic Maori phase probably began *c.* 1650 and continued until the period of European settlement. Indeed we possess valuable eye-witness accounts of Maori life written in the eighteenth and nineteenth centuries, beginning with the description of Cook's landing in 1769. Maori society was based on the *whanao*, or ex-

TINT SHOWS LAND ABOVE 1,000 M

A B C D E F

a

Mt Camel
Onepu   Moturoa
Bay of Islands
Huruiki

Moutapu
Galatea Bay (Ponui)

b

Kaipara Harbour
Otakanini
Hamlin's Hill
Auckland
Mangere
Waikato River
Lake Ngaroto
Pirongia Mountain
Kawhia Harbour
Waipa River

Opito
Mercury Bay
Tairua
Oruarangi
Kauri Pt &
Ongari Pt
Lake Mangakaware

c

Kumarakaiamo

Lake Tutira
Poukawa

d

Lake Horowhenua
Heaphy River Mouth Wellington
Wairau Bar

e

Redcliffs
Christchurch
Rakaia River Mouth

f

Oturehua   Waitaki Mouth
Nenthorn   Shag River
Dunedin

g

Riverton
Sand Hill Pt   Pounawea
Wakapatu   Papatowai
Tihaka   Tiwai Pt

h

0   300
KILOMETRES

0   200
STATUTE MILES

208   *New Zealand*

tended family. Several families comprised one *hapu*, an extended kinship group, and several *hapu* made up an *iwi*, or tribe. The Maori lived in permanent or semi-permanent villages and *pa*, or hill-forts. They possessed neither metal nor pottery. They were skilled carpenters. Nephrite, used for personal ornaments such as *tiki* (anthropomorphic amulets) and ceremonial weapons, was traded from outcrops in South Island to the more densely populated North Island.

FURTHER READING

BELLWOOD, P. 1971. Fortifications and Economy in Prehistoric New Zealand. *Proceedings of the Prehistoric Society* 37, 56–95.
COUTTS, P. and C. HIGHAM 1971. The seasonal factor in Prehistoric New Zealand. *World Archaeology* 2, no. 3, 266–77.
DAVIDSON, J. 1969. *The First Settlement of New Zealand*, Auckland.
DUFF, R. 1950. *The Moa Hunter Period of Maori Culture*, Wellington, N.Z.
GOLSON, J. and P. W. GATHERCOLE 1962. The last decade in New Zealand Archaeology. *Antiquity* XXXVI, 168–74.
New Zealand Archaeological Association Newsletter 1957– .

Early sites in the Pacific

see map pp. 210/211

The islands of the Pacific formed the last large habitable region of the earth to be colonized by man. Between the second millennium BC and *c*. AD 1000 settlements were established over a huge area, from the Solomon group to Hawaii and the Galapagos Islands. Two factors hindered colonization: (1) the islands, though numerous, are widely scattered and many are invisible from their nearest neighbours, and (2) the prevailing trade winds blow from east to west, whereas most settlers came from the west. Indeed, although the voyage of the Kon-Tiki showed that one *can* sail from the Americas to Polynesia (and sherds from the Galapagos Islands seem to show that some

early voyagers *did*), it is abundantly clear that the islands were settled from south-east Asia. For example, the physical features of the Polynesians show no trace of Amerindian characteristics; the languages of Polynesia and Melanesia are related to those of the south-east Asian islands and to Thai and other mainland tongues; domesticated plants and animals include no American species; the European explorers found leprosy in Polynesia but not in America, while veneral disease, indigenous to the Americas, was unknown in the Pacific.

The scattered pattern of islands made systematic colonization impossible, for the largest boats used in the Pacific were catamarans designed for short voyages. Nevertheless, Cook and other explorers reported that islanders did occasionally embark on voyages of discovery, although more often they discovered new islands by accident. John Williams, a missionary in Raiatea (1817–39), described how a vessel from Raivivae in south Polynesia was driven off course and after three months made a landfall at Manua in the Samoan group, 2400 km. from home.

It is hardly surprising that many communities developed in near-isolation, with distinctive culture traits. Nevertheless, in west Polynesia (Tonga, Samoa and the Ellice Islands) pottery and other features derived from Melanesia and southeast Asia occur. In east Polynesia (which extends from New Zealand to Easter Island) a coherent group of cultures emerged before AD 1000. The most prominent features were monumental earth and stone structures: terrace plazas (*tahua*) in the Marquesas, funerary platforms with large stone figures (*ahu*) on Easter Island.

FURTHER READING

FREEMAN, J. D. and W. R. GEDDES (eds) 1959. *Anthropology in the South Seas*, New Plymouth, N.Z.
MÉTRAUX, A. 1957. *Easter Island*, London and New York.
OLIVER, D. I. 1951. *The Pacific Islands*, Cambridge, Mass.
SHARP, A. 1957. *Ancient Voyagers in the Pacific*, Harmondsworth.
SUGGS, R. C. 1960. *The Island Civilization of Polynesia*, New York.

Peking

Ishigaki/Okinawa
Iriomote/Yonaguni

Hong Kong

+Batan
+Fuga

Calatagan   ⊘ Bato/Cagrary
Tres Reyes   * Kalanay

+ Tabon
+ Jolo   + Palau
⊘ Niah

⊘ Gua Sirih

Kalumpang   Ocean Is.(Te Aka)

                        Waghi Valley (Manton/Kuk)
                        Batari/Aibura/Kafiavana/Niobe
                        Anuru River/Silop
Maros ⊘ Banta Eng/Batu Edjaja/Toala   Buka
     Salajar   Bougainville
Ngandong/Trinil   Lie Siri   Nebira4 Trobriand Is.
+ Buni + Bali Bui Cero Uato   Nuamata Santa Ana
Pacitan   Budiawa/Liang Momer/ Wanigela
               Liang Toge Timor   Bellona

                                       Shepherd Is.   Fanga (Tau Is.)
                                       Efate   Tutuila

                                                       Vanua Levu
                                                       Viti Levu/Sigatoka
                              Lapita   Moindou
                              Noumea   Ile des Pins   Tonga
                                       (St Maurice)

Sydney

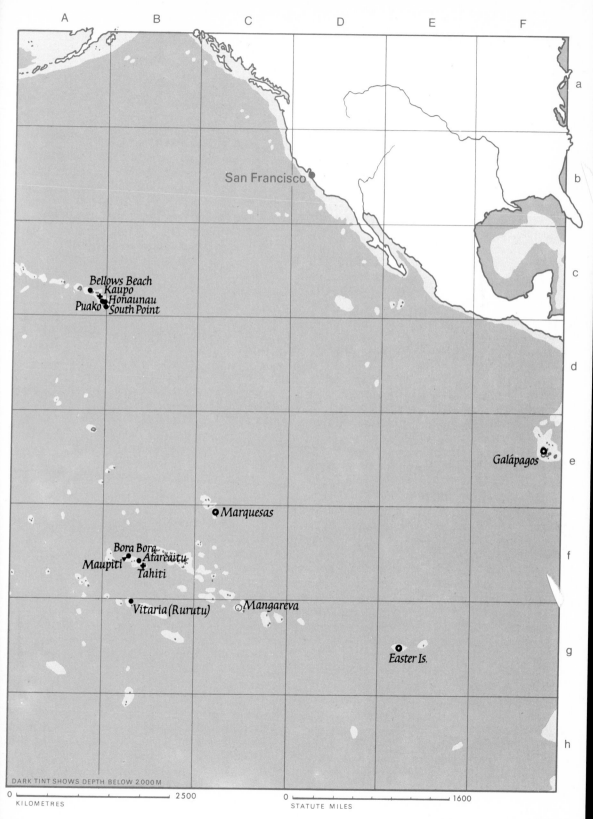

DARK TINT SHOWS DEPTH BELOW 2,000 M

San Francisco

Bellows Beach
Kaupo
Honaunau
Puako South Point

Galápagos

Marquesas

Bora Bora
Maupiti Afareaitu
Tahiti

Vitaria (Rurutu)

Mangareva

Easter Is.

0 ———————————— 2500
KILOMETRES

0 ———————————— 1600
STATUTE MILES

The Americas

Man's first presence in the Americas can be traced to the late Pleistocene period and the earliest sites belong to the technological stage known as the Upper Palaeolithic in the Old World and the Palaeoindian in the New. The earliest inhabitants arrived from north-east Asia at a time when a fall in sea level created a land bridge across the Bering Strait, probably between c. 25,000 and 10,000 bc. American archaeologists have repeatedly sought evidence for an even earlier Palaeoindian stage, but its existence is uncertain and the earliest completely reliable C^{14} dates from sites in the Americas post-date 10,000 bc. These first Americans hunted large mammals using weapons armed with projectile points comparable with those of the Leptolithic in Siberia. The best known hunting groups are those of the High Plains east of the Rocky Mountains. Early groups in this region used projectile points named after the site of Clovis; later groups used points named after another New Mexican site, Folsom.

Developments after the Palaeoindian stage were exclusively – or almost exclusively – of local origin. Contrary to formerly-held diffusionist views, we now believe that events in the Americas followed a very different course from those in the Old World and, while rare contact across the Pacific may have occurred (for example where the Intermediate area between Mesoamerica and Peru is concerned), American civilization was a fundametally indigenous growth.

After c. 7000 bc the inhabitants of the Americas had to adapt to changing climatic conditions. Regional adaptations emerged: two of the best known are the Desert Culture of the Great Basin, where increasingly arid conditions compelled communities to concentrate on small game and plant foods, and the Archaic culture of eastern North America, where the spread of forests provided a less harsh environment and the toolkit included polished stone tools and, after c. 5000 bc, implements of hammered native copper.

The most significant development of the period c. 7000–2000 bc, sometimes known as the Meso-indian phase, was the beginning of food produc-

tion. Agriculture in the New World, as in the Old, provided the subsistence base on which the higher civilizations developed, but American farming was radically different from that of Eurasia. In America animals were never important: dog, llama, alpaca and guinea pig were domesticated, but either were not used as food, or did not play a significant role. The domesticated plants, a great variety of which was cultivated, were of different species from those in the Old World. The earliest evidence of food production comes from the Tehuacán valley of central Mexico. Here in the El Riego phase, dated by C^{14} to c. 7000–5000 bc, many wild plants, including maize, were collected and chilis, squash and avocado pears were first cultivated. In the next phase (c. 5000–3400 bc) a primitive, but undoubtedly domesticated, strain of maize was introduced, but cultivated plants still formed only 10% of the vegetable diet. By 3700 BC (3000 bc) however, the percentage of cultivated plants had risen to 25%. After 2900 BC (2300 bc) an improved hybrid form of maize was developed and, on the basis of efficient farming, long-term settlements became possible. The emergence of permanent villages is usually taken to mark the beginning of the Pre-Classic, or Formative, period.

Experimental agriculture also took place in other areas of the New World, although nowhere as early as in Mesoamerica. The Orinoco–Amazon basin, for example, was the home of manioc cultivation, though its incidence cannot yet be dated closely. In Peru pumpkins, chilis, two species of bean and cotton, all thought to be local domesticates, were being grown well before 3200 BC (2500 bc), considerably earlier than the introduction of maize from Mesoamerica, c. 1800 BC (1500 bc). The cultivation of the potato probably originated in Bolivia, but we know little about its early history. In the south-west United States local gourds, squashes and sunflowers were being cultivated before maize was introduced from Mesoamerica c. 3700 BC (3000 bc). In the Mississippi valley sunflowers and Jerusalem artichokes, probably domesticated locally, were cultivated in the first millennium bc.

Civilization emerged in the New World in two of the areas in which early agriculture developed: Mesoamerica and Peru. Just as New World farming differed radically from that of the Old, so American civilizations differed from the city states of Eurasia. For example, technological innovations such as the plough and the wheel, which were basic to Old World development, were either lacking or scarcely used in the Americas.

In Mesoamerica the latter part of the Formative period (c. 1000 bc–AD 300) saw the emergence of civilizations characterized by ceremonial centres containing large temples, hieroglyphic writing and elaborate calendars. This development reached its peak in the Classic period (c. AD 300–900), during which the civilization of the Maya flourished. The Maya devised the most elaborate and accurate calendar of all ancient peoples and, despite their lack of metal tools, they raised enormous pyramids faced with dressed and mortared masonry. During the Post-Classic period (c. AD 900–1520) the leading role in Mesoamerica was assumed by the inhabitants of central Mexico, prominent among whom were firstly the Toltecs and later the Aztecs, whose state was destroyed by the conquistadors under Cortes in the years 1519–21.

In Peru civilization with a character different from that of Mesoamerica emerged, although contacts between the two areas existed. Whilst the Peruvians never developed a system of writing or an accurate calendar, they did practise a more advanced technology than that of their contemporaries in Mesoamerica, notably in their mastery of gold, silver, copper and alloy metallurgy. Although highly developed cultures existed in many regions, it was only in the century before the arrival of the Spaniards that the Incas of the Cuzco valley were able to incorporate much of modern Peru, Ecuador, Bolivia, northern Argentina and Chile in a single empire, held together by a tightly controlled economic and social organization – an organization which was, however, wholly unable to resist the Spaniards under Pizarro in 1532.

In North America no civilization developed, but farming cultures flourished in two main areas: the south-west, which was the territory of the Basket-maker and Pueblo cultures, while the Woodland culture occupied many of the eastern states. These cultures were based on maize cultivation, presumably introduced from Mesoamerica. The Middle Mississippi culture, which developed c. AD 1000, was with its large temple mounds the closest approach in North America to civilization, but was none the less only a pale reflection of Mesoamerican development.

Throughout the rest of North America and at the southern extremity of South America hunting, fishing and gathering communities survived until the arrival of the Europeans.

FURTHER READING

Bushnell, G. H. S. 1968. *The First Americans*, London and New York.

Clark, G. 1969. *World Prehistory: a New Outline*, London and New York.

Coe, M. D. 1962. *Mexico*, London and New York.

Katz, F. 1972. *The Ancient American Civilisations*, London.

Willey, G. R. 1966 and 1971. *An Introduction to American Archaeology. I. North and Middle America* (1966); *II. South America* (1971). Englewood Cliffs, New Jersey.

A B C D E F

a

b

Kogruk

Engigstciak
(British Mountain)

Columbia

Vancouver

d

Ottawa

Fort Rock Cave

Horner

Missouri

Mississippi

St. Lawrence

Bull Brook
New York

Eden

Hell Gap

Scottsbluff

Meserve

Shoop

Danger Cave

Lindenmeier

Graham Cave

Williamson

Ohio

e

Farmington

Tule Springs

Dent

Arkansas

Madoc Cave

Tolchaco

Sandia

Gypsum Cave

Lucy

Folsom

Quad

Tennessee

Santa Rosa Is.

Lake Manix

Clovis

La Jolla/San Diego

Ventana

Red

Naco

Lewisville

f

Lake Chapala

Scharbauer

Friesenhahn Cave

Rio Grande

Havana

Tamaulipas
Caves

g

Tequixquiac

Mexico City

Valsequillo

h

0 |___|___|___|___| 1200   0 |___|___|___|___| 800

KILOMETRES   STATUTE MILES

The earliest Americans *for map of South America turn to p. 216*

Man arrived late in the New World. No convincing traces of human occupation are known from Early or Middle Pleistocene deposits and all the human fossils are of *Homo sapiens sapiens*. Despite eccentric suggestions that man evolved independently in the Americas, or arrived from the west by boat, it is abundantly clear that the earliest inhabitants migrated from Asia by land. During the glacial phases of the Pleistocene, when large masses of water were converted to ice, the sea level fell, exposing a land-bridge across the Bering Strait between Siberia and Alaska. This bridge, however, only afforded access to the Americas when a gap existed between the glaciers of the Rocky Mountains and the great Laurentide ice sheet of the Hudson's Bay region. Between *c.* 25,000 and 10,000 bc, ice formed an impenetrable barrier across northern Canada and it follows that man can have penetrated southward only before or after that time-span. Finds from sites in both North and South America are quoted in support of an early date for man's arrival, but none is unequivocal. Thus, tools (or tool-like objects) are said to occur with signs of burning at Lewisville, Texas (with a C^{14} date of *c.* 38,000 bc) and on Santa Rosa Island, California (*c.* 27,650 bc). However, the Lewisville site appears to be disturbed and the 'tools' from Santa Rosa may be natural pebbles. Indeed, the evidence available at present suggests that the earliest inhabitants of the Americas – bands of hunters of mammoth and other big game – arrived soon after 10,000 bc, although an earlier date is by no means ruled out. They spread rapidly in pursuit of abundant game and the remains of horse- and sloth-hunters from Fell's Cave in Patagonia have a carbon date of 8760 bc. Archaeologists divide these early hunting communities into several groups, usually on the basis of distinctive types of stone spearhead: Cascade points in western North America, Lerma points in South America and Mexico, and Clovis and Folsom points on the North American plains.

FURTHER READING

BUSHNELL, G. H. S. 1968. *The First Americans*, London and New York.
WILLEY, G. R. 1966 and 1971. *An Introduction to American Archaeology. I. North and Middle America* (1966); *II. South America* (1973). Englewood Cliffs, New Jersey.

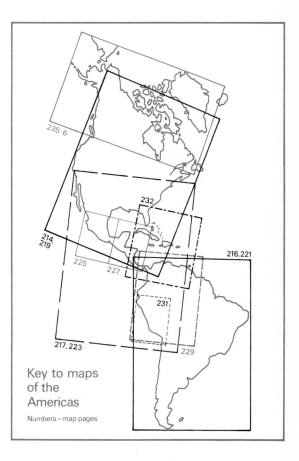

Key to maps
of the
Americas

Numbers – map pages

TINT SHOWS LAND ABOVE 1625M

Muaco
El Manzanillo
El Jobo
Caracas

Orinoco

Bogotá

El Inga

Negro

Amazon

Marañón
Ucayali
Madeira
Tapajós
Xingu
Tocatins
San Francisco

Lima

La Paz
Viscachani

Brasília

Paraguay
Paraná

Lagoa Santa

Rio de Janeiro

Ghatchi

Ampajango

Ayampitín
Santiago
Intihausi

Buenos Aires

Tandilense

Oliviense

Palli Aike
Fell's Cave
Rio Chico

0   1200
KILOMETRES

0   800
STATUTE MILES

216   *The earliest Americans (South)*

A   B   C   D   E   F

Talus   South-West United States   a
Shabik Eshchee
Bluff
Snaketown   Bat Cave   Washington
Su   Tularosa
San Simon   Cienega/Crooked Ridge

Rio Grande   b

Southern
Tamaulipas   Mississippi

Sierra Madre ✪   ✪ Sierra de Tamaulipas   Havana   c

Mexico City
Tehuacán
Valley

Caracas   e

Bogotá

Tehuacán   Tehuacán
Valley   Amazon   f

El Riego   San Marcos   Marañon
Tecorral   Ajalpán   Huaca Prieta
Quachilco +   Coatepec/Las Canoas   Coastal Peru   Kotosh   g
●Coxcatlán   Playa Culebras   Rio Seco
✪Coxcatlán   Lima   El Paraíso (Chuquitanta)
Abejas/Purron ○   Chilca   La Paz
●Teotitlán   Ancón/Pampa   h
Rio Salado   Asia Valley

0 ┣━━━━━━━━┫ 20 Kms
0 ┣━━━━━━━━┫ 10 Mls

TINT SHOWS LAND ABOVE 1625M

0 ┣━━━━━━━━━━━━━━┫ 1200   0 ┣━━━━━━━━━━┫ 800
KILOMETRES   STATUTE MILES

The first farmers in the Americas   **217**

The first farmers in the Americas

see map p. 217

The early development of farming in the Americas did not follow the same course as in the Old World. In at least four areas, groups of semi-nomadic hunters and gatherers gradually domesticated a variety of food plants, most of which were unknown in Eurasia. They included squashes (*Cucurbita*), gourds, beans and, later, maize. At all times domesticated animals were few. The period of 'incipient domestication' lasted a considerable time: an estimated 1500 years in Peru and parts of Mexico.

The four main areas of early agriculture in the Americas were: (1) coastal Peru, (2) south-central Mexico, (3) north-east Mexico, (4) the south-west United States.

In *coastal Peru* groups of fishers and shellfish-gatherers began to experiment with the cultivation of gourd (*Lagenaria*) and Lima bean (*Phaseolus lunatus*) *c.* 4000 bc. In the Huaca Prieta phase (*c.* 2500–1200 bc) large villages came into existence. Although sea-food was still important, villagers also depended on their crops, which included cotton, chilis and squash. Maize (*Zea mays*) was introduced in the period *c.* 1500–750 bc.

In *south-central Mexico* (Tehuacán valley) the first definite evidence of domestication belongs to the El Riego phase (*c.* 7000–5000 bc), when crops included chilis, squash and avocado pears. Although the amount of agriculture increased in the Coxcatlán period (*c.* 5000–3400 bc), cultivated plants still provided only 10% of the vegetable diet. However, one important development took place: the introduction of maize. By the Abejas phase (*c.* 3400–2300 bc) 25% of the diet was cultivated and domesticated dog was also eaten. In the Purron phase (*c.* 2300–1500 bc) new hybrid varieties of plant food were developed and by 200 bc more than half of the vegetable part of the diet was cultivated.

A similar process took place in the Tamaulipas area of *north-east Mexico*. The period of incipient cultivation lasted from *c.* 7000 to 5500 bc. Subsequently, in the Ocampo, Nogales and La Perra groups (*c.* 5000–2200 bc), the proportion of domesticated plant foods increased and maize cultivation began.

Finally, in the *south-west United States* domesticated plants *may* have been used at San José on the Rio Grande *c.* 4000 bc. At Bat Cave seasonal nomads grew maize, gourds, squashes and sunflowers (*c.* 3600–2000 bc) and bean cultivation began in the south-west *c.* 1000 bc. The first permanent villages, however, did not occur until the early first millennium A D.

FURTHER READING

BUSHNELL, G. H. S. 1968. *The First Americans*, London and New York.
MACNEISH, R. S. 1961–62. *Tehuacan Archaeological-Botanical Project. First and Second Annual Reports*, Andover, Mass.
———— 1965. The Origins of American Agriculture, *Antiquity* XXXIX, 87–94.
WILLEY, G. R. 1966. *An Introduction to American Archaeology. I. North and Middle America*, Englewood Cliffs, New Jersey.

TINT SHOWS LAND ABOVE 1625 M

Vancouver Fraser Canyon
Cattle Point/Victoria
Cold Springs/Hat Creek
Five Mile Rapids/Indian Well
Netarts/Willamette
Catlow/Fort Rock/Paisley
Black Rock/Dead Man/Promontory Pt
Humboldt/Leonard/
Lovelock
Borax L./Emeryville/
Windmiller
Danger Cave
Fulton Co
Cahokia
Hopi Area
Anasazi Region
Canaliño/Cape Mendocino/
Oak Grove
Zuñi Area
New Madrid Sites
Ozark Bluffs
L. Mojave/Pinto Basin
Patayan Region
Fourche Maline/Spiro
Harris/La Jolla
Mimbres
Hohokam
Region
Mogollon Region
Poverty Pt
Davis
Marksville
Coles Creek
Comondú
Cerro Cuevoso

Ellsworth Falls
Ottawa
Lamoka
New York
Oconto
Aztalan
Adena/Hopewell
Baumer/Faulkner/Kincaid
Green River
Eva
Candy Creek/Watts Bar
Piedmont Sites
Hiwassee Is.
Pickwick Basin
Stallings Is.
Irene
Lamar/Macon/Swift Creek
Kolomoki
St Johns River
Moundville
Troyville
Fort Walton
Tchefuncte
Crystal River/Weeden Is.

Parkin
Walls

Havana

Mexico City

Little Sycamore/Malaga Cove/
Topanga

Columbia
Missouri
Mississippi
Colorado
Arkansas
Red
Rio Grande
Ohio
St Lawrence

0   1200
KILOMETRES

0   800
STATUTE MILES

Later collectors and farmers in the Americas (North) **219**

Later collectors and farmers in the Americas

for map of North America turn to p. 219

The maps on pp. 219, 221 cover the Americas after the period of early hunting and gathering, except those areas of advanced farming culture or higher civilization shown in the maps on pp. 223–9 and the Eskimo, shown in the map on pp. 234/5.

In North America this includes three main cultural regions: the eastern area, the south-west and the north-west. In the eastern United States the Archaic culture developed into the Woodland stage (*c.* 1000 bc–AD 500). Within this general tradition two particular developments have been recognized: the Adena and the Hopewell cultures. These were characterized by stamped and impressed pottery and burial mounds; they were based on the cultivation of plants, including maize, which was presumably introduced from Mesoamerica. In the period *c.* AD 500–1500 they developed into the Mississippian cultures, which were almost urban in organization and showed many Mesoamerican traits, including ceremonial centres with rectangular temple mounds.

The south-west was the only other North American area where maize cultivation was practised. Here three main farming cultures emerged out of a generalized Desert culture background: the Hohokam, Mogollon and Anasazi cultures. The Anasazi is divided into a Basket-maker period (*c.* AD 0–700) and a Pueblo period (*c.* AD 700–1540).

Elsewhere in North America hunting cultures survived. Particularly well known are those of the north-west coast, where the unusually abundant uncultivated food supplies allowed permanent, fairly large settlements and complex social systems, as exemplified by the historical Nootka and Kwakiutl.

The parts of South America considered here fall into four main regions: the east Brazilian, the Chaco, the Pampean and the Fuegian areas. In the east Brazilian region an early 'Upland' tradition of inland hunting and gathering and a coastal variant of the same survived into the present era. In addition there were pottery-using groups in the first millennium AD, perhaps earlier, who may or may not have been farmers. After *c.* AD 500 tropical forest agriculture based on manioc was introduced by groups known as Tupí-Guaraní. Farther south hunting and gathering groups predominated, although tropical forest agriculture reached both the Chaco and the Pampean areas in late prehistoric times. In the Fuegian area hunting and gathering groups alone existed, preserving ancient traditions into modern times in the tool-kit and way of life of the Yahgan, Ona and Alacaluf peoples.

FURTHER READING

CALDWELL, J. R. 1962. Eastern North America. In Braidwood, R. J. and G. R. Willey (eds), *Courses toward Urban Life*, Edinburgh and Chicago.

HAURY, E. W. 1962. The Greater American Southwest. In Braidwood, R. J. and G. R. Willey (eds), *Courses toward Urban Life*, Edinburgh and Chicago.

WILLEY, G. R. 1966 and 1971. *An Introduction to American Archaeology. I. North and Middle America* (1966); *II. South America* (1971), Englewood Cliffs, New Jersey.

Caracas

Orinoco

Bogotá

Negro

Amazon

Marañón

Ucayali

Madeira

Tapajós

Xingu

Tocantins

San Francisco

Lima

Pedro Oca

La Paz

Brasília

Paraguay

Arica/Azapa/Conanoxa

Arani/Chullpa Pampa/Mizque

Paraná

Lagoa Santa

Pichalo

Tamboara/Umuarama Caloré

Rio Claro

Ciudad Real/
José Vieira

Estirão
Comprido

Rio de Janeiro

Guaratiba

Barracão

Gomes/Saquarema/Macedo/
Porto Mauricio

Taltal

Humaita/Camuri/Camboatá/
Taquara/Maquiné/Monjolo

Guanaqueros

Ayampitín/Ongamira

Vieira

Santiago

Cerro Grande

Las Cenizas/Concón/
Sitio Alacranes/Longotoma

Intihausi

El Cerrillo/Rio Matanzas/Arroyo/Sarandi

Buenos Aires

Concepción

Punta Piedras

Angol/El Vergel/Cueva de los Catalanes

Puerto Montt

San Blas Region

Oliviense Region

Toldos Region

Fell's Cave/Palli Aike

Englefield Is.

Beagle Channel

0 · · · · · 1200
KILOMETRES

0 · · · · · 800
STATUTE MILES

Later collectors and farmers in the Americas (South) **221**

Urban civilization in the Americas

Urban civilization in the New World was restricted to Mexico, central America and part of the Pacific seaboard of South America. Thus, the conquistadors encountered urban societies in central Mexico (the Aztecs), southern Mexico, Guatemala and Honduras (the Maya) and Peru (the Incas). All were agricultural societies with simple technologies. They offered little resistance to the invaders and between 1519 and 1533 the Spaniards virtually destroyed all three civilizations.

Civilization developed in the Americas in the first millennium BC. On the Gulf of Mexico, in Vera Cruz and Tabasco, the Olmecs emerged c. 800–400 bc. They were literate, using hieroglyphics for writing, but their script has yet to be deciphered. The most famous Olmec site is the ceremonial centre at La Venta, where temples, ball-courts and massive stelae were erected in the Formative period. Farther north, in Oaxaca, the Zapotecs emerged as another literate society with large ritual sites, such as Monte Albán. Cultures at a similar stage of development existed in the Valley of Mexico and in the Maya region. By the beginning of our era the most impressive centre in Mesoamerica was Teotihuacán near Mexico City, a complex of 18 sq. km. dominated by the pyramids of the Sun and Moon, the former no less than 64 m. high. Despite the destruction of Teotihuacán c. AD 600, the region continued to support civilization and the Spaniards were deeply impressed by the Aztec capital Tenochtitlán, the forerunner of Mexico City. The Maya period spanned some eight centuries from c. 500 BC to AD 300. While most of the population lived in dispersed rural settlements, the Maya congregated at great ceremonial centres, including Chichén Itzá, Tikal and Palenque. The Maya were literate and possessed a calendar based on accurate astronomical observation. The Maya year, for example, was 365·2420 days long – closer to the actual value of 365·2422 than the corrected Gregorian calendar of 365·2425 days. In Peru the Classic period, represented by the sites of Nazca and Tiahuanaco, began about the same time as the Christian era. In the Post-Classic period the city of Chanchán occupied an area of 29 sq. km. During the fifteenth century the Incas established a large, but ephemeral empire ruled from Cuzco in Peru.

Civilization in the Americas differed markedly from civilization in the Old World. Most of the 'cities' lacked the high population densities found in Eurasia. Civilization was based on a virtually non-metallic technology. It used neither wheeled vehicles nor machinery requiring the wheel. Although agriculture was the mainstay of the economy, all American societies possessed only the simplest agricultural implements (ploughs were unknown) and domesticated animals were for the most part few.

FURTHER READING

BUSHNELL, G. H. S. 1963. *Peru* (revised edn), London and New York.
COE, W. R. 1965. Tikal. *Expedition* VIII, no. 1, 1–56.
MILLON, R. 1967. Teotichuacan. *Scientific American* 216: 6, 38–48.
THOMPSON, J. E. S. 1966. *The Rise and Fall of Maya Civilisation*², Oklahoma.
VAILLANT, G. C. 1950. *The Aztecs of Mexico*, Harmondsworth.

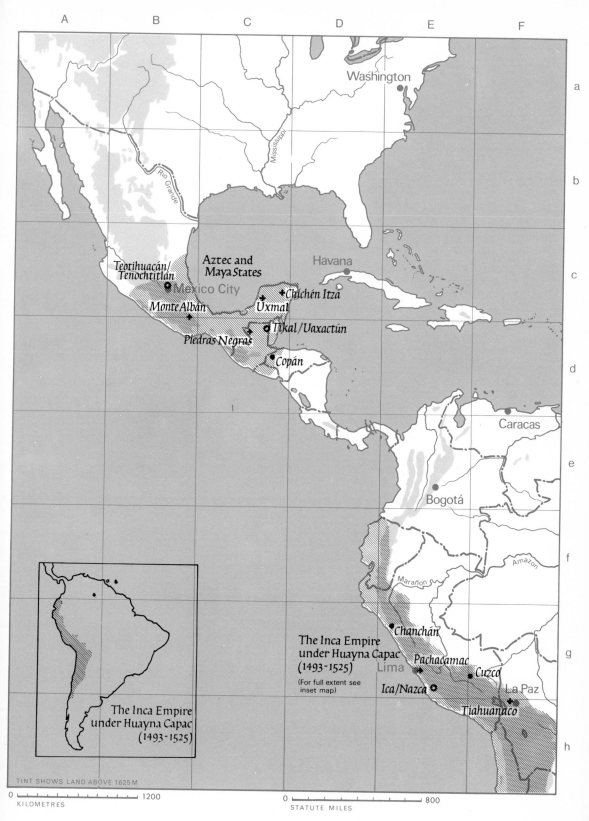

A B C D E F

a

Washington

b

Mississippi

Rio Grande

Teotihuacán/
Tenochtitlán

Aztec and
Maya States

Havana

c

Mexico City

Chichén Itzá

Monte Albán

Uxmal

Piedras Negras

Tikal/Uaxactún

Copán

d

Caracas

e

Bogotá

f

Amazon

Marañon

g

Chanchán

The Inca Empire
under Huayna Capac
(1493-1525)

(For full extent see
inset map)

Pachacamac

Lima

Cuzco

Ica/Nazca

La Paz

Tiahuanaco

h

The Inca Empire
under Huayna Capac
(1493-1525)

TINT SHOWS LAND ABOVE 1,625 M

0 ⊢──────────────────┤ 1200
KILOMETRES

0 ⊢──────────────────┤ 800
STATUTE MILES

Urban civilization in the Americas **223**

The Aztecs and their predecessors

The Aztecs moved into the Valley of Mexico from the north or north-west *c.* AD 1160, occupying the area formerly held by the Toltecs, who had become prominent in the tenth century. In the fifteenth century the Aztec city of Tenochtitlán (modern Mexico City) joined the cities of Texcoco and Tlacopán to form a league, which was still functioning at the time of the Spanish invasion. Under Montezuma I (1440–69) the Aztecs adopted a policy of expansion. Ahuitzotlo (1486–1502) pushed the frontiers of the Aztec 'empire' to the shores of the Pacific and the Gulf of Mexico and pressed southwards into Guatemala. The empire was still growing when Cortes landed in Vera Cruz in 1519.

The Aztec economy was based on the cultivation of maize (*Zea mays*). Other crops included a variety of squashes, gourds, peppers and tomatoes. The Aztecs grew cotton, tobacco, and agave which they used mainly for making a fermented drink. In low-lying parts of the Valley of Mexico fields were drained and irrigated by an ambitious system of canals. The Aztecs had few domesticated animals; they did, however, keep turkeys (and perhaps other birds) and dogs. One product of the European invasion of the Americas was to enlarge the range of domesticated plants and animals used in the Old World: turkeys, potatoes, tomatoes and tobacco, for example, were unknown in Europe before the conquistadors.

The Aztecs possessed only a simple technology. Metal-workers used copper and gold (sometimes an alloy of both), but were ignorant of bronze. Objects were cold-hammered or cast by the *cire perdue* (lost wax) technique. They excelled in other crafts, notably the manufacture of 'mosaic' masks and the like, and pottery.

Despite their limited technology, the Aztecs were great builders and the Spanish conquistador Bernal Diaz wrote an impressive account of Tenochtitlán, the Aztec capital. It was an island city approached by causeways from the mainland and supplied with pure water by means of a long aqueduct. It was walled and contained pyramids, temples, a huge plaza, and the palaces of the later Aztec rulers. The Spaniards were, however, horrified by one aspect of Aztec life: the human sacrifice which their religion required.

FURTHER READING

BRAY, W. 1968, 1969. *Everyday life of the Aztecs*, London and New York.

BUSHNELL, G. H. S. 1968. *The First Americans*, London and New York.

CASO, A. 1967. *The Aztecs, people of the sun*, Oklahoma.

VAILLANT, G. C. 1950. *The Aztecs of Mexico*, Harmondsworth.

WEAVER, M. P. 1972. *The Aztecs, Maya and their predecessors, archaeology of Mesoamerica*, New York and London.

TINT SHOWS LAND ABOVE 2,000 M

+ Durango
+ Chalchihuites

+ El Pueblito
+ Llera

+ Venado   + Tula
La Quemada

Tampico
● San Luis Potosí   + Pánuco
Panuco

+ Ixtlán
+ Léon

S. Marcos / Etzatlan +

+ Papantla

● Guadalajara /
Itzépetl   Rio Grande de Santiago
+ El Opeño
+ Zamora   + Tulancingo
Tepeji   + Teotihuacán   Veracruz
+ Tzintzuntzan   Mexico / Tenochtitlán   Cempoala
Apatzingán +   Mexico   Puebla   Paso de Ovejas
Gualupita   Cholula
+ Huetamo   + Atlihuayan   + Chalcatzinco   + Orizaba
Balsas   Iguala +   + Tres Zapotes
Zacatollan +   + Tlacotepec   Olinala   Ioapan   + La Venta
+ Coyuquilla   Zumpango   + Huamelulpan   San Lorenzo +
San Jerónimo ● Acapu + Monte Negro MonteAlbán
+ Monte Negro   + Mitla
Oaxaca   + Juchitán
+ Jamiltepec + Tehuantepec +
+ Tututepec   + Tonalá

Teoloyucan +
Tepotzotlan +
Lake
Xaltocan
+ Teotihuacán
+ Tepexpan
Azcapotzalco / Lake
Tlatilco   Texcoco + Texcoco
+ Tlacopán + Chapingo / Huexolta
Chapultepec   + Coatlinchan
Acachinanco   + Mexico / Tenochtitlán
Coyoacan
Ixtapalapa Lake Tlahuac Lake Chalco + Texmelucan
Xochimilco   + Chalco
Ayotzingo   + Tlalmanalco
Tenango   + Xalitzintla + Huexotcingo
Amécameca + Tlamácaz
Ozumba +
✳ Popocatepetl
Volcano
Gualupita +   Kms 0   20
Mls 0   10

0 ⊢—————————————— 400
KILOMETRES

0 ⊢————————————— 250
STATUTE MILES

The Aztecs and their predecessors **225**

The Maya and their predecessors

The development of Mesoamerica is usually divided into three stages: the Pre-Classic or Formative stage (*c.* 2000 bc–A D 300), the Classic (A D 300–900) and the Post-Classic (A D 900–1520). Here we are concerned with the Pre-Classic and Classic periods in southern Mexico, Honduras and British Honduras. The first millennium of the Pre-Classic was characterized by simple village farming; only after *c.* 1000 bc did the first Mesoamerican civilization – that of the Olmecs – emerge. Olmec civilization is known chiefly from large ceremonial centres, which contain pyramid-like mounds and colossal sculpted stone heads. The best known sites are La Venta, Tres Zapotes and San Lorenzo.

In the late Pre-Classic period (*c.* 300 bc–A D 300) there were several regional cultures, all to some extent derived from the civilization of the Olmecs. In the main Olmec area, Tres Zapotes continued to be occupied and hieroglyphic signs and mathematical symbols came into use. To this period, too, belongs the culture of Monte Albán I in the highlands of Oaxaca, with large, flat-topped mounds and monumental reliefs.

The Maya lowlands had been occupied since the middle Pre-Classic period, but civilization emerged only in the Classic phase. Typical features of Mayan civilization were hieroglyphic writing, the so-called 'long count' calendar, a distinctive art style, characteristic pottery and the corbelled masonry vault. Towns in the normal sense of the word were unknown and the settlement pattern consisted of scattered hamlets surrounding massive ceremonial centres. The greatest, and earliest, centres existed in north-east Petén: Tikal and Uaxactún were particularly splendid. Here pyramidal mounds and platforms rose from large open spaces. Tall, steep mounds were surmounted by small 'temples'; low broad platforms supported larger 'palaces'. In the late Classic period ball-courts were added to the complexes. Maya building was remarkable: without metal tools, these people produced coursed ashlar, which they bonded with mortar. More remarkable still was the elaborate and extremely accurate Maya calendar, devised to ensure that religious ceremonies were carried out at the prescribed dates.

At the end of the Classic period the great Maya centres were abandoned, for either military or ecological reasons. Indeed, in the Post-Classic period the leading role in Mesoamerica passed from the Maya lowlands to various groups in central Mexico.

FURTHER READING

COE, M. 1966. *The Maya*, London and New York.
KATZ, F. 1972. *The Ancient American Civilizations,*London
WILLEY, G. R. 1966. *An Introduction to American Archaeology. I. North and Middle America*, Englewood Cliffs, New Jersey.

TINT SHOWS LAND ABOVE 2,000 M

Havana

Dzibilchaltun
Mérida • Kabáh Labná ♦ Chichén Itzá
Uxmal ♦ Maní Cenote
Jaina ♦ Sayil ♦ Cobá
♦ Etzná

♦ Xpuhil
♦ Calakmúl

♦ Bellote
Comalcalco
Palenque
Piedras Negras ♦ Uaxactún
Toniná ♦ Tikal ♦ San José
Altar de Sacrificios ♦ Yaxchilán
Chinkultic ♦ Seibal
Quen Santo ♦ Lubaantún
Zaculeu ♦ Pusilhá
San Agustín ♦ Quiriguá ♦ Playa de los Muertos
Kaminal-Juyú ♦ Guatemala ♦ Yojoa
Santa Lucía ♦ Copán ♦ Las Vegas
Cozumaluapa ♦ Lo de Vaca ♦ Tegucigalpa
Las Victorias ♦ Yarumela ♦ Tenampua

Managua

Papagayo ♦ Las Mercedes
♦ Guapiles
Las Huacas ♦ Las Pacayas
San José

Venado
Palmar ♦ Cocé
Sitio Conte
Barriles ♦ Girón
Pueblo Nuevo
Cerro Mangote
Monagrillo

•—•— Approximate extent of Classic Maya culture

0 ⊢⊢⊢⊢⊢⊢⊢⊣ 400
KILOMETRES

0 ⊢⊢⊢⊢⊢⊢⊢⊣ 250
STATUTE MILES

The Maya and their predecessors **227**

The Intermediate area and Amazonia

This map comprises the so-called Intermediate area, Amazonia and part of the Caribbean, which is shown in full in the map on p. 229. The first European settlers found groups practising three different forms of subsistence economy: hunting and gathering (the exponents of which are known as marginal groups), tropical forest agriculture (i.e. slash-and-burn cultivation with bitter manioc as the staple crop) and intensive agriculture, often with irrigation. Exponents of the last-named economy, sometimes known as the Circum-Caribbean groups, either practised 'seed farming' with maize as the staple, or 'vegetative farming' of manioc, sweet potato, etc., sometimes supplemented by maize. It is thought that the three types of economy – marginal, tropical forest and intensive agriculture – may recapitulate the sequence of development in pre-colonial times.

Hunting and gathering communities are poorly documented in the archaeological record. The El Jobo complex in Venezuela is a Pleistocene group, while to the Neothermal period belongs a series of coastal middens, typical of which is the Manicuare complex of eastern Venezuela.

By contrast, the remains of communities based on tropical forest agriculture are abundant. Archaeologists suppose that cultivation of this type was developed in the Orinoco–Amazon area; the earliest securely dated sites belong to the Saladero culture of the lower Orinoco (c. 900/800 bc). Groups using 'Saladoid' pottery occur widely in Amazonia and Venezuela, some with C14 dates in the early second millennium bc; these may well have practised tropical forest agriculture, but we have no direct evidence. In the succeeding phase, groups with 'Barrancoid' pottery (named after Barrancas, another site on the lower Orinoco) were even more wide-spread. They were almost certainly tropical forest cultivators.

While tropical forest agriculture was eventually practised throughout the area shown on the map, intensive farming developed only in the Intermediate and Caribbean areas, with a brief occurrence in the Marajoan culture of the Amazon delta. Communities in the Intermediate area acquired the knowledge of maize from Meso-america, sometime after c. 1000 bc. At the Colombian site of Momíl, a community of vegetative (manioc) farmers was succeeded c. 500 bc by seed farmers specializing in maize. The highest level of culture in the region was achieved by the Tairona Indians of northern Colombia after c. AD 1000. The Tairona lived in urban settlements with stone-built ceremonial centres. Their technology included gold and copper metallurgy. However, they never attained literacy and should not be regarded as possessing a civilization comparable with those of Mesoamerica and Peru.

FURTHER READING

LATHRAP, D. W. 1970. *The Upper Amazon*, London and New York.

MEGGERS, B. J. and C. EVANS 1957. Archaeological Investigations at the Mouth of the Amazon. Washington (Smithsonian Institution, Bureau of American Ethnology, Bulletin 167).

REICHEL-DOLMATOFF, G. 1965. *Colombia*, London and New York.

ROUSE, I. 1962. The Intermediate Area, Amazonia and the Caribbean Area. In Braidwood, R. J. and G. R. Willey (eds), *Courses toward Urban Life*, Edinburgh and Chicago.

WILLEY, G. R. 1971. *An Introduction to American Archaeology. II. South America*, Englewood Cliffs, New Jersey.

TINT SHOWS LAND ABOVE 500M

Malambo　+Pueblito
+Crespo/Hormiga/Barlovento
San Nicolas/Tolú
Ciénaga del Oro +
+Momil
Betancí
+Rio de la Miel
+El Palito
Caracas
+Rio Guapo
Apostadero/
Barrancas/
+Saladero
+Tamalameque/Zapetosa Lagoon
+Ronquín
+Arauquín
+Mabaruma
Georgetown
Panama

+Cupica
Bogota

+Corobal
+Nericagua

Atacames/Rio Tiaone
+La Tolita
El Inga/Quito
Nueva Armenia
+Nuevo Rocafuerte
Yasuni
Chorrera
Alausi
+Macás
Cerro Narrío
Milagro
Santa Elena Pen./Valdivia
Mangueiras
Pirapitinga
Paredaõ
Manacapurú
+Mamía
Oriximiná
Itacoatiara
+Miracanguera

La Plata Is.
Guangala/Machalilla
Maranon
Napo
Amazon
Ucayali

+Huayurco
+Quelap

+Gran Pajatén (Abiseo)
+Hupa Iya/Nueva Esperanza/Tutishcainyo
Tournavista +Caimito/Cumancaya
Tantamayo
+Ichu/Kotosh
+Casa de la Tía
+Chacra de Giacomotti/Naranjal
+Tarma

Lima

Oriximiná
+Iauarí
+Santarém
Amazon
Pacoval+
Belém

on the same scale

+Trenchera
+Chimay
+Mascito/Velarde
+Markopata
Chullpa Pampa
La Paz
+Rio Palacios

0 ⊢━━━━━━━━┤ 800
KILOMETRES

0 ⊢━━━━━━━┤ 500
STATUTE MILES

The Intermediate area and Amazonia **229**

Peru: the Incas and their predecessors

The map of Peru is dominated by the Andes, large areas of which are too high to sustain permanent habitation. However, there are fertile and well-watered valleys, including the Cuzco plain, between 2400 and 3400 m. above sea level and these supported many of the major sites of the Incas, Peru's empire-building civilization. East of the Andes, the Pacific coast is an arid strip, much of which is desert; to the west lies the *montaña*, covered with tropical forest.

The Inca empire was short-lived. It first expanded under Pachacuti (whose reign began *c.* 1438) and reached its greatest extent under Topa Inca (1493). At its zenith *c.* 1500, it extended from northern Ecuador to central Chile and had an area of about 900,000 sq. km. The Incas ruled from Cuzco, recruited their troops from subject tribes and consolidated their conquests by transporting populations *en masse*. In 1532–3 the Spaniards, led by Pizarro, destroyed the Incas, seized enormous quantities of gold and silver and reduced the population to slavery.

The Incas were mainly vegetarian. Their agriculture was based on maize, which grows at altitudes of up to 3400 m. They also grew potatoes, beans, tomatoes and cotton. Tobacco was little used, but coca was chewed as a stimulant. The Incas also brewed *chicha*, an intoxicating drink. They had few domesticated animals, but kept llamas, dogs, guinea pigs and ducks, and hunted vicuña, which they sheared and then released.

Inca smiths worked gold, silver and copper, using the techniques of hammering, *cire perdue* casting, annealing and gilding. Inca textiles, many of which have survived in the arid conditions of coastal Peru, show wide variations of pattern and weave and at their best are very fine indeed.

We know from Spanish accounts and other sources that the basic unit of Inca society was the *ayllu*, or extended family. Several *ayllus* made up each administrative region and several regions comprised a *guaman*, or province. Each province was governed by an Inca nobleman, who ruled from a local capital. The provinces were divided into the Four Quarters (*Suyu*) of the empire. The governors of the four *Suyu* formed a high council in the imperial capital at Cuzco. The ruler, however, had almost absolute power and was regarded as a lineal descendant of the Sun.

FURTHER READING

BUSHNELL, G. H. S. 1963. *Peru* (revised edn), London and New York.

MASON, J. ALDEN 1957. *The Ancient Civilizations of Peru*, Harmondsworth.

WILLEY, G. R. 1953. *Prehistoric Settlement Patterns in the Virú Valley, Peru*, Washington (Smithsonian Institution, Bureau of American Ethnology, Bulletin 155).

——— 1971. *An Introduction to American Archaeology. II. South America*, Englewood Cliffs, New Jersey.

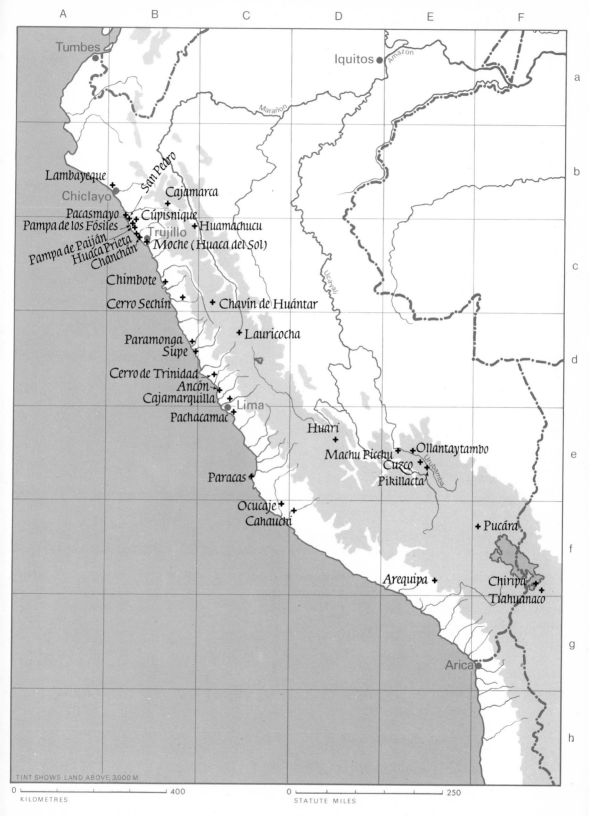

Tumbes

Iquitos   • Amazon

Marañon

Lambayeque

Chiclayo   Cajamarca

San Pedro

Pacasmayo   Cúpisnique

Pampa de los Fósiles

Pampa de Paiján   Trujillo   Huamachuco

Huaca Prieta   Moche (Huaca del Sol)

Chanchán

Chimbote

Cerro Sechín   Chavín de Huántar

Paramonga   Lauricocha

Supe

Cerro de Trinidad

Ancón

Cajamarquilla   Lima

Pachacamac

Huari

Machu Picchu   Ollantaytambo

Cuzco

Paracas   Pikillacta

Ucayali

Ocucaje

Cahuachi   Pucára

Arequipa   Chiripa

Tiahuanaco

Urubamba

Arica

TINT SHOWS LAND ABOVE 3,000 M

0   400
KILOMETRES

0   250
STATUTE MILES

Peru: the Incas and their predecessors   **231**

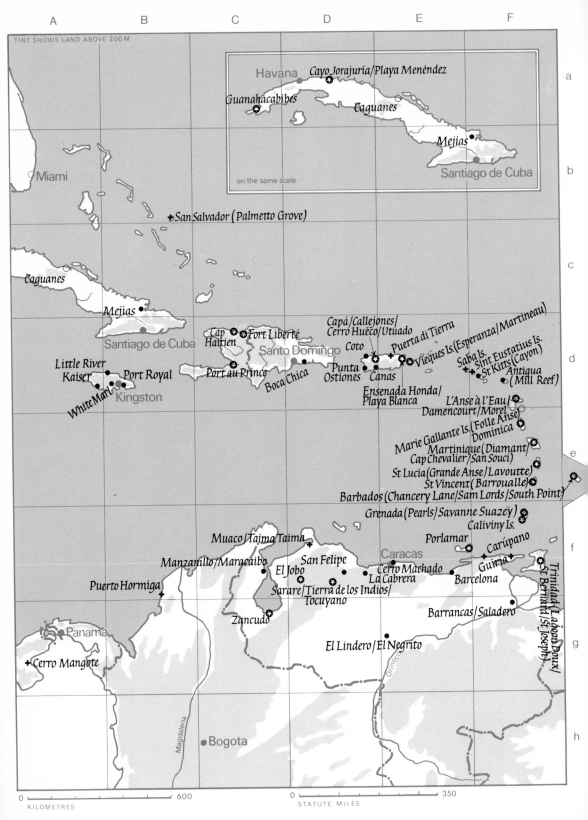

TINT SHOWS LAND ABOVE 200M

A   B   C   D   E   F

a

Havana   Cayo Jorajuría/Playa Menéndez

Guanahacabibes   Caguanes

Mejías

on the same scale   Santiago de Cuba

b

Miami

Caguanes

Mejías

Little River   *Santiago de Cuba*   Cap   Fort Liberté   Capá/Callejones/
Kaiser   Haitien   Santo Domingo   Coto   Cerro Huéco/Utuado   Puerta di Tierra
White Marl   Port Royal   Port au Prince   Boca Chica   Punta   Canas   Vieques Is.(Esperanza/Martineau)   Saba Is.
Kingston   Ostiones   Ensenada Honda/   Sint Eustatius Is.
Playa Blanca   St Kitts (Cayon)
Antigua
(Mill Reef)
L'Anse à l'Eau/
Damencourt/Morel
Marie Gallante Is.(Folle Anse)
Dominica
Martinique(Diamant/
Cap Chevalier/San Souci)
St Lucia(Grande Anse/Lavoutte)
St Vincent(Barroualle)
Barbados (Chancery Lane/Sam Lords/South Point)

San Salvador (Palmetto Grove)

Grenada (Pearls/Savanne Suazey)
Caliviny Is.
Porlamar   Carúpano
Muaco/Taima Taima   Caracas   Guiria   Trinidad (Laboab Doux/
Manzanillo/Maracaibo   San Felipe   St Bernard (St Joseph)
El Jobo   Cerro Machado
Puerto Hormiga   Sarare/Tierra de los Indios/   La Cabrera   Barcelona
Tocuyano
Zancudo   Barrancas/Saladero
Panama   El Lindero/El Negrito
Cerro Mangote

Bogota

0 ———————————— 600   0 ———————————— 350
KILOMETRES   STATUTE MILES

232   *The Caribbean*

The Caribbean

To the archaeologist the 'Caribbean area' means the islands of the Caribbean and the Orinoco river region – Guyana and part of Venezuela. Its cultures did not develop in the same way as those in the tropical forests of Amazonia and adjacent regions. The first Europeans found the Caribs in the Lesser Antilles and on the Venezuelan coast, while the Taino occupied the islands of the Greater Antilles. The Taino grew manioc, lived in large permanent villages and sometimes erected monumental architecture; neither they nor the Caribs built towns.

The earliest inhabitants of the Caribbean area were hunters of big game on the mainland of South America. The best known site is El Jobo, while the disturbed site of La Vela del Coro yielded a C¹⁴ date, presumably suspect, of *c*. 14,000 bc.

Subsequent developments in the Caribbean area may be divided into four phases. Period 1 is represented almost exclusively by coastal middens in Venezuela. Similar sites occur also in central America. The middens yield remains of fish and shellfish, bone points and chipped shell artifacts. We have no evidence of agriculture and little trace of wild plant collecting. Sites in Venezuela and elsewhere yield dates between 4850 bc (Cerro Mangote in Panama) and 1020 bc (Barlovento in Colombia).

Food production began in Period 2, for which we have carbon dates between *c*. 1000 bc and AD 200. Communities on the Venezuelan llanos probably domesticated manioc and, to judge by the discovery of manioc pounders, cultivation had spread to the lower Orinoco (e.g. at Barrancas and Saladero) by 800 bc. Typical of Period 2 is 'Saladoid' white-on-red painted pottery. This was developed in the Orinoco valley, became common in eastern Venezuela and, in the early centuries AD, was carried to the islands of the West Indies. Indeed Period 2 saw wide-spread exploration and settlement of the islands. Among several insular variants is the Cuevas culture of Puerto Rico.

In Periods 3 (*c*. AD 200–1000) and 4 (*c*. 1000–1500 and later) influence from Mesoamerica brought maize and ceremonial structures to the islands of the Caribbean. The earliest ball-courts, for example, were built in Period 3, while in Period 4 maize became a secondary crop among the Taino. Throughout these periods, however, manioc remained the staple food plant for village communities and many groups never developed beyond the hunting and gathering stage; coastal middens, for example, were common.

FURTHER READING

LOVÉN, S. 1935. *Origins of the Tainan culture, West Indies*, Göteborg.

Proceedings of the International Congresses for the study of pre-Columban culture in the Lesser Antilles, 1962.

ROUSE, I. 1952. Scientific survey of Porto Rico and the Virgin Islands, *New York Academy of Sciences, XVIII*, parts 3 and 4, New York.

——— 1962. The Intermediate area, Amazonia and the Caribbean area. In Braidwood, R. J. and G. R. Willey (eds), *Courses toward Urban Life*, Edinburgh and Chicago.

ROUSE, I. and J. M. CRUXENT 1963. *Venezuelan Archaeology*, New Haven and London.

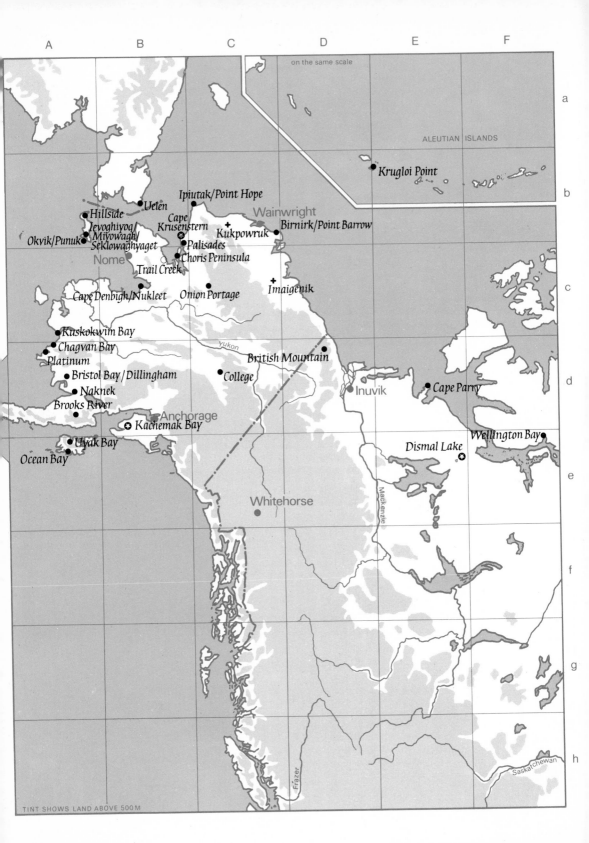

Krugloi Point

Ipiutak/Point Hope

Uelen

Hillside
Ievoghiyoq/
Miyowagh/
Seklowaghyaget

Cape
Krusenstern

Wainwright

Okvik/Punuk

Kukpowruk

Birnirk/Point Barrow

Nome

Palisades

Trail Creek

Choris Peninsula

Cape Denbigh/Nukleet

Onion Portage

Imaigenik

Kuskokwim Bay

Yukon

Chagvan Bay
Platinum

British Mountain

Bristol Bay/Dillingham

College

Cape Parry

Naknek

Inuvik

Brooks River

Anchorage

Kachemak Bay

Wellington Bay

Uyak Bay

Dismal Lake

Ocean Bay

Mackenzie

Whitehorse

Frazer

Saskatchewan

TINT SHOWS LAND ABOVE 500 M

on the same scale

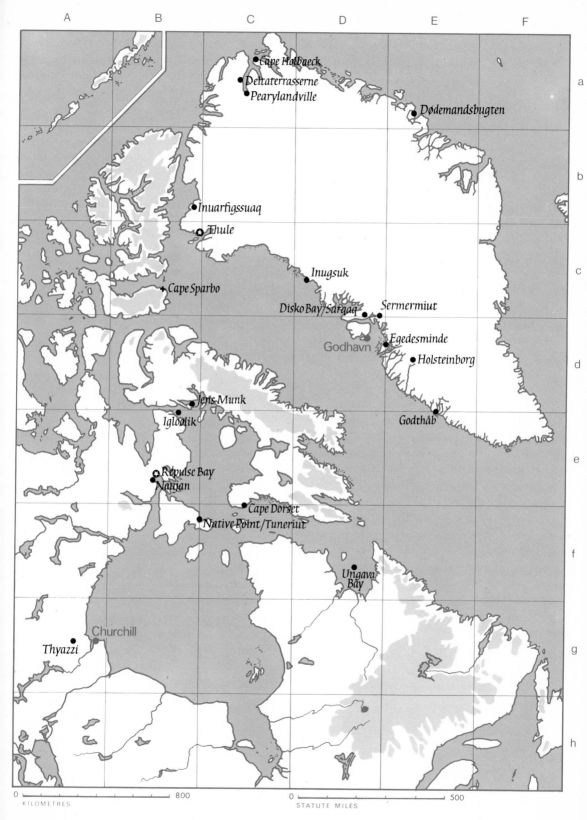

Map labels:

Cape Holbaeck
Deltaterrasserne
Pearylandville
Dødemandsbugten
Inuarfigssuaq
Thule
Cape Sparbo
Inugsuk
Disko Bay/Sarqaq
Sermermiut
Godhavn
Egedesminde
Holsteinborg
Jens Munk
Igloolik
Godthåb
Repulse Bay
Naujan
Cape Dorset
Native Point/Tuneriut
Ungava Bay
Churchill
Thyazzi

A   B   C   D   E   F

a
b
c
d
e
f
g
h

0 ———————————— 800
KILOMETRES

0 ———————————— 500
STATUTE MILES

Eskimo prehistory 235

Eskimo prehistory

see map pp. 234/235

We have already discussed (p. 215) the scattered evidence for the arrival of the earliest Americans, bands of late palaeolithic hunters who travelled from Siberia by way of a land bridge across the Bering Strait. Groups of hunters spread rapidly through the Americas, reaching even Patagonia by the ninth millennium bc. In the arctic regions of North America we have little evidence of occupation before *c.* 4000 bc, when the Denbigh culture, named after a site in Alaska, is first attested. Besides Alaska, camp sites of the Denbigh culture are known in arctic Canada and even the Sarqaq region of west Greenland.

The Denbigh culture – and its successors – were well adapted to their extreme environment. Coastal groups practised a subsistence economy based on hunting large sea mammals (whale, walrus and seal) and fishing. Farther inland, some communities hunted caribou. In most groups, houses were generally semi-subterranean, with walls of stone and sods, occasionally reinforced with whale ribs and jaws; the igloo, or snow-house, was *not* the universal form of dwelling. Denbigh communities fished with harpoons consisting of slotted bone points (paralleled in arctic Eurasia) armed with microliths.

In the Hudson's Bay region, the Denbigh culture was succeeded by the Dorset culture, named after Cape Dorset on Baffin Island. It has C^{14} dates of up to *c.* 800 bc, developed out of the Denbigh tradition and is remarkable for its bone and ivory figurines, both incised and carved in the round.

Although the Denbigh and Dorset cultures were ancestral to the Eskimo groups that have survived in diminishing numbers to the present day, the earliest truly Eskimo assemblages belong to the Old Bering Sea culture of Alaska and north-east Siberia. Farther east, the Thule culture achieved a distribution from Hudson's Bay to Greenland, where Eskimo groups came into contact with Viking settlers from Iceland in the tenth century A D.

FURTHER READING

BANDI, H. G. 1969. *Eskimo Prehistory*, London.
BIRKET-SMITH, K. 1959. *The Eskimos²*, London.
GIDDINGS, J. L. 1967. *Ancient Men of the Arctic*, London and New York.
MATHIASSEN, T. 1927. *Archaeology of the Central Eskimos*, Copenhagen.

ACKNOWLEDGMENTS
The authors wish to express their grateful thanks to those specialists who checked the maps for accuracy, among them Dr Daniel Bruce, Mr John Chapman, Mr Desmond Collins, Miss Susan Frankenstein, Mr Peter Gathercole, Mr Howard Hawkes, Dr Arthur Irvine, Miss Ann Kendall, Mr Ronald J. Lampert, Miss Leong Sau Heng, Professor Vincent Megaw, Mr James Mellaart, Miss Marion Oakeshott, Professor Colin Renfrew, Mr Michael Roaf, Miss Sheila Robinson, Mr Mohammed Salim, and Dr Trevor Watkins. For any errors that may remain the authors take full responsibility.

Ashara 77Fc
Asia Valley 217Eg
Aşıklı Hüyük 62Cc; 73Cd
Asine 99Bc
Askalon 101Df; 103Bf
Askola (Porvoo) 147Ee
Aspendus 109Dd
Asprochalico 39Af
Assos 107Ed
Assur (Qala't Sharqat) 71Bb
Asta Regia 130Cg
Astacus 109Dc
Astrakhan 82Cd
Aşvan 73Fc
Aswan 59Dg
Asyut 59Cd
Atacames 229Ad
Atalaia 126Bf
Ataniya (Adana) 75Dd
Atarneus 107Fe
Atchana (see also Tell Atchana
    and Alalakh) 75De; 77Cb;
    101Dd; 103Cb
Athenae (see also Athens) 109Cd
Athenopolis 108Eb
Athens (see also Athenae) 98De;
    107De; 153Bf
Athgreany 155Be
Athienou 95Dc
Atlihuayan 225Dd
Atlit 103Be
Atranjikhera 191Dc
Attirampakkam 25Df
Auchagallon 155Cc
Auchin-depe 185De
Auchnacree 167Db
Aulnay-les-Planches 165Dd
Aurillac 183Ce
Auvernier 141Ee
Auvers 183Cd
Avaricum 174Ad
Avaris 59Da
Avdeevo 37Bc; 39Cc; 47Cc
Avebury 142Aa; 143Df; 155Df
Aveline's Hole 38Bc
Avetrana 111Fe

Awan 69Fe
Aweinat 53Dc
Ayampitín 216Cf; 221Cf
Ayia Irini 95Bb
Ayia Triadha 96Fd
Ayios Iakovos 95Db
Ayios Sozomenos 95Cc
Aylesford 179Ef; 183Cc
Ayotzingo 225Bg (inset)
Ayudhya 204Cd
Azaila 131Bc
Azapa 221Bd
Azcapotzalco 225Ag (inset)
Aztalan 219Dd

Baba Jan 79Bd; 81Bd
Babaköy 72Bc; 91Ec
Bab edh-Dhra 77Bg
Babięty Małe 168Ed
Babilim (Babylon) 69Ce; 71Ce
Babya Guba 185Ba
Babylon (Babilim) 69Ce; 71Ce
Bac Son 202Ea
Bada 200Ef
Badakhshan (Sang-i Sar) 87Fb
Badari 53Ec; 57Cd; 59Cd
Badden 167Cc
Baden (Königshöhle) 156Fd
Badjawa 210Af
Bad Nauheim 172Dc
Bad Tibira (Tell Medina) 69Df
Bagendon 179Df
Baghdad 69Cd
Bagneux 141Bd; 149Cd
Bagor 25Cc
Baguia 200Fh
Bahal 191Cd
Bahawalpur state, sites in 189Dc
Bahrain 84Fb
Bahrija 122Cd
Bahriyat (Isin) 69Cf
Bahurupa 191Cd
Baia (Hamangia) 136Ef
Baia de Fier 39Ad
Baia Farta 28Cf
Baierdorf 171Dg

Băile Herculane 49Ad
Bäk 168Cd
Baker's Hole 32Cc
Bala Kot 189Ad
Balangoda 25Dg; 191Bh (inset)
Balata (Eski Mosul) 71Aa
Balawat (Imgur-Bel) 71Ba
Balestra 117Cc
Bali 210Af
Balkåkra 168Cc
Balkh 87Db
Ballinderry 167Bd
Ballymeanoch 155Cc
Ballynamona 155Be
Ballynoe 155Cd
Ballyvourney 167Ae
Balmallock 143Cc
Balver Höhle 42Dc
Bambata 28Dg; 53Dg
Bamiyan 87Dc
Bampur 65Eg; 87Ag
Ban Chieng 202Dc
Bandarawela 25Dg; 191Bh
    (inset)
Bandibal 67Fe
Bandung 26Bh
Banff 167Db
Bani Surmah 79Bd
Bankälla 181Da
Ban Kao 202Cd
Bankinang 200Ag
Banon 204De
Banta Eng 210Ae
Banteai Srei 204Dd
Bara 189Fa; 191Cb
Bara-Bahau 40Af; 44Dc
Barasimla 25Dd
Barawa 55Fe
Barbados (Chancery Lane/Sam
    Lords/South Point) 232Fe
Barca, Czechoslovakia 161Bd
Barca, Libya 109Be
Barcelona 232Ef
Barche di Solferino 113Bb
Barclodiad y Gawres 143Ce
Bardal 147Bd